The Singer on the Shore
Essays 1991–2004

GABRIEL JOSIPOVICI was born in Nice in 1940 of Russo-Italian, Romano-Levantine parents. He lived in Egypt from 1945 to 1956, when he came to Britain. He read English at St Edmund Hall, Oxford, graduating with a First in 1961. From 1963 to 1996 he taught at the University of Sussex, where he is now Research Professor in the Graduate School of Humanities. He has published over a dozen novels, three volumes of short stories and a number of critical books. His plays have been performed throughout Britain and on radio in Britain, France and Germany, and his work has been translated into the major European languages and Arabic. In 2001 he published *A Life*, a biographical memoir of his mother, the translator and poet Sacha Rabinovitch (London Magazine editions). His most recent novels are *Goldberg: Variations* (Carcanet, 2002) and *Only Joking* (Zweitausendeins, Germany, 2005).

Also by Gabriel Josipovici

Fiction
The Inventory (1968)
Words (1971)
Mobius the Stripper: Stories and Short Plays (1974)
The Present (1975)
Four Stories (1977)
Migrations (1977)
The Echo Chamber (1979)
The Air We Breathe (1981)
Conversations in Another Room (1984)
Contre Jour: A Triptych after Pierre Bonnard (1984)
In the Fertile Land (1987)
Steps: Selected Fiction and Drama (1990)
The Big Glass (1991)
In a Hotel Garden (1993)
Moo Pak (1995)
Now (1998)
Goldberg: Variations (2002)
Only Joking (2005)

Theatre
Mobius the Stripper (1974)
Vergil Dying (1977)

Non-fiction
The World and the Book (1971, 1979)
The Lessons of Modernism (1977, 1987)
Writing and the Body (1982)
The Mirror of Criticism: Selected Reviews (1983)
The Book of God: A Response to the Bible (1988, 1990)
Text and voice: Essays 1981–1991 (1992)
(ed.) *The Modern English Novel: The Reader, the Writer and the Book* (1975)
(ed.) *The Siren's Song: Selected Essays of Maurice Blanchot* (1980)
A Life (2001)

GABRIEL JOSIPOVICI

The Singer on the Shore

ESSAYS 1991–2004

CARCANET

in association with

The European Jewish Publication Society

First published in Great Britain in 2006 by
Carcanet Press Limited
Alliance House
Cross Street
Manchester M2 7AQ

in association with
The European Jewish Publication Society
PO Box 19948
London N3 3ZJ

www.ejps.org.uk

The European Jewish Publication Society is a registered charity which gives grants to assist in the publication and distribution of books relevant to Jewish literature, history, religion, philosophy, politics and culture.

A CIP catalogue record for this book is available from the British Library
ISBN 1 85754 844 2
978 1 85754 844 0

The publisher acknowledges financial assistance from Arts Council England

Typeset in Monotype Centaur by XL Publishing Services, Tiverton
Cover design by Ornan Rotem
Printed and bound in England by SRP Ltd, Exeter

For Dick and Ally

&

For Ornan and Num

Contents

Preface   ix

1   The Bible Open and Closed   1
2   Vibrant Spaces   25
3   Singing a New Song   46
4   The Opinion of Pythagoras   60
5   I Dream of Toys   78
6   In Time: Rembrandt's Self-Portraits   99
7   Escape Literature: Tristram Shandy's Journey
      Through France   104
8   Dejection   119
9   Kierkegaard and the Novel   130
10   Kafka's Children   149
11   The Wooden Stair   179
12   Listening to the Voice in *Four Quartets*   183
13   Borges and the Plain Sense of Things   208
14   Aharon Appelfeld: Three Novels and a Tribute   221
15   Andrzej Jackowski: Reveries of Dispossession   254
16   The Singer on the Shore   260
17   Memory: Too Little/Too Much   275
18   This Is Not Your Rest   290
19   Writing, Reading and the Study of Literature   308

Acknowledgements   337
Index   341

List of Plates

Plates 1–5 will be found between pp.102 and 103; Plates 6–9 between pp.262 and 263.

1 Rembrandt van Rijn, *Artist in his Studio*, c.1628, 24.8 × 31.7cm, oil on panel. Photograph © 2006, Museum of Fine Arts, Boston, MA. Zoe Oliver Sherman Collection, given in memory of Lillie Oliver Poor, 38.1838

2 Rembrandt van Rijn, *Portrait of the Artist at his Easel*, 1660, 111 × 90cm, oil on canvas. Paris, Musée du Louvre. Photo RMN / © Hervé Lewandowski

3 Rembrandt van Rijn, *Self-Portrait with Two Circles*, c.1665, 114 × 94cm, oil on canvas. Kenwood, The Iveagh Bequest © English Heritage Photographic Library

4 Rembrandt van Rijn, *Self-Portrait at the Age of Sixty-Three*, 1669, 86 × 70.5cm, oil on wood. Photo © The National Gallery, London

5 Rembrandt van Rijn, *Self-Portrait*, 1669, 63.5 × 57.8cm, oil on canvas. By permission of the Royal Cabinet of Paintings, Mauritshuis, The Hague

6 Andrzej Jackowski, *Refuge/Refugee*, 1982, 137.2 × 122 cm, oil on canvas. Private collection © Andrzej Jackowski

7 Andrzej Jackowski, *The Tower of Copernicus*, 1980, 136.6 × 117 cm, oil on canvas. Arts Council Collection, South Bank Centre © Andrzej Jackowski

8 Andrzej Jackowski, *The Burying*, 1994, 152 × 162.5 cm, oil on canvas. The collection of the artist © Andrzej Jackowski

9 Andrzej Jackowski, *Beneath the Tree*, 1994, 152.4 × 162.5 cm, oil on canvas. Private collection © Andrzej Jackowski

Preface

THE ESSAYS COLLECTED HERE were nearly all written in response to specific requests: by publishers to write introductions to works they knew I admired; by editors to contribute to volumes on specific themes in which they thought I might be interested; by institutions inviting me to lecture. I like the idea of miscellaneous collections and enjoy reading those of writers I admire: a whole book on one topic can have a somewhat wilful feel to it, whereas an essay is never wilful, and it is (or should be) what Montaigne understood it as: an *essai*, an attempt, which should retain its transient and momentary quality: this is how it seems to me, now (and I may feel differently next year).

At the same time a volume of such *essais* will, one hopes, add up to more than the sum of its parts, will convey to the reader that 'secret signature' which Proust rightly held to be what we most treasure in art, and which cannot be found in any one passage but rather emerges between the different *essais* of any artist, be they pieces of music, sketches and paintings, books or essays proper. No artist, should, however, attempt to sum up what that secret signature is, just as no person should try to be what he or she thinks they 'really are' — that is the recipe for self-parody, a topic I deal with in 'The Singer on the Shore'.

For that reason I have resisted tinkering with the texts (except occasionally to correct a mistake of fact or an obvious clumsiness of style). This means that I have left those essays delivered as lectures in the lecture format, and resisted the temptation to remove the occasion of their delivery; and it means, inevitably, that there is some repetition, since one's repertoire of examples is naturally limited. To try and eliminate this, however, would have meant producing a quite different kind of book, and I feel that more would have been lost than gained.

At the same time, finding the same issues dealt with in different contexts may help the reader understand them better. I am thinking, for example, of the discussion of contingency in 'The Bible Open and Closed' and in the essay on Borges, or of patience in the essay on *Twelfth Night* and in that on some recent paintings by Andrzej Jackowski. I also rather like the idea of returning to the same issues in slightly different ways, as happens in 'Dejection' and in both the essay on Borges and the one on 'Kierkegaard and the Novel'. It suggests that the critic, unlike the scholar, is not putting forward a thesis or delivering a truth, but is more like the artist, struggling to articulate something which is difficult to put into words, something which, as Eliot says in *Four Quartets*, is lost and found and lost again, and which reveals the critical enterprise as a journey on which critic and reader embark together, not as a terrain to be mapped by a specialist in the 'field'.

The essays that follow are not, of course, the only writing I did between 1991 and 2004, and not even the main form of writing; but I put as much into each one as I did into the novels, short stories and books I wrote in that time, and one or two of them seem to me more successful (in the sense that I got closer to what I wanted to say) than the more extended pieces of work.

One final point: the concluding essay was delivered as my inaugural lecture as Professor of English at the University of Sussex, where I spent my professional life. I hesitated to include it in my previous volume of essays, *Text and Voice: Essays 1981–1991*, feeling that it was too personal. It seeemed to fit in better this time, so I have included it, though it was delivered in March 1986.

Gabriel Josipovici
Lewes, 1 January 2005

1. The Bible Open and Closed

THE BIBLE IS FROM FIRST TO LAST – from 'In the beginning God created the heaven and the earth' to Cyrus's decree ordering the exiles to return to Jerusalem, from Matthew's genealogy to the end of Revelation – a series of narratives, perhaps a single narrative made up of many pieces. Narrative was clearly how these ancient Semitic peoples made sense of the world, as it was the way the Greeks of the time of Homer, and so-called primitive peoples all over the world did. Yet we in our culture have a problem with narrative. What does it *mean?* we ask. What is the guy trying to *say?* And if the book in question is a sacred text the problems grow even more acute. For then it is even more important to understand clearly what it is saying, since our very lives may depend upon it. We need to feel we are dealing with a text that is closed, in the sense that its meaning can be clearly understood and translated into other terms; yet the Bible, like all narratives, but, as I hope to show, even more than most, is open, that is, it resists translation into other terms and asks not so much to be *understood* as *lived with*, however puzzling and ambiguous it may seem.

Let me try to flesh out this rather stark opposition between open and closed by giving you some examples of what I have in mind. I will confine myself for the moment to the Hebrew Bible, what Christians call the Old Testament. Rather than arguing this point in general terms, let me take you straight to some specific examples of what I mean. When it becomes clear that David has become a rebel leader and will not be persuaded to return to court, Saul gives his daughter Michal, who had been David's wife, to a certain Phalti, the son of Laish (1 Sam. 25:44). We hear nothing more of this man, who had not previously been mentioned, until after the death of Saul and his son Jonathan, when Abner, the commander of Saul's army, makes peace overtures to David, now king in Hebron. David, however, is only prepared to listen if Abner hands over Michal. This is of course no romantic tale of lovers re-united; Michal stands for the Saulide succession, as Ishbosheth, Saul's sole surviving son, now clinging to the kingship of Israel, and Abner and David well know. But since the power now rests with David, there is nothing Ishbosheth can do about it:

> And Ishbosheth sent, and took her from her husband, even from Phaltiel the son of Laish. And her husband went with her along weeping behind her to Bahurim. Then said Abner unto him, Go, return. And he returned. (2 Sam. 3:15–16).[1]

We never hear of this Phalti or Phaltiel again. He is a mere pawn in the game being played out between Saul and David and David and Saul's descendants, only one tiny cog in the chain of history unfolding in the Hebrew Bible, the history of God's relations with Israel. It would have been perfectly easy for the narrator to say: 'And David took again his wife Michal, daughter of Saul, which Saul had given to Phalti, the son of Laish.' But no. He chooses instead to bring this man momentarily to life, to make his pain, whether wounded pride or anguished love, all the more palpable for remaining unspoken. And then he makes him disappear: 'Then said Abner to him, Go, return. And he returned.'

---

1 For ease of reference I have used the Authorised Version (AV) throughout.

What are we to make of this? What, we ask, is this silent Phalti's role in the history of Israel's relations with God? How much importance, if any, are we to allot to him? We might let these questions pass in a novel (though we can be sure that if this novel becomes the object of academic study they will sooner or later be raised), but in a sacred text like the Bible the lack of an answer is deeply troubling, so troubling that someone at some point will seek to provide answers to them. I don't wish to engage with this issue at the moment, but want instead to pass on to another example. Chapter 38 of Genesis concerns Judah and his daughter-in-law Tamar. He gives her one of his sons, who dies shortly after, then a second son, who also dies. Anxious to protect the life of his youngest son, he withholds him from Tamar, although he should by rights now let him marry her. She, however, dresses up as a temple prostitute and accosts Judah as he passes on his way to the sheep-shearing. The encounter leads to her becoming pregnant, and, when her father-in-law arraigns her before the court, she turns the tables on him and proves that he is the father. Once this is made clear Judah does not try to hide: 'She is in the right and I am not; because that I gave her not to Shelah my son. And he knew her again no more'(38:26).[2] However, she bears him twins, Pharez and Zarah, and with their birth the chapter ends and we return once again to the story of Judah's younger brother, Joseph. In Chapter 46 we read that among those who went down with Jacob to Egypt were the sons of Judah, Shelah and Pharez, and the sons of Pharez, Hezron and Hamul. Much later, in Numbers, we learn that the Pharzites, the Serahites, the Hezronites and the Hamulites are still going strong (26:20–21). Then in the Book of Ruth we learn that Boaz, whose own son,

---

2 I have changed the wording of the AV here ('She hath been more right-eous than I') because, as Jan Fokkelman has pointed out to me, it is misleading.

Jesse, is the father of David, is himself a descendent of Pharez. Finally, at the start of the New Testament Matthew tells us that 'Judas begat Pharez and Sara of Thamar; and Pharez begat Esrom... and Obed begat Jesse; and Jesse begat David the king; and David begat Solomon... and Jacob begat Joseph the husband of Mary, of whom was born Jesus, who is called Christ' (Mat. 1:1–16).

In both instances, the brief story of Phalti and the story of Judah and Tamar, we can safely say that the Bible does not conform to our expectations of how narrative should be constructed, and, especially, of how this most important narrative of all should be constructed. If we look for a common denominator we can say that in both cases the narrative is too open for our comfort. No self-respecting creative-writing teacher today would allow a student to bring in a character like Phalti only to drop him again for ever. We want him either developed or excised altogether. The Bible does not do this. Is it because of the clumsiness of the writer? Or because something has dropped out of our text?

As for the second example, it too seems to us to be a blatant case of clumsy writing. Why has the chapter about Judah slipped in to the Joseph story? If the point is that while Joseph imagined himself to be the centre of the universe he was, all the time, a mere side-show in the larger story of Israel, in which Judah and *his* sons are to play the major role, why is this not made clear? Is it that the scribes or compilers were not aware of this? Or that they simply failed to make the connection? Or that they lacked the skill to integrate the stories of Joseph and Judah?

We could describe our frustration with both examples as due to a failure on the part of the writers to tell a story as it should be told. More neutrally, we could say it stems from the extraordinary *reticence* of the writers. We find such reticence not simply puzzling but intensely frustrating. We want to shake them, to scream at them: 'What are you trying to say, you oafs, what is the point, the point, the point? If Phalti has a role in this story then for God's sake tell us what it is! If the birth of Judah's twins is that important, then don't just slip it in at the end of the chapter and go on to something completely different!'

The strategies adopted by readers in the past to cope with this frustration have been various. So long as the text was held to be sacred, the word of God, readers either filled in the silences by elaborating the stories so as to bring out their point, or else they explored the psychology of the protagonists, filling in the inner lives of the characters, as it were. By and large the first of these approaches led to Hebrew midrash and early Christian narrative elaborations, while the latter led to Protestant exegesis. When, at the time of the Enlightenment, the text began to be studied like any other, as the product of men, whether the initial impulse came from God or grew out of social needs, the silences of the text began to be attributed either to a failure on the part of the writers or to lacunae in the tradition. But what if we were to start from the other end, so to speak, and ask what our frustration has to say about *us as readers*? What if we were to start with the assumption that the text (let us not speak about authors) knows exactly what it is doing, and that it is *we* who have been found wanting, either because we lack the critical tools to do it justice or because we lack the cast of mind and spirit to respond as the text asks us to respond?

Instead of trying to answer this question straight away let us stay with our frustration for a little longer. Let us look at one or two other examples of the biblical mode of narration and see how earlier readers, both Christian and Jewish, dealt with it, and what this has to teach us about both the characteristics of biblical narrative and the nature of its readers.

After their exile from the Garden of Eden Adam and Eve have two children, first Cain and then Abel. Cain, we learn, was a 'tiller of the ground', while Abel was a 'keeper of sheep'. It comes to pass that Cain brings 'the fruit of the ground' as an offering to the Lord, while Abel brings 'the firstlings of the flock'. We are then told: 'And the Lord had respect unto Abel and his to offering: But unto Cain and to his offering he had not respect'(Gen. 4:4–5). We all know what happens next: Cain is furious, the Lord rebukes him, but that does not stop him 'rising up against' his brother as they are talking in the field, and killing him. The Lord now asks him where his brother is, and he answers: 'I know not: Am I my brother's keeper?' (9). Whereupon the Lord curses him and makes him 'a fugitive and a vagabond... in the earth' (12). Cain responds mysteriously to the Lord's curse: 'My punishment is greater than I can bear'(13), he says, but he has no option but to accept his lot. He settles in the Land of Nod, east of Eden, where he marries, begets children, and builds a city called Enoch, after his eldest son. Adam and Eve meanwhile have another child, Seth, to replace the murdered Abel.

From the first the commentators were exercised by this stark narrative. The traditional Jewish commentators felt that gifts should not be rejected arbitrarily. The rejection of a gift needs to be justified. So what had Cain done wrong? Had he perhaps offered God a sacrifice from some inferior portions of the crop while Abel chose the finest of the flock? Or was Abel accepted because he offered with an open heart while Cain begrudged God every bit of what was offered? Or was Cain perhaps inherently evil? The Septuagint, the Greek translation of the Hebrew Bible, is so sure that it had to do with the wrong kind of sacrifice that it renders Genesis 4:7: 'If thou doest well, shalt thou not be accepted? And if thou doest not well, sin lieth at the door' as: 'If you have properly brought it [i.e. your sacrifice] but have not properly divided it, have you not sinned?' And that is the view of the Jewish Platonist philosopher, Philo of Alexandria: '[I]t is not proper to offer the best things to that which is created, namely oneself,' he writes 'and second best to the All-knowing'. The Midrash Tanhuma, an early medieval compilation of rabbinic midrash on the Torah, glosses 'And Cain brought to the Lord an offering of the fruit of the ground': '[W]hat does this imply? The ordinary fruit [rather than the first fruits reserved for God].' The notion that Cain was inherently evil, on the other hand, is the one favoured by John in his first epistle: 'By this it may be seen,' he writes,

> who are the children of God and who are the children of the devil; whoever does not do right is not of God, nor he who does not love his brother. For this is the message which you have heard from the beginning [i.e. the book of Genesis]: that we should love one another and not be like Cain, who was of the Evil One and murdered his brother. (1 John 3:10–12)[3]

St Augustine combines the two approaches:[4] while arguing that Cain sacrificed wrongly and kept the best for himself, he built upon the episode the entire argument of his *City of God*. Cain, the builder of cities, is the ancestor of the men of Thebes and Rome, he argues, those conglomerations of men where each is for himself and what your neighbour acquires leaves that much less for you; while Abel is the ancestor of the Christian way of life, of that city of God where what we give we receive back a hundredfold, and where, as Dante puts it, 'in his will is our peace'.

This is powerful and suggestive both as a philosophy of history and as a psychological insight into the motivations of men. Unfortunately it has no basis whatever in the biblical story. There is nothing in the Hebrew text as we have it that suggests either that Cain sacrificed wrongly or that he was inherently evil. But this is intolerable to us. For the corollary would then be that it is God who has behaved arbitrarily in condoning

---

3   See James L. Kugel, *Traditions of the Bible*, Cambridge, MA, 1998, p.150.
4   *The City of God*, Book xv.

Abel's sacrifice and condemning Cain's. That, of course, is the position taken by those who dismiss the Bible as a wicked and pernicious book. For the moment, though, I want to stay with the reader who in some way believes in and trusts the God of the Bible, but who cannot square that with what he reads in Genesis 4. For such a reader there *must* be a reason for God's actions, otherwise the whole book becomes worthless. So he looks for explanations of the kind I have been outlining.

Let us look at one further example, much less outrageous than the Cain and Abel story, but nevertheless instructive. At the end of Genesis 11, after a list of the genealogies of Shem, Noah's son, we are told that

> Terah begat Abram, Nahor and Haran; and Haran begat
> Lot... And Abram and Nahor took them wives: the name
> of Abram's wife was Sarai; and the name of Nahor's wife,
> Milcah, the daughter of Haran... (Gen. 11:27–9)

Terah takes Abram and Lot and their wives and they 'went forth with them from Ur of the Chaldees, to go into the land of Canaan; and they came unto Haran, and dwelt there' (31). In Haran Terah dies. 'Now,' we read at the start of the next chapter (but the chapter divisions, remember, are medieval editorial additions), 'Now the Lord had said unto Abram, Get thee out of thy country, and from thy kindred, and from thy father's house, unto a land that I will shew thee.' He promises Abram innumerable offspring and that he will make his descendants a great nation in whom all the earth will be blessed. 'So Abram departed, as the Lord had spoken unto him; and Lot went with him; and Abram was seventy and five years old when he departed out of Haran' (Gen. 12:1–4).

This of course is the founding story of Israel, God's holy people. This is the moment when those who will later be called Israelites (after the name given to Abraham's grandson Jacob by the angel) separate themselves off from the other sons of

Shem; and the story does not end, in the Hebrew Bible, till many thousands of pages later, when the decree of Cyrus, King of Persia, sends the Israelite exiles back to what is now their land (2 Chronicles 36:23).

The question is: Why Abraham? The rabbis pored over the text for an answer and, not finding one, patched one together out of a few hints in the Bible. The start of Chapter 11 tells the story of the Tower of Babel. The ruler of Babel, they said, was Nimrod. Nimrod was an idol-worshipper and a cunning astrologer.[5] He had foretold Abram's birth, 'and it was manifest to him that a man would be born in his day who would rise up against him and triumphantly give the lie to his religion'. He sent out a decree that all male children were to be killed, but Terah's wife got out of the city and gave birth in a cave, which was immediately filled with the splendour of the sun. She wrapped her cloak round him and left him there to the mercy of the Lord. The child began to wail and 'God sent Gabriel down to give him milk to drink, and the angel made it to flow from the little finger of the baby's right hand, and he sucked at it until he was ten days old.' Then he got up and left the cave. Outside he was struck by the beauty of the stars and decided they were gods and he would worship them. But at dawn they disappeared and he thought: 'I will not worship these, for they are no gods.' The same thing happened with the sun and the moon. Then Gabriel appeared again and told Abraham he was the messenger of God and led him to a spring where he washed his hands and feet and then prayed to God. Later Nimrod caught up with him and threw him into a burning fiery furnace because he denied the godliness of the idols he himself worshipped. Abraham, however, remained steadfast in his faith, and was miraculously drawn out of the flames alive and well.

5   See Louis Ginzberg, *The Legend of the Jews*, tr. Henrietta Szold, Baltimore and London, 1998, Vol. 1, pp.183–308.

All in all, the rabbis say, Abraham was tempted with ten temptations, and he withstood them all, for God was always with him.

It is possible that the rabbis who compiled these stories were influenced by the accounts of the childhood of Jesus to be found in the Gnostic Gospels and traces of which survive in Matthew and Luke, as well as by the stories of the early years of Moses at the start of Exodus. But it is also possible that these stories, like those associated with the infant Jesus, all emerged out of the same cultural climate. In both cases startling claims are made for the protagonist, and in both cases it is easy to see why. As in the case of Cain and Abel, the question: Why is X chosen (or Y not chosen)? is answered by asserting that X had striking qualities, chief among which was the ability to recognise the true God and be recognised in turn by him in turn, while Y had striking defects, chief among which was the refusal to recognise the true God.

I will come to the Gospels in due time. For the moment let us stay with the Hebrew Bible. In both stories, that of Cain and Abel and that of Abraham, we are dealing with the problem of *election*. Why was Abel chosen and Cain rejected? Why was Abraham chosen? In neither case can election be explained, either theologically or morally, by the text as we have it. To explain it we have either to posit incompetence on the part of the writers, or the disappearance of crucial pieces of information; or else to go outside the text and invent a scenario which will makes sense of the apparently arbitrary choices of God.

This problem of election, as we have seen, deeply troubled the rabbis and the early Christians. It became, as we all know, a major source, if not *the* major source of controversy, in the time of the Reformation. Writers across the entire spectrum, from Catholic to Lutheran to Calvinist, probed the Bible, and especially the key text in the Bible on the problem of election, Paul's Epistle to the Romans, for an answer to the question:

Who is chosen? (and its corollary: How do I know if *I* am chosen?). On this issue alone wars were fought and thousands brutally slaughtered, as well as the greatest poetry written, in the course of the sixteenth and seventeenth centuries. And though the Enlightenment brought an end to the bloodshed, the continuing importance of Romans in Protestant theology testifies to fact that it remains a central issue in Christian thought. In the light of this it might appear casual, to say the least, to suggest that the question has been wrongly posed, but that is what I propose to do. What if, I want to ask, instead of forcing the biblical text to provide an explanation, we ask: Why should election, in the Hebrew Bible, appear to be so arbitrary?

The answer, I would suggest, must run something like this. The Hebrew Bible is above all realistic. It is realistic in its assessment of the human condition, and it is realistic in its assessment of how men and women react to that condition. It starts from the position that it is a fact of life that some are more fortunate than others, that fathers, for example, love some of their children more than others. This may not be fair, but then why should life be fair? The Hebrew Bible, accepting this premise, concentrates rather on the question: How do we *respond* to the unfairness of life? How do we respond to the privilege of being chosen, of being the favourite child, say, and how do we respond to the disappointment of being rejected, of not being the parents' favourite? In the case of Abraham, the response is immediate and does not even require words: God asks him to leave his city, his home and his family, to face an uncertain future, and he promptly does so. We cannot and must not ask why, for perhaps Abraham does not know himself. Perhaps there is a moment in everyone's life when a call of a certain kind comes and they either respond or don't. Of course there is no certainty that the call is from God or that it is genuine. This is the question that haunted Kierkegaard, who responded to a call in his early manhood and then spent the rest of his life alternately pondering whether he had been mistaken and trying to explain to himself why he had had to do what he did. We know that in extreme conditions people make choices which in some cases, such as that of Gandhi or Nelson Mandela, subsequently look heroic, but there must be many millions who have also made choices which cannot be confirmed in this way by outward events. In the case of Cain the response is also immediate. Filled with jealousy, he kills his privileged brother, and then shrugs off responsibility for his deed: 'Am I my brother's keeper?' A proper reading of Genesis 4 will have to recognise the anger and even anguish of Cain, and it is indeed easy to do so, for who has not felt such anger and anguish, even if they have not carried their anger into action in the way Cain does. Cain's answer to God is also something it is easy to understand, and in fact we have already seen an example of such a response in the Bible itself. When God, in the garden, asks Adam if he has eaten of the forbidden fruit, he replies: 'The woman whom thou gavest to be with me, she gave me of the tree and I did eat' (Gen. 3:12). Later in Genesis we find a much more elaborate example of fraternal jealousy: Joseph, their father's darling, makes himself intolerable to his brothers by his conceit, which culminates in his recounting to them a dream in which they will all bow down to him in homage. Like Cain they plan to kill him, but this time the plan goes wrong and in the long aftermath of the bungled and half-hearted murder the brothers gradually come to different understandings of what they have done. It is Judah who comes closest to admitting his fault (we have already seen him admitting that he is the culprit in the story of Tamar), and accepting that it is the way of the world for parents to love their offspring in unequal measure (Gen. 44:33). With this recognition on his part comes the possibility of a comic rather than a tragic outcome, and it does indeed come to pass that in Egypt the brothers and their father bow down to Joseph – though even that situation, as I have suggested, is only temporary, and in a longer perspective, a perspective vouchsafed only to God and the patient reader, Joseph's descendants will in turn have to bow to Judah's.

To move on to Abraham. The mystery of Abraham's election merges into the mystery of the election of the Israelites. The old rhyme says it all: 'How odd of God/To choose the Jews'. There is no reason for it. But again, to look for the reason is to look for the wrong thing. The important point is: How does one react to the favour of election? It could have been anyone; it happened to be Abraham. It could have been any group; it happened to be the Israelites. How will Abraham cope? How will the Israelites?

In fact the second book of the Bible, Exodus, deals with precisely this question. It is an exploration of how Israel responds to the call, how it comes, in the course of many adventures, to understand that what is important is not, as in the Greek philosophical tradition, to know yourself, but to walk in God's way, not to ask the meaning of the call, but to respond to it. That is a hard lesson to learn and in a sense it is never fully learned.

In memory the Book of Exodus is divided in two at the point of the crossing of the Red Sea and Moses' triumphant song. But that is not how it is. No sooner are the Israelites free, with the Egyptian army drowned behind them, than they begin to long for the assurances of their previous life, when, though slaves, they at least knew they would not die of hunger and thirst:

> And all the congregation of the children of Israel journeyed from the wilderness of Sin... and pitched in Rephidim: and there was no water for the people to drink... And the people thirsted there for water; and the people murmured against Moses, and said, Wherefore is this that thou hast brought us up out of Egypt, to kill us and our children and our cattle with thirst? And Moses

cried unto the Lord, saying, What shall I do unto this people? They be almost ready to stone me. (Exod. 17:1–4)

The Hebrew Bible, I said, deals with reality; and the reality is that we are weak and uncertain; that we long for clarity and certainty and find it difficult to go on without them. But that is precisely what we have to do, unless we wish to pass our lives as slaves, automata simply obeying orders in return for the comfort of knowing that we are protected from cold and hunger and danger. And though we are weak and uncertain God is there, to listen to our groans and help us if we will only turn to him. This help, however, is conditional on our acting in certain ways. By the end of Exodus it seems that at some deep level the people have learned these lessons. Now they are ready to receive the laws of God: Leviticus can begin. As the subsequent history of the Israelites will show, however, even armed with the rules and precepts of Leviticus, the temptations of certainty and slavery are never far away.

We are now in a position to return to my opening examples and to ask whether the openness I have hitherto discussed in negative terms can be seen in a different light if we trust the text rather than criticising it for not doing what we expect it to do.

In both cases the modern reader is disorientated by the reticence of the narration. This often has to do with brevity, but not necessarily. The text can be prolix and yet deny us information we feel we cannot do without. We want the text to say more, to explain, to take sides; but what if this non-explanation, this not taking sides, were, like the inexplicability of the call, the mystery of the father's love, part of what this book is about and not a weakness or a lack? Phalti's sudden and disconcerting eruption into the story, saying nothing but going weeping behind his wife to Bahurim before turning back, still without speaking, when told to do so – this helps make us aware of the fact that the story teems with silent figures, some mere names in genealogical lists, yet each no doubt with his or her own life and joys and sorrows. Even more, though, it makes us aware of the fact that even though the story told here is that of the Israelites, there are other stories which we might have entered had we not entered this one. In other words, just as the various stories of election alert us to the *contingency* of life – it needn't have been me, but it *is*, – so the story of Phalti alerts us to the contingency of stories, even stories which, like this one, start with the creation of the world.

But even that is not quite right. It makes contingency sound too much like relativity. Relativity is rather a safe concept, at least in the abstract. It says that there are other ways of seeing things than ours, other worlds than ours. But we can easily accept this and yet remain locked up in *our* world, merely imagining other worlds *like* ours, only, somehow, different. Contingency, however, is radical. To experience it is to experience the frailty of life and also its wonder: this, now, and not something else. Contingency decentres one, and the Phalti episode shows how the Bible is a radically decentred book: it seems to go in a straight line from Adam to David to exile to return, but every now and again it opens a window onto another landscape, even if, as here, only for a moment. We are thus made to feel that we are not, as Joseph imagines himself to be, the centre of the universe, but only a tiny part of it.

Of course, as the story of Joseph and his descendants itself shows, it is folly to imagine that we are ever at the centre, for what is central one day will be peripheral the next. And if Judah and his line triumph in the long run, who is to say that this will hold true in the *longest* run? That is why the narrator does not alert us to this fact when describing Joseph's triumph, for to do so would be to suggest that we stand outside and above time. But that, for the Hebrew Bible, is to commit an unpardonable folly, the folly of Adam and Eve, the folly of the builders of the Tower of Babel – wanting to be like God.

Most narratives we are familiar with – novels, that is – take it upon themselves to reach clear conclusions. That is what attracts us to them. In Sartre's famous example, in the early pages of *La Nausée*, I open the pages of a novel and am taken into the life of the hero. He is walking down the street; his life, like mine, is open before him; but I know, because that is what novels are about, that before long this man will plunge into an *adventure*, that his life will fill with *meaning*. Otherwise there would be nothing for the novel to do. That is its task. But it is also a sleight of hand. A magnificent sleight of hand, but a sleight of hand nonetheless. For the duration of the novel I too then feel that life has a meaning, and therefore that *my* life has a meaning, that in some sense I am at the centre of the universe.

But the classic novel is not the only form of narrative. In a famous essay Walter Benjamin drew a sharp contrast between the narratives of the storyteller and of the novelist. The story-teller is the spokesman of tradition, the novel the utterance of the solitary individual. The storyteller is not interested in character or morality but in pure narrative. We can see, from our perspective, that the novel grows out of midrash and allegory, while the stories of the storyteller are akin to the biblical narratives. Only occasionally, in our Western tradition, has anyone challenged the power of the novel, a power which stems from its providing us with the illusion that we are at the centre of an adventure, that our lives are imbued with meaning. Sartre and Camus did so in their first novels, but we can go back to the origins of the novel and already find a challenge being mounted. Rabelais, Cervantes and Sterne all, in their different ways, question the assumptions of the classic novel, and, in our own time, Proust does so in *A la recherche*. In fact *A la recherche* is the only extended narrative known to me which operates on the same principle as the Bible and it does so, like the Bible, in the interests of *reality*. We think we have grasped who Saint-Loup is, only to discover a few pages later that we were wrong. However, a thousand pages after that we learn that we were right the first time, and there is always the likelihood that a few pages on this verdict too will be overturned. In other words, in Proust as in the Bible, narrative is a means of showing us *how things are* rather than of making us feel better. The openness of the Hebrew Bible, like that of *A la recherche*, is hard to take. It requires a willingness to stay with uncertainty and with what we will often feel to be an unfair world; but that, after all, is what is required of all men and women *in* the Hebrew Bible, and it is what is required of the nation of Israel.

Of course there are places in the Hebrew Bible where such openness is missing, where we are assured that good will triumph and evil be destroyed; that God's world is a just and relatively simple one. But this tends to be in the prophetic books and in some of the Psalms, and in the work of the Chronicler. What has always been conceived as the centre of the Hebrew Bible, the Torah (Pentateuch), and the books of Judges and Samuel, are nearly always 'open' in the ways I have been describing.

But what of the Christian Bible? It would seem at first sight to be working with principles directly opposed to those of the Hebrew Bible. Modern critics like Northrop Frye and Frank Kermode have in fact argued for the Christian Bible as a supreme example of closure.[6] It begins with Creation and ends with Revelation. And the Book of Revelation ends with an injunction not to add or subtract a word from what has been written. Jesus saw himself and was seen by the Evangelists and the writers of the Epistles as the capstone of the arch, that which

6 Northrop Frye, *Anatomy of Criticism*, Princeton, NJ, 1957; *The Great Code*, New York, 1982; Frank Kermode, *The Genesis of Secrecy*, London, 1979; *The Sense of an Ending*, New York, 1967.

binds both parts together and gives meaning to what came before. The notion of *figura*, so central to the theology and art of the Middle Ages, the idea that what was shadow in the Old Testament becomes reality in the New Testament, was already part of Jesus's message to his disciples: 'For as Jonas was three days and three nights in the whale's belly; so shall the Son of Man be three days and three nights in the heart of the earth' (Mat. 12:40). This meant that where before there was no way of standing outside time and space and grasping the essential story of mankind, now there is such a way: belief in Jesus Christ the Son of God. Armed with such belief Christians could now claim to understand both themselves and the universe, both the past and the future.

This was an extremely powerful message. Meaning is suddenly introduced where before there were only injunctions, certainty where before there was only the ambiguity and uncertainty of human life. A prophet might exhort, but who was to say that he was right? The exodus from Egypt might be celebrated at Passover, but how exactly did that impinge upon the present? Now, however, certainty and meaning were to hand for those who had eyes to see. A fine example of the power of this message is to be found in the episode of the Ethiopian eunuch in Acts 8. 'A man of great authority', he is sitting in his chariot reading 'Esaias the prophet', that is, Isaiah:

> Then the Spirit said unto Philip, Go near, and join thyself to this chariot. And Philip ran thither to him, and heard him read the prophet Esaias, and said, Understandest thou what thou readest? And he said, How can I, except some man should guide me? And he desired Philip that he would come up and sit with him. The place of the scripture which he read was this, He was led as a sheep to the slaughter; and like a lamb dumb before his shearer, so opened he not his mouth... And the eunuch... said, I pray thee, of whom speaketh the prophet? Of himself, or of some other man?

Then Philip opened his mouth, and began at the same scripture, and preached unto him Jesus. And as they went on their way they came unto a certain water; and the eunuch said, See, here is water; what doth hinder me to be baptized? And Philip said, If thou believest with all thine heart, thou mayest. And he answered and said, I believe that Jesus Christ is the Son of God. And he commanded the chariot to stand still: and they went down both into the water, both Philip and the eunuch; and he baptized him. (Acts 8:29–38)

If that were the norm non-Christian readers would have the right to feel disappointed. But of course it is not. The books of the New Testament, and the Gospels in particular, while in some ways flying in the face of everything the Hebrew Bible stood for, are in other ways deeply imbued with its spirit, and, as the makers of the Christian canon recognised, form a continuum with it. The kind of openness I have been exploring in the Hebrew Bible is there at the heart of the New Testament. I want to end by looking at two great examples of what we might call the real biblical mode of narration, the mode of openness, in the New Testament.

The Bible, as I have said, is above all a realistic book. In *The Book of God*[7] I described the pattern followed by many of the lives of the key figures in scripture as starting out as fairy-tale and then at some point encountering a shattering reality. It happens with Adam, born in the Garden of Eden, growing up immortal, then (as he would see it) only transgressing momentarily and mildly, but finding suddenly that he has been exiled forever and forced into a different and harsher life and with the prospect of death always before him; it happens to Jacob, who gets his own way until the day he wakes up and finds he has

7   New Haven and London, 1987, pp.193–4.

slaved for seven years not for his beloved Rachel but for her plain sister Leah; it happens to David, who has led a charmed life from the moment he emerged as a young shepherd boy and defeated the giant Goliath until the death of Saul and his assumption of the kingship, who one day sees a woman he desires, sends for her, sleeps with her, and suddenly his whole life turns tragic: he finds himself committing not just adultery but murder by proxy, and there follow the death of his child, then the death of a grown son after he has raped his sister, and finally the death of his favourite son Absalom in an ill-fated rebellion against his father. And it happens to Jesus:

> Then cometh Jesus with them unto a place called Gethsemane, and saith unto the disciples, Sit ye here, while I go and pray yonder. And he took with him Peter and the two sons of Zebedee, and began to be sorrowful and very heavy. Then saith he unto them, My soul is exceeding sorrowful, even unto death; tarry ye here, and watch with me. And he went a little further, and fell on his face, and prayed, saying, O my Father, if it be possible, let this cup pass from me; nevertheless not as I will, but as thou wilt. And he cometh unto the disciples, and findeth them asleep... (Mat. 26:36–40; cf. Mark 14:32–7)

This is Matthew. Jesus, who seems to have been aware of his destiny at least since his baptism, and who is, of all the figures in the Bible (for obvious reasons) the one who seems most sure of himself, is suddenly 'very sorrowful and very heavy' (*lupeisthai kai ademonein*) (in Mark he is described as 'sore amazed' (*ekthambeisthai*) and 'very heavy'. He confesses his anguish to his most trusted disciples, but then goes forward alone to commune with God. And for the first time he begs to be released from his calling, just as Moses and many of the prophets had begged. Even as he says this, though, he accepts that the world may have to go on in ways that conflict with his own wishes: 'O my Father, if it be possible let this cup pass from me; nevertheless, not as I will but as thou wilt.' Nineteen words in the Greek and then it is all over. God does not answer, as he does Moses or Isaiah, but for the moment the crisis is past. Yet, we realise, even Jesus had to learn Freud's harsh lesson that 'what is painful may nonetheless be true' (*Auch das schmerzliche kann wahr sein*), a lesson we all keep hoping we never have to learn.

John leaves the episode out altogether, and one can see why: his Jesus could never entertain any doubts, could never find his own desires at odds with what must be. Luke, on the other hand, elaborates: Jesus prays to God to 'remove this cup from me':

> And there appeared an angel unto him from heaven, strengthening him. And being in an agony he prayed more earnestly: and his sweat was as it were great drops of blood falling down to the ground... (Luke 22:43–4)

This is a disaster. Luke introduces the angel to reassure, to make us feel that God is in control all the time; then he adds the drops of sweat to crank up the mood. The result is the opposite of what he wanted: the intensity of Mark and Matthew's narrative vanishes and we are left with a scene from a bad play.

The power of Matthew's narrative stems from the combination of two elements we have already seen at play in the Hebrew Bible: the deadpan of narration, its refusal to comment on the action from some position outside and above it; and (what follows from this), its depiction of man as a being existing in time, its refusal of teleology. This I have called 'openness'. It is open because we are forced, as we read, to experience Jesus's anguish, his sense that what he desires and what has to be are not one and the same, and his sense that he does not know how things will turn out. Nevertheless, after a moment, he accepts things as they are and must be. But that acceptance would have been a sham had Jesus (and we) had the assurance that all would, in the end, turn out for the best. This is what I mean by openness; and only out of that openness can Jesus's remarkable acceptance be grasped for what it is: a gesture of trust. Luke does what we have seen Augustine and the midrashim do with the Old Testament narratives: he takes us to some vantage point from which we can look down, reassured that all is for the best, that there is a meaning in the world after all, and we can know it. Matthew's narrative denies us that, it remains open to the end and therefore demonstrates what trust *means*.

There is of course one more moment in the Gospels when this clash between the deep desire of the individual not to suffer and 'what must be' come into conflict. And there again the different ways in which the Evangelists treat the scene are most revealing. Here is how Mark and Matthew give it to us:

> And about the ninth hour Jesus cried with a loud voice, saying, Eli, Eli, lama sabachthani? that is to say, My God, My God, why hast thou forsaken me?... Jesus, when he had cried again with a loud voice, yielded up the ghost. (Mat. 27:46,50; cf. Mark 15:34,37)

And here is Luke:

> And it was about the sixth hour, and there was a darkness over all the earth until the ninth hour. And the sun was darkened, and the veil of the temple was rent in the midst. And when Jesus had cried with a loud voice, he said, Father, into thy hands I commend my spirit: and having said thus, he gave up the ghost. (Luke 23:44–6)

As with Luke's account of Gethsemane, nature itself takes part in the event, thus assuring us it has a cosmic meaning; Jesus is allowed to 'cry', but the substance of what he says is elided, presumably as being too shocking and negative. Instead, when Jesus is given speech, it is pious and reassuring: 'Father, into thy hands I commend my spirit.' John too removes the human tension, as we might expect, and he closes the scene with Jesus himself pointing us to its meaning: 'When Jesus therefore had received the vinegar, he said, It is finished: and he bowed his head, and gave up the ghost' (John 19:30).

One can see the problem for the Evangelists. Although they go on to describe the Resurrection (or, at least, the empty tomb), they cannot end Jesus's life with his despairing words. The fact that those words would have been well known to all Jews, being the opening words of Psalm 22, would not have been enough to nullify the horror. For Jesus seems here, even more than in the Garden, to doubt. As Mark and Matthew give it to us, the moment of death is not calm, not resigned. Jesus feels at this moment that God, in whom he trusted, has abandoned him.

The scene surprises and shocks us. It does more: it opens up an abyss which no amount of reasoning, no amount of theology, can ever close. It is as though pure narrative were like a band of steel around which reason and understanding flutter hopelessly. That is how it was, we feel, that is how it is. We try desperately to make sense of it but all we can do is reiterate: that is how it was, that is how it is.

It is remarkable that a religious document should place narrative above theology, reality above consolation in this way. But the Bible does. And it does so, it seems to me, because it recognises that in the end the only thing that can truly heal and console us is not the voice of consolation but the voice of reality. That is the way the world is, it says, neither fair not equitable. What are you going to do about it? How are you going to live so as to be contented and fulfilled? And it contains no answers, only shows us various forms of response to these questions. And from Adam to Jesus it is constant in its reliance not on teaching, not on exhortation, not on reason, but on the one human form that can convey the truth that we are more than we can ever understand, the only form that is open, the form of pure narrative.

Narrative is the easiest thing in the world to read, but when so much appears to be at stake, when what we long for are answers and certainty, it is fatally easy to misread. The history of Bible interpretation could be said to be the history of such misreadings. Yet the history of religious communities, both Jewish and Christian, tells quite a different story. For what we have in the liturgies of the Jewish and Christian faiths is the living witness of the blessing conferred by placing communal reading out loud above the needs of interpretation, and the trust that such speaking out loud is a key to the good life. Few of us today belong to such communities, few of us still partake of the liturgy in this way. But all of us can purchase a Bible and simply start to read.

2. Vibrant Spaces

in memory of Robert Carroll

IN HIS GREAT ESSAY ON READING, 'Journées de lecture',[1] which he wrote as an introduction to his translation of Ruskin's own meditation on reading, *Sesame and Lilies*, Proust makes a number of absolutely fundamental points which have, alas, not been taken on board by subsequent professional readers, that is, by critics and scholars. Every page of the essay, even the asides and subsequent insertions, bristles with observations which, when we fully grasp them, seem both obvious and revolutionary. Early on, for example, he remarks:

> I have to admit that a certain use of the imperfect indicative — that cruel tense which portrays life to us as something at once ephemeral and passive, which, in the very act of retracing our actions, reduces them to an illusion, annihilating them in the past without leaving us, unlike the perfect tense, with the consolation of activity — has remained for me an inexhaustible source of mysterious sadness. Still today I can have been thinking calmly about death for hours; I need only open a volume of Sainte-Beuve's *Lundis* and light, for example, on this sentence of Lamartine's (it concerns Mme d'Albany): 'Nothing about her at that time recalled (*rappelait*)... She was (*c'était*) a small woman... etc.' to feel myself at once invaded by a profound melancholy. (57–8)

1 Translated as *On Reading* by John Sturrock, London, 1994.

As with so many passages of *A la recherche*, this strikes the reader as both slightly comic and, when we think about it, absolutely true. Long before Sartre and Barthes, Proust grasped that all narrative has a hold on us, and that the nature of that hold depends on *how* something is narrated much more than on *what* is narrated. Late in his life he would begin his essay in defence of Flaubert,[2] an author he admits he does not much care for, but whom he feels called on to defend against his academic detractors, by making a similar claim:

> I was astounded, I have to admit, to see treated as one who has few literary gifts a man who, by the entirely original and personal use he has made of the *passé défini*, of the *passé indéfini*, of the present participle, of certain pronouns and prepositions, has renewed our vision of things almost as much as Kant, with his categories and his theories of knowledge and the reality of the external world.[3]

Why does thinking about death leave us completely unaffected, while the reading of a narrative which is couched in the imperfect causes us the most profound melancholy? Why is Flaubert's work on syntax and grammar the equivalent of Kant's philosophical revolution? In what sense can we say that it has 'renewed our vision of things'? *A la recherche* explores these questions within the context of life as a whole, not just syntax and grammar. Its central theme is the way external events can shock us into a recognition of how things are, which even the most concentrated thinking will fail to do. Marcel has grown tired of life with Albertine and decides to end their relationship. He comes home determined to tell her that their affair has come to an end and that she should leave his house for ever, only to find

2 'A propos du "style" de Flaubert', in *Contre Sainte-Beuve*, ed. Pierre Clarac, Paris, 1971, pp.586–600.
3 *Ibid.*, p.586; translations are my own.

that she has already left. The shock turns his life and feelings upside down. *Now* he recognises that he cannot let her go, that she means more to him than anything else in his life, and that his earlier thoughts were completely beside the point, predicated as they were on the fact that he knew Albertine was safely his. But once that fact has been blown away by her departure it is as though his very body had at last understood something which had been hidden from it before, or as though his body had been given voice when before only his mind had spoken. Or, again, Marcel's grandmother dies. He grieves for her, mourns her, and slowly recovers. Then one day, years later, he bends down to tie his shoelace and it is as if his grandmother, who used to perform the task for him when he was a child, had been buried in the folds of his body, and was now suddenly resurrected. The violent sense of her presence, of her *livingness*, shakes him to the core, and it brings with it the equally powerful sensation of her death, of the fact that she is no more. Suddenly, unexpectedly, he is racked by an agony greater than any he had ever imagined.

In precisely this way the use of a tense in a book we are reading, or of a preposition or conjunction, seems to force upon us truths we had hitherto protected ourselves from, or which we could never have experienced if left to our own thoughts. That is why, Proust goes on in his wonderful essay on reading, great writers prefer ancient books, 'the classics', to those of their contemporaries. For ancient books open up for us vanished worlds; they not only possess the beauty which their creator endowed them with,

> they receive another beauty, more affecting still, from the fact that their substance, I mean the language in which they were written, is like a mirror of life. Something of the happiness one feels when walking in a town like Beaune, which has preserved intact its fifteenth-century hospice, with its well, its wash-house, the painted panel of its

27

> wooden ceiling, the tall gables of its roof broken by
> dormer windows

in the midst of the busy modern town, a fragment of a past that
has disappeared but is here, miraculously, still present. So
ancient works of literature contain 'all the lovely forms of
language that no longer exist, the persisting traces of the past
that nothing in the present resembles, and whose colours time,
as it passed over them, has been able only further to enhance'
(52–3). That is why no good writer is satisfied with anthologies, with *morceaux choisis*, as the French say. For anthologies give
us what we know and expect, they are like Marcel thinking that
he would feel happier without Albertine, thinking that he has
come to terms with his grandmother's death. But reading the
entire works of ancient authors, attuning our ears to their way
of thinking and speaking, we are given entry into worlds which,
but for these writers and their works, would have been lost
forever; we are made to leave the prison-house of ourselves and
are touched by the world.

But, Proust goes on, 'it is not the sentences alone that trace
out for us the forms of the ancient soul. Between the sentences
– and I have in mind,' he says, 'those very ancient books that
were originally recited – in the interval separating them, there
is still contained,' today, if we are prepared to listen, the silence
of centuries long gone:

> Often in Saint Luke's Gospel, meeting with the colons that
> interrupt it before each of the almost canticle-like passages
> with which it is strewn, I have heard the silence of the
> worshipper who had just ceased reading it out loud in
> order to intone the verses following like a psalm that
> reminded him of the more ancient psalms in the Bible.
> (53–4)

In those pauses two thousand years are, as it were, made palpable
to us, just as, he goes on, in the Piazzetta in Venice the two

ancient columns, brought from far away so long ago, alert the modern visitor to the way Time erupts into the present.

Many years later, at the very end of his great novel, Proust is clearly still thinking of those two dots which have, by an easy imagistic transition, given way to those two columns, when he writes of the way human beings exist in time, like a man who walks on stilts and whose two long legs reach down into the depths of the past. Indeed, the entire essay on reading can be seen, formally and thematically, as a model and blueprint for the novel to come.

But also, though he does not pursue it, Proust's intuition here about the Bible is, as so often with this wonderful reader, absolutely right. More than any other ancient book, the Bible depends on pauses, on the space and silence between phrases, a space and a silence which are alive, as Proust grasped, and which I want to call 'vibrant'.

That is not all. Though the way the Bible proceeds, its use of tenses and conjunctions, is quite as original as Flaubert's, what is really extraordinary about the Bible is that one of its central themes, if not *the* central theme, concerns the nature of pauses, of 'in between'. In what follows I want to try and tease out some of the implications of this and, by so doing, to sketch in some of the key elements of what is a unique attitude to and conception of space.

Though Proust, in a way typical of assimilated Jews at the end of the nineteenth century, talks only about the New Testament, what he has to say is particularly illuminating about the Hebrew Bible. For one of the most striking things about biblical Hebrew is its use of parataxis. Though Hebrew has a number of conjunctions, the biblical authors nearly always opt for the simple 'and', *wa*. '*And* Boaz took Ruth *and* she was his wife *and* he went in unto her *and* the Lord gave her conception *and* she bore a son'

(Ruth, 4:13). The English Authorised Version (AV) is on the whole faithful to such constructions, and refuses to subordinate. That is in large part why it is such a great and distinctive translation. But the desire to subordinate in our Western culture, profoundly influenced as it is by Latin, is so powerful, that in passages like the above even the AV translators succumb: '*So* Boaz took Ruth, *and* she was his wife; *and when* he went in unto her, the Lord gave her conception, *and* she bare a son.' It is the same with Luther: '*Also* nahm Boas die Ruth, *dass* Sie sein Weib ward. *Und da* er bei ihr lag, gab ihr der Herr, *dass* Sie Schwanger ward, *und* gebar einen Sohn.' Modern translations are even more prone to this, under the mistaken impression that modern readers want something that runs smoothly and in the manner to which they are accustomed. Thus the Jerusalem Bible has: '*So* Boaz took Ruth *and* she became his wife. *And when* they came together, Yahweh made her conceive *and* she bore a son.' Simple 'and' is used five times in the Hebrew, twice only in the three translations. But it isn't just a question of numbers. In the Hebrew each phrase is separate and of equal weight: Boaz took Ruth; Boaz went in unto her; the Lord gave her conception; she bore a son. As Proust would say, the space between the phrases is an important part of the meaning; to introduce temporal markers such as 'when' or '*da*' is to compress time, when what the Bible does is to keep it flowing evenly and smoothly; and to stress causality where the Bible does not. The effect of course is cumulative, and an isolated verse cannot give an adequate sense of what the consistent use of *wa* does for the Hebrew. But in some cases meaning is directly involved. In my book on the Bible[4] I looked at another passage where translation away from *wa* has rather important implications for interpretation. This is the passage which concludes the episode of David dancing before the ark and being rebuked by his wife Michal. The final

---

4 *The Book of God*, New Haven and London, 1987, pp.22–3.

sentence reads, literally: '*And* to Michal, daughter of Saul, there was not to her a child till the day of her death.' The AV, however, reads: '*Therefore* Michal the daughter of Saul had no child unto the day of her death'(2 Sam. 6:23). (Luther, for some reason, has '*Aber* Michal etc.') The AV translators naturally knew that Hebrew has a term for 'therefore', *al ken*, but they instinctively chose that term as a translation of *wa* since to them it was obvious that Michal's childlessness was the result of her criticism of David. But the Hebrew does not say that. It says that Michal rebuked David, *and* that she was barren till the day of her death. Whether that is the Lord's doing or not, whether there is a connection between the two or not, is left to us to decide.

I don't say that the Hebrew is deliberately ambiguous. I say that the greater precision of modern languages, especially Latin-derived languages, may come at a cost; the wise haziness is replaced by a false precision.

That 'wise haziness' is, as this example has suggested, bound up with the effect of the insistent parataxis: elements are laid side by side, and a whole is built up which is more than the sum of its parts, but which does not rush towards conclusion or fit all the parts into one large box on which the lid may eventually be placed. Christians, who see the Old Testament as constantly prefiguring the New, as *leading up to* the Gospels and Revelation, are more prone than others to ignore the spaces between; but if we would get close to the Hebrew Scriptures we must be more respectful.

Of course this is not just a matter of being alert to syntax. For in this book, as in Flaubert, syntax reflects thematics. This is most obvious at the very beginning:

> In the beginning God created the heaven *and* the earth. *And* the earth was without form, *and* void; *and* darkness was upon the face of the deep. *And* the Spirit of God moved upon the face of the waters. *And* God said, Let there be

light: *and* there was light: *And* God saw the light, that it was good: *and* God divided the light from the darkness. *And* God called the light Day, *and* the darkness he called Night. *And* the evening *and* the morning were the first day. *And* God said... (Gen. 1:1–6)

The verses roll on, as day is added to day, and element of creation to element of creation, each separated from the other by *wa*; and it is right that they should be so separated, since the act of creation is an act both of addition and of separation: 'And God divided the light from the darkness'; 'And God said, Let there be a firmament in the midst of the waters, and let it divide the waters from the waters'; 'And God said, Let there be lights in the firmament of the heaven to divide the day from the night.' (1:4, 6, 14) At first the earth was *tohu vavohu*, 'without form and void', a chaos lacking boundaries. Chapter 1 of Genesis shows how this is transformed into the orderly cosmos we know today.[5]

For Christians the creation ends on the sixth day: '*And* God saw every thing that he had made, *and*, behold, it was very good. *And* the evening and the morning were the sixth day.' That is where, in the Middle Ages, the Christian scholars placed the end of the first chapter. But in the Jewish tradition the section does not end till 2:3. Why? What is it that follows? First of all, a recapitulation: 'Thus [actually, another *wa*, *and*] the heavens *and* the earth were finished, *and* all the host of them. *And* on the seventh day God ended his work which he had made; *and* he rested on the seventh day from all his work which he had made. *And* God blessed the seventh day, *and* sanctified it; because that in it he had rested from all his work which God created *and*

5 Mary Douglas long ago pointed out that the key to Leviticus is the act of separation, the making of distinctions. See *Purity and Danger*, Harmondsworth, 1966.

made.' On the seventh day God ended his work, and he rested. But that is not all. On the fifth day God had created the creatures of the sea and air and blessed them; on the sixth day he had created man and woman, and blessed them; on the seventh he creates the Sabbath and not only blesses it but sanctifies it (*yebarek wayekadesh*). The Sabbath, the day of rest, the day of pause in the onward rush of life, is that which divides week from week, but it is also, in a sense, the embodiment of the ubiquitous *wa*. It is as though that which underlay the rhythm of the preceding six days of creation had been brought out into the open, given a place and a name, and blessed; the day of rest, of pause, we are made to understand, is not simply a gap, a hiatus; it is a holy thing, the holiest of all creation.

The Hebrew God is a God who makes it a sacred injunction to pause, to rest. This has profound ethical implications. This is a God who wants to stop man thoughtlessly or selfishly marching across space as though it weren't there. As the remainder of the Hebrew Bible will make clear, *when you stop*, not *how you go on*,[6] shows what you are and where you belong. This of course is a very different attitude to life from that which prevails in the West today, and one it is rather difficult for us to come to terms with. Nevertheless, the Bible will help us do so.

God reserves his most severe punishments for those who try to breach boundaries, to annihilate space. We see this happening in the very next chapters, Genesis 2–3. Adam, told that he must keep his distance from the tree of the knowledge of good and evil, breaches that injunction. It is as though he tries to attain the godhead mechanically – rather as Proust said

6 I owe this lapidary formulation to Bernard Harrison, in conversation.

the bad reader is the one who imagines the books in the library are jars of honey from which he can feed at will and in passivity, instead of recognising that books can only lead us to a threshold, after which it is up to us – and is punished for it by being expelled from the sacred space of the Garden of Eden. A short while later, in the episode of the Tower of Babel, the whole of mankind is in similar breach of sacred space, again trying mechanically to reach up to God instead of talking to Him, and as a result is scattered over the face of the earth.

The breaching of established boundaries or, on the contrary, the acceptance of them, is in fact the key to distinguishing acts which are pleasing to God or otherwise. Saul, for example, is someone who has no sense of where the boundaries are, and in the end he is driven to calling up a mere image to seek its help, a final proof of his refusal to walk in God's way; while David, for all his faults, seems to have an instinctive sense of where boundaries lie. And we could go on multiplying examples. Fundamentally, 'walking in God's way', which means keeping the commandments, but also being mindful of space and its vibrancy, is seen to be the only true path, and those who do not do so lay themselves open to chaos and destruction.

A number of important consequences for interpretation and reading flow from this. First of all there is the issue of mysticism and the Bible. Various mystical texts, Gnostic or otherwise, have grown up round both the Hebrew and the Christian Bibles. Commentators, both ancient and modern, have argued that these texts give us the hidden truth of the Bible, which those who read only superficially will miss. But if I am right and the central injunction of the Bible is to respect boundaries, then it is perfectly easy to understand why the central tradition of commentary, in both the Hebrew and the Christian traditions, is wary of such texts, for what they do is to deny boundaries, to claim to lead us to a hidden truth which we can, if we are initiated, possess. This runs counter, I would suggest, to the central thrust of the Bible as we have it, and Gnostics and cabbalists, as well as their modern champions, from crazed interpreters of Genesis and Revelation to sober scholars such as Elaine Pagels and Margaret Barker, are not so much finally revealing the hidden truth of the Bible as branding themselves the descendants of the men of Babel and the wretched Saul.[7]

Secondly there is the question of the sacred geography of the Bible. Of course the geography of the region resonates symbolically throughout this book: Egypt, the place of bondage, versus the mountain of Sinai, the place of freedom in willing servitude; Sinai and the desert versus Zion and the city; Red Sea and Jordan; Babel and Babylon; and so on. A structural anthropologist such as Mary Douglas[8] has shown how the sacred mountain of Sinai is mirrored not just in the sacred space of the tabernacle, but also in the sacred space of the body of the sacrificial animal and, finally, even in the structure of the Book of Leviticus itself. She has also shown, convincingly in my view, how the disposition of the twelve tribes round the mountain, as described in the Book of Numbers, is itself profoundly symbolic.[9] But my criticism of this kind of work when applied to the Bible, rests on the fact that, while correctly stressing spatial oppositions, it ignores the temporal dimension, that it presents us with static and, as it were, timeless oppositions. But the Bible is a narrative, it moves forward in time from creation to slavery in Egypt to the wandering in the desert to the establishment and disintegration of the state. At each stage memory of the past is a crucial factor. Memory as nostalgia, whether for a lost paradise or the pleasures of Egypt, is to be condemned. But memory as the recalling of God's saving acts is central to

7 Elaine Pagels, *The Gnostic Gospels*, New York, 1979; Margaret Barker, *The Revelation of Jesus Christ*, London, 2000.
8 Mary Douglas, *Leviticus as Literature*, Oxford, 1999.
9 *In the Wilderness*, Sheffield, 1993.

the survival of the people. To recall is to recognise that we are creatures who exist in time, but that we are not simply driven by time; recalling is in fact an instance of the Sabbath motif, the motif of pause and the acceptance of distance, except that in this case it is distance in time, not space.

Recalling, in the Hebrew Bible, is a question of speaking out loud and listening to what is spoken. In that sense the person who listens is like the reader, who also moves forward in time, but pauses, recalls, repeats. In fact the rhythm of the creation of the world and the rhythm of the wandering of the Israelites and their eventual arrival in a (temporary) homeland, is mirrored in the very rhythm of reading – if only we obey Proust's injunction and listen as we read, allow an alien and distant world to penetrate our senses.

So far I have drawn attention to the pausal or paratactic element in biblical syntax; to the moral dimension of the institution of the Sabbath; and to how an awareness of this can keep us from some frequent errors of reading. I want now to look a little more closely at the way space is made vibrant in the course of biblical narratives. I will look at three examples, but before I do so I myself want to pause and ask you to listen to a seaman's description of the element in which he lives and works:

Seen from the cliffs, the sea might have looked as evenly arranged as the strings on a harp – the lines of white-caps running parallel at intervals of sixty feet or so. Seen from the wheel of a small boat, it presented quite a different aspect. Each wave in the train carried a multitude of smaller deformities – nascent waves bulging, heaping, trying to break as they rode the back of the senior waves in the system. Many-angled, climbing every which way, they turned each square yard of water into an unruly brew of shifting planes and collapsing hillocks. Wherever the wind found an exposed surface, it raised tiny wrinkles of waves awaiting birth.

This, from Jonathan Raban's *Passage to Juneau: A Sea and Its Meanings*,[10] provides the best description I know of one aspect of the Hebrew Scriptures: the broad expanse of scripture we look down on from above, when we are merely thinking about it or remembering it, turns, on closer inspection, into myriads of waves, each slightly different from the others. Let us look closely at three such 'waves'.

The first is in stark contrast to the stately march of Genesis 1–2:3. This is 2 Samuel 18–19, the narrative of David's discovery of the death in battle of his beloved son Absalom. We learn first of David's injunction to the commander of his forces, Abner, not to harm 'the lad' – an ironic description of Absalom, given that he is the leader and instigator of a rebellion against David – but of course, in spite of everything, that is still David's view of him. Then we learn of the battle in the wood and of how Absalom is caught by his long hair – another irony, given his pride in his hair – in the branches of a tree and how Abner 'took three darts in his hand, and thrust them through the heart of Absalom, while he was yet alive in the midst of the oak' (2 Sam. 18:24). We then move to David, waiting for news of the outcome of the battle: 'And David sat between the two gates: and the watchman went up to the roof over the gate unto the wall, and lifted up his eyes and looked, and behold a man running alone' (24).

The watchman tells the king: 'And the king said, If he be alone, there is tidings in his mouth. And he came apace, and drew near'(25). Now the watchman sees another man running, and he tells the porter, who tells the king. 'And the king said,

10 Quoted in Frank Kermode, *Pleasing Myself*, London, 2001, pp.232–3.

He also bringeth tidings'(26). The watchman now is able to make out the first man, and he tells the king it seems to be Ahimaz, the son of Zadok. 'And the king said, He is a good man, and cometh with good tidings' (27). Note that we are not told how David felt, only what he said, yet we have no difficulty in realising that what for David as father is 'good tidings' may not be that for David the commander of the army which is fighting a civil war, or, of course, for the army itself. Conversely, what is 'good tidings' for the commander may not be that for the father. The next verse has Ahimaz coming up to within shouting distance of the waiting king:

> And Ahimaaz called, and said unto the king, All is well. And he fell down to the earth upon his face before the king and said, Blessed be the Lord thy God, which hath delivered up the men that lifted up their hand against my lord the king. And the king said, Is the young man Absalom safe?' (28–9)

The difference between the two points of view, the public and the personal, is now out in the open. The king only wants to know if his son is safe, the messenger, perhaps knowing that Absalom has been killed out of political and military necessity, but also knowing how the king feels, does not directly answer the question. The knowledge, which we and Ahimaz have, of how things have turned out for Absalom, has not yet become David's knowledge: the space between the two is vibrant with tension, both for the reader, who waits to see how David will react to the news and what effect this will have on the army, and for David, whose question has not yet been answered. The narrative will maintain this for a short while longer:

> And Ahimaaz answered, When Joab sent the king's servant... I saw a great tumult, but [wa again] I knew not what it was. And the king said unto him, Turn aside, and stand there. And he turned aside, and stood still. (29–30)

Now the second messenger comes running up:

> And, behold, Cushi came; and Cushi said, Tidings, my
> lord the King: for the Lord hath avenged thee this day of
> all them that rose up against thee. And the king said unto
> Cushi, Is the young man Absalom safe? And Cushi
> answered, The enemies of my lord the king, and all that
> rise against thee to do thee hurt, be as that young man is.
> And the king was much moved, and went up to the
> chamber over the gate, and wept: and as he went, thus he
> said, O my son Absalom, my son, my son Absalom! would
> God I had died for thee, O Absalom, my son my son! (31–3)

David is the great lamenter of the Bible, more so even than
Jeremiah. The first part of his life ends with the defeat of Saul
and Jonathan, leaving him in sole possession of the Kingdom,
and he greets their death with a formal lament of great beauty,
but one which makes it impossible to decide if he is really moved
or not. He had loved Jonathan, and he had had a love–hate relationship with Saul, his father-in-law, but their deaths are also
to his advantage. Now too the death of the leader of the revolt
leaves him once again in complete control, but this time there
is no doubting the nature of his feelings.

For the reader, the time it takes for the news to arrive and to
enter David's consciousness is made palpable. We are both
inside David and outside him, and both the time and the space
traversed is brought fully alive by the narrative: the distance
between Joab and David, between the war zone and the king's
residence, between ignorance and knowledge, is made vibrant
by the constant deferral of meaning. In the end Absalom's death
is made all the more unbearable by its never being explicitly
mentioned. We only get the messenger's circumlocution, which
is partly perhaps common practice on the part of a courtier and
partly his way of protecting himself from the news he brings;
and David's final recognition that what he had feared all along

has come to pass. His outburst is both release and acknowledgement, and all the more moving for being so brief.

The second 'wave' I want to examine briefly is one which encompasses one of the best-known episodes in the Bible, Moses' first encounter with God, in Exodus 3. At the end of Chapter 2 the Israelites, oppressed in Egypt by a new and cruel Pharaoh, set up a groan, 'and they cried, and their cry came up unto God by reason of the bondage' (Exod. 2:23). 'And God heard their groaning,' we are told, 'and God remembered his covenant with Abraham, with Isaac, and with Jacob' (24).

The Israelites may be the chosen people, but it is they who have to initiate events. It is because they cry unto God that he responds. He 'remembers' his covenant with their fathers, 'And God looked upon the children of Israel, and God had respect unto them' (25). At this point we switch from Egypt and from God to Moses, in a specific space: 'Now Moses kept the flock of Jethro his father in law, the priest of Midian: and he led the flock to the backside of the desert (*ahar hamidbar*), and came to the mountain of God, even to Horeb' (3:1). Why did Moses lead the flock to just this place? Did God have a hand in it? Was it just chance? We are not told. Only that now the angel of the Lord appears to Moses 'in a flame of fire out of the midst of a bush: and he looked, and behold, the bush burned with fire, and the bush was not consumed' (2). That phrase, 'and behold', which we have met before, is the Bible's way of placing us at the point of view of the beholder – but again, note the effect of this ancient way of putting it: the simple phrase puts us in a particular position and establishes the act of looking, the act of bridging a gap through sight, as the key fact. Moses looks, Moses sees, and now Moses speaks – to himself, but nevertheless, it is an act of speech, it is an *act*: 'And Moses said, I will now turn aside, and see this great sight, why the bush is not burned' (3). So once again the encounter requires two partners: God and man. God makes the bush burn, but the man is roused to try and understand what is being shown him: 'And when the Lord saw that he turned aside to see, God called unto him out of the midst of the bush, and said, Moses, Moses. And he said, Here am I.' Encounter, the making vibrant of the space between two beings, depends upon acknowledgement. God acknowledges Moses, 'calls' him, utters his name, twice, and Moses in turn acknowledges the presence of Another by saying: *hineni*, 'here, present before you in all my openness, am I.' At this point God establishes the need for a more formal space between them: 'And he said, Draw not nigh hither: put off thy shoes from off thy feet, for the place whereon thou standest is holy ground'(5). God then reveals himself as the God of the fathers, the God of Abraham, Isaac and Jacob. On hearing this Moses covers his face, 'for he was afraid to look upon God' (6). The conversation that follows, in which God promises that he 'will be with' Moses and gives his name as 'I will be that I will be', is an encounter that makes space even more vibrant, for it is no longer crossed by Moses' sight, which is a passive thing, but by words.[11] And since that encounter is *relayed to us* by words, the words of this book we are reading, we too experience it in its fullness.

The Bible is not unique in its way of making space sacred. Sophocles' *Oedipus at Colonus* is also about an encounter of man and God in a sacred space, and the space is created for us all the more powerfully in that the man we see on stage is blind.[12] But it is worth pointing out that in Sophocles the space was sacred before Oedipus arrived, and will go on being so after he has gone. His death, so beautiful and mysterious, merely reinforces its sacred status. In the Bible, on the other hand, though the

---

11 Actually, sight is at once both more passive and more a matter of the will than hearing: the eyes have lids, which we can close at will, unlike the ears.

12 See my discussion in Gabriel Josipovici, *Touch*, New Haven and London, 1996, pp.52–7.

encounter takes place somewhere at the foot of Mount Horeb, the place is only made sacred temporarily, for the duration of the encounter, *by* the encounter. That is why the later Christian sacralisation of the space, the erection of the 'burning bush' as an object of pilgrimage and worship (it is now in the confines of the monastery of Saint Catherine at the foot of Gebel Musa, the mountain of Moses) is completely misguided (and, one might add, why Jewish fundamentalist claims to portions of the ancient land of Israel are equally, and much more tragically, misguided).

My last example is, if anything, even better known than this. But there is much that is frequently overlooked even in discussion of the best-known biblical episodes, and it may be worth while to examine this from the point of view adopted here.

I am thinking of the episode of Jacob wrestling with the angel (Genesis 32). The scene is quickly set: hearing of the approach of Esau, the brother he had tricked all those years before, and who is advancing with a great force to meet him, Jacob sends his camels, sheep and cattle, along with the rest of his family over the brook Jabbok to meet Esau, while he himself stays behind.[13] As always, the action moves swiftly: 'And he took them, and sent them over the brook, and sent over that he had. And Jacob was left alone; and there wrestled a man with him until the breaking of the day' (23–4). The next eight verses recount what happened. But it is never explained why 'the man' wrestled with him, or whether Jacob was prepared for this or not. Unlike the encounter of Moses and God in Exodus 3, here distance appears to be immediately abolished; instead of talking, the two wrestle. Yet out of the wrestling, which seems

13 Barthes has pointed out the ambiguity of the narrative at this point: on which side of the ford is Jacob when the wrestling takes place? See Roland Barthes, 'La Lutte avec l'ange: Analyse textuelle de Genèse 32, 22–32', in *Analyse structurale et exégèse biblique*, Neuchâtel, 1971.

to result in stalemate, a dialogue does ensue: 'And when he [the angel or man, that is] saw that he prevailed not against him, he touched the hollow of his thigh; and the hollow of Jacob's thigh was out of joint, as he wrestled with him' (25). At the end of this sentence the pronouns are indeed interchangeable: wrestling in the dark, the two become indistinguishable: *behe'avku 'imo*, says the Hebrew, 'in his show of strength against him'. 'And he [the 'man' again] said, Let me go, for the day breaketh. And he said, I will not let thee go, except thou bless me'(26). The 'man' who has come upon Jacob so suddenly in the dark has enough power to inflict damage on Jacob's body, but he cannot overpower him. Indeed, it is Jacob who has him in his grip and won't let go. But dawn approaches and the 'man' has to beg Jacob to let him go, for it seems that he cannot remain there in daylight. Jacob now appears to have the upper hand, and extracts a promise from the man: I will only let you go if you bless me. 'And he [the man] said unto him, What is thy name? And he said, Jacob. And he said, Thy name shall be called no more Jacob, but Israel: for as a prince hast thou power with God and with men, and hast prevailed'(28). Jacob, Ya'akov, was the name given him at his birth, a name related both to the word *ekev*, 'heel', for Jacob came forth from the womb holding his brother's heel, and to *akav*, 'crooked', a word probably related to the other. Jacob, in other words, is what the Americans call 'a heel'. Now, says the man, you will no longer be called a heel, but the one who stood up to God. Jacob proceeds to ask the man his own name, just as Moses had asked, and, as with Moses, the answer is a kind of riddle: 'And Jacob asked him, and said, Tell me, I pray thee, thy name. And he said, Wherefore is it that thou dost ask after my name? And he blessed him there' (29). The man does not answer, but blesses Jacob, and that blessing *is* the answer: the one who fought with him is the one with the power to bless: that is his name: *the power to bless*. Man need know no more. To ask for more is to ask to cross boundaries which may not be crossed, to imagine that one can take away an essence, a 'name' instead of an epithet, a phrase which is verbal: 'I will be that I will be', 'I am the one who blesses', etc.

'And Jacob called the name of the place Peniel: for I have seen God face to face, and my life is preserved'(30). He has not actually seen God, nor has he really talked to him, as Moses will; rather, they have wrestled together and each has acquired a sense of the other which is deeper than words. The story ends: 'And as he passed over Penuel the sun rose upon him, and he halted upon his thigh' (31). He has a new name, Israel, and a new mark on his flesh: he limps. And the narrator, having pulled the camera back, so to speak, and given us a long shot of the lonely limping figure, now moves even further away, in both time and space, speaking to the reader directly and telling him about a current practice amongst the Hebrews:

> Therefore ['al ken here, for causality needs to be stressed] the children of Israel eat not of the sinew which shrank, which is upon the hollow of the thigh, unto this day: because he touched the hollow of Jacob's thigh in the sinew that shrank. (32)

His body has been altered, the God has touched him. That is not something he has *learned* from the encounter, it is the *mark* of the encounter, a mark which signifies both proximity and distance from the God. To this day, the text says, we commemorate the event, without needing to understand it – just as to this day we read the episode, without needing to go behind it and extract its meaning. Space extends into time and commemoration returns us to the initial encounter, mysterious, vibrant: the narrative of *something happening*.

These are some of the waves which make up the ocean of the text, when we get down to eye-level. In each case the reader is forced to participate by the form of the syntax, the rhythms and pauses. It is important to understand the sacred geography of the Bible, but even more important to grasp that we can only understand the space of the Bible by walking through it, in other words, by the act of reading. History and theology abound in the Bible, but why we go on reading it, as Proust understood, is because only the act of reading can lead us into its world and make us experience that world not just in our minds, but with our bodies.

3. Singing a New Song

IT IS DIFFICULT FOR US TO GRASP the sense of shock the opening of Genesis would have conveyed to its first hearers and readers. We are so familiar with its contents and cadences that it strikes us as perfectly natural, a kind of 'given'. But while the Ancient Near East was familiar with creation myths, and a number of narratives of such creations have come down to us, from Ugarit and Egypt and elsewhere, these were always in verse, and they always entailed ferocious battles between the gods, until one emerged as the supreme deity. By contrast the quiet, regulated prose of the biblical account, in which God speaks and the orderly world of light and dark, sea and land, beasts, birds and fish comes into being, is shocking in its very restraint and dignity.

This does not last, of course, but the use of prose does, and, as scholars like Cassuto and Alter have demonstrated,[1] it is not an arbitrary choice but intimately bound up with the unique Hebrew conception of a single creator God, to whom all is subservient, including the chaotic sea and even death itself, but whose relation to mankind, and in particular to his chosen people, the Israelites, is that of a loving father, protective,

---

1 Umberto Cassuto, *A Commentary on the Book of Genesis*, tr. Israel Abrahams, 2 vols., Jerusalem, 1964; Robert Alter, *The Art of Biblical Narrative*, London, 1981.

yet just; slow to anger yet tolerating no dissimulation and no evasion of responsibility.

Given this central place of prose and of simple consequential narration, the next big shock to the reader or hearer would have come in the middle of Exodus. We have had a detailed account of the slavery of the Israelites in Egypt, of the rise of Moses, of his leading the people out of Egypt and of the sudden destruction of Pharaoh's army in the Sea of Reeds, while before the Israelites the waters parted and they crossed over as on dry land:

> And Israel saw that great work which the Lord did upon the Egyptians: and the people feared the Lord, and believed the Lord, and his servant Moses. Then sang Moses and the children of Israel this song unto the Lord, and spake, saying, I will sing unto the Lord, for he hath triumphed gloriously: the horse and his rider hath he thrown into the sea [*ashir le'adonai ki ga'oh ga'ah sus verokeku ramah bayam*] (Exod. 14:31–15:1)[2]

There had, it is true, been moments of poetry in the narrative up to then: the brief outburst of Lamech, the extended deathbed utterance of Jacob, blessing his sons, but *song* is something

---

2 I have used the Authorised Version (AV) throughout. Its verse numberings often differ from those of the Hebrew Bible because the superscription of Psalms is not included. So those with the Hebrew text should simply add one – i.e. Psalm 4:1 in my text is 4:2 in the Hebrew (but 1:1 in my text is 1:1 in the Hebrew since Psalm 1 has no superscription).

Scholars argue about the way the text should be laid out; the latest to join the debate is Jan Fokkelman, whose *Major Poems of the Hebrew Bible* (four volumes published so far, by Royal van Gorcum in the Netherlands) is a typically radical and impressively backed plea for a total rethinking of the lay-out of the poetry of the Bible. I have stuck to the AV, except where I have felt that Nahum Sarna presented a more satisfactory alternative (*On the Book of Psalms*, New York, 1993).

new. And it does not occur very frequently in the remainder of
the Bible. There is the Song of Deborah in Judges, and there
are formal laments, such as the lament of David over Saul and
Jonathan, which one can imagine being set to music. Poetry
takes over from prose as the main vehicle for the prophetic
utterances and for many of the *ketubim* or miscellaneous collection of pieces which make up the last portion of the Hebrew
Bible: most of Job, Lamentations, and, of course, the Psalms.
But the Book of Psalms is the only extended portion of the Bible
which consists not only of poetry, but, quite explicitly, of song.
'O sing unto the Lord a new song [*shir hadash*]: sing unto the
Lord, all the earth./Sing unto the Lord, bless his name; shew
forth his salvation from day to day./Declare his glory among
the heathen, his wonders among all the people' (96:1–3). That
is Psalm 96, and the whole collection ends with five poems
which do not simply call out to the people to sing, but *become*
that song, introduced by a word that means 'praise the Lord'
but which is also onomatopoeic: *Halleluja.* (It is significant, I
think, that there is an onomatopoeic word in classical Greek
which is derived from a kind of choric singing, the word from
which the English 'ululation' derives, but that is the word for
choric lamentation, not choric rejoicing.) And from the Psalms
themselves we learn that many musical instruments were used
to accompany at least some of them: harps, cymbals, trumpets,
and a host of instruments that remain unidentified.

Scholars have of course for a long time been arguing about
the precise *sitz im leben* of the Psalms, both the Psalms as a whole
and individual groups of them: were they pilgrim chants sung
on the way to the Temple, or were they sung within the Temple,
by the Temple choir? Was the bulk of them composed after the
exile or before? Some of them have superscriptions, such as 'A
Psalm of David, when he was in the wilderness of Judah', and
'Shiggaion [whatever that means] of David, which he sang unto
the Lord, concerning Cush, a Benjamite', but scholars agree that

these were added later, and they are of little help in locating either the authors or the place in which they were written or sung. However, I don't think it's important, in this case as in other parts of the Bible, to establish a precise *sitz im leben*. What is important, to my mind, is what it means that a great many if not all the Psalms seem to ask to be sung, and sung communally – what it means to our *understanding* of them.

The early rabbis who commented on the Bible often saw patterns in it that eluded those intent solely on discovering how factually accurate the Bible is and how it came to be written. One thing the rabbis noted was that the Psalms have, since early times, been divided into five books, to mirror, they suggested, the five books of the Torah. And one reason why Psalm 1 heads the collection is perhaps that it includes, in its second verse, the word *torah*: 'Blessed is the man that walketh not in the counsel of the ungodly, nor standeth in the way of sinners, Nor sitteth in the seat of the scornful./But his delight is in the law [*torah*] of the Lord; and in his law [*torato*] doth he meditate day and night' (Ps. 1:1–2). The whole of this short Psalm, in fact, is, like Psalm 119, the longest in the Psalter, a meditation on the virtues of studying *torah*.

Let me read it out to you. I will use the Authorised Version or King James Bible of 1611, here, as I do throughout this lecture:

Blessed is the man that walketh not in the counsel of the
ungodly,
Nor standeth in the way of sinners,
Nor sitteth in the seat of the scornful.
But his delight is in the law of the Lord;
And in his law doth he meditate day and night.
And he shall be like a tree planted by the rivers of water,
That bringeth forth his fruit in his season;
His leaf also shall not wither;
And whatsoever he doeth shall prosper.

The ungodly are not so:
    But are like the chaff which the wind driveth away.
Therefore the ungodly shall not stand in the judgement,
    Nor sinners in the congregation of the righteous.
For the Lord knoweth the way of the righteous:
    But the way of the ungodly shall perish.

As Nahum Sarna, in a splendid exposition of this Psalm, says: '[T]he study of the sacred and revered text itself constitutes a pious act, a profoundly religious experience, and is an important mode of worship.'[3] What Sarna shows, though, is that our modern conception of what 'studying a text' means falls far short of the rich experience early readers of the Bible would have taken from their encounter with it, and that this Psalm inducts us into that experience.

He begins with the first word, *ashrei*, which the AV renders as 'blessed' but which is usually translated as 'happy'. 'Although,' he says,

> the English translations imply a verbal sentence underlying the original Hebrew text, this opening phrase contains no verb at all. The Hebrew *'ashrei* is a noun in the construct state, that is, in the form it takes when joined to another noun on which it is dependent. Hence the phrase is really an exclamation meaning 'O for the happiness of that person…!' It is the discriminating judgement of an observer who expresses wonderment and admiration over another's enviable state of being.

More than this, *'ashrei* is in the plural, the inflectional form denoting intensity. This "plural of intensity", as it is called, communicates energetic focusing upon the basic idea inherent in the Hebrew root. It is the highest form of happiness that the

3 Sarna, *On the Book of Psalms*, p.29.

psalmist has in mind.' And happiness, Sarna notes, is different from pleasure.[4] Pleasure is 'an instinctive response to a particular stimulus that gratifies the senses; and it may be frivolous and illusory. By contrast, happiness is deep-rooted; it penetrates the very depths of one's being, and it is serious and enduring.'

It is because he takes delight in the *torah* of the Lord and studies it day and night, as opposed to the wicked, the sinners, the insolent, that a man is happy. But once again the English translation lets us down. The happy man is not 'studying' or 'meditating on' the first five books of Moses. For one thing, there is no mention of a 'book' of the Torah. 'Torah' here means teaching, but 'the Lord's teaching' must define, as Sarna says, 'a recognizable, established, and crystallized text that can be committed to memory and recited.' Secondly, we must rid ourselves of the notion that the activity mentioned is a purely inner one. '[T]he Hebrew verb, usually mistranslated "meditates",' Sarna points out,

> carries a decidedly oral nuance... The verbal form [of the root *h-g–h*] is used for the moaning of a dove, and the growl of a lion; it takes as its subject the mouth, the tongue, and the palate. The action of the verb obviously has an acoustical effect because the throat can be its instrument.[5]

So the happy man of our Psalm is not engaged in meditation and contemplation, but in rote learning and verbal repetition, such as we find prevalent in many ancient traditions. Our own culture finds this hard to understand, because centuries of educational theory have persuaded us that rote learning is a bad thing, but that is our loss. This form of *torah* study was, as Sarna points out, 'seen as not only an act of piety but also as a fundamental mode of worship, both it and prayer being accorded in

4 *Ibid.*, pp.29–30.
5 *Ibid.*, p.38.

rabbinic literature the designation *'avodah*, the standard term for the sacrificial system in the Temple in Jerusalem.'[6]

We can now see why the Psalm goes on to say of this happy man: 'And he shall be like a tree planted by the rivers of water, That bringeth forth his fruit in his season; his leaf also shall not wither; and whatsoever he doeth shall prosper' (Ps. 1:3). Reciting *torah* is an *activity* that *roots* him, gives him the strength to fulfil his potential, to grow into himself. By contrast the wicked 'are like the chaff which the wind driveth away'(4), taking their moment of pleasure, but without roots and without water, and so incapable of real fulfilment.

Psalm 1, then, like Psalm 119, helps fill in the human consequences of 'walking in the way of the Lord'. It shows that this is not just a matter of being good, or of doing good, but of happiness and rootedness; and it also shows what happens to those who do not do so. Nevertheless, if what we treasure in the narratives of the Hebrew Bible is that they are never merely pious, that they see the complexity and confusion of human aims, desires and motives, we have to ask whether something of that can be found in the Psalms as well. Samuel Beckett, who was as rooted in scripture as any Hebrew writer, called his only radio play *All That Fall*. The reference is to Psalm 145:14: 'The Lord upholdeth all that fall, and raiseth up all those that be bowed down.' The reference is ironic; more than that, like so much of Beckett it is bitter, a bitter denunciation of a tradition that seemingly offers hope only to dash it, for the play concerns a boy who falls from a train and is killed. Do the Psalms, then, only consist of such pious injunctions as to study *torah* day and night, or of such uplifting but clearly false statements as that the Lord upholdeth all that fall, or do they, like the narratives of the Hebrew Bible, provide, if not an answer to Beckett's anguished cry, at least a response to it?

6   *Ibid.*, p.39.

Let us return for a moment to the opening of Genesis. God speaks and an orderly world is created, a world in which each element respects its boundaries. But in the next two chapters we discover that language is a double-edged sword. First the serpent and then Adam and Eve use language to deceive, or to try to lessen their guilt. 'The woman... gave me..., and I did eat,' says Adam to God, trying to pass the buck. 'Am I my brother's keeper?' asks Cain of God in the next chapter. Language, it seems, is a slippery thing, which carries no guarantee within it of good usage. The establishment of the covenant at Sinai and the giving of laws to the Israelites provides a blueprint for the good life, but it does not stop lying, hypocrisy and deceit, as the stories in Judges, Samuel and Kings abundantly demonstrate. The Psalms too recognise the prevalence of hypocrisy and duplicity in civic life: 'The words of his mouth were smoother than butter, but war was in his heart; his words were softer than oil, yet were they drawn swords' (Ps. 55:21). 'Hide me from the secret counsel of the wicked; from the insurrection of the workers of iniquity:/Who whet their tongue like a sword, and bend their bows to shoot their arrows, even bitter words:/That they may shoot in secret at the perfect; suddenly do they shoot at him, and fear not./They encourage themselves in an evil matter; They commune of laying snares privily; they say, Who shall see them?' (Ps. 64:2–5). Are those the alternatives, then, to recite the Torah of the Lord all the days of our life, or to whet our tongue like a sword and aim our poisoned words at others?

The answer is no, there many other ways in which we use speech, and in the Psalms we can see many of those in action. In the first place there is a high, an enormously high premium, put on the simple human ability to utter words. We can see this at work in Psalm 32: 'When I kept silence, my bones waxed old through my roaring all the day long./For day and night thy hand was heavy upon me: my moisture is turned into the drought of summer. Selah./I acknowledged my sin unto thee, and mine iniquity have I not hid. I said, I will confess of my transgressions unto the Lord; and thou forgavest the iniquity of my sin. Selah' (3–5). The speaker here, like David after his sin with Bathsheba and the murder of Uriah, has tried to repress his guilt, but the more he does so the more it burdens him. At last he confesses to the Lord, and at once he is forgiven: 'Many sorrows shall be to the wicked: but he that trusteth in the Lord, mercy shall compass him about' (10).

This is fairly straightforward, though we should note that there is a psychological as well as a moral dimension to this, as the Roman Church, with its institution of Confession, well understood. But the Psalms explore this aspect of speech, of what I would like to call utterance, at an even deeper level.

'The dead praise not the Lord, neither any that go down into silence' (Ps. 115:17). On one level that is a truism: of course the dead do not praise the Lord – but what does it mean, 'neither any that go down into silence'? It could be a mere synonym for 'death', but Hebrew parallelism often works in more interesting ways, as Alter has shown,[7] the second limb enriching and even questioning the first. The Psalmist is perhaps suggesting that silence, the inability or refusal to speak, is a kind of death, a psychological death. Such a psychological death is given many metaphors in the Psalms: silence, desert, being overwhelmed by the sea. 'O God, thou art my God; early will I seek thee: my soul thirsteth for thee, my flesh longeth for thee in a dry and thirsty land, where no water is' (Ps. 63:1). 'Thou holdest mine eyes waking,' says the speaker of Psalm 77, 'I am so troubled that I cannot speak' (4). 'Save me, O God; for the waters are come in unto my soul,' cries the speaker of Psalm 69. 'I sink in deep mire, where there is no standing: I am come into deep waters, where the floods overflow me. /I am weary of my crying: my throat

---

7 Robert Alter, *The Art of Biblical Poetry*, New York, 1985, Ch. 1.

is dried: mine eyes fail while I wait for my God' (2–3). Most terrible of all perhaps is the devastatingly simple remark of the narrator of Psalm 88: 'I am shut up, and I cannot come forth' (three words in the Hebrew: *kalu velo ezeh*; 8).

The most interesting example from our point of view is the prayer or psalm in Jonah 2, which is close to Psalm 69, from which I have just quoted, and to Psalm 120:

> I cried by reason of mine affliction unto the Lord, and he heard me; out of the belly of hell cried I, and thou heardest my voice./For thou hadst cast me into the deep, in the midst of the seas; and the floods compassed me about; all thy billows and thy waves passed over me... The waters compassed me about, even to the soul: the depth closed me round about, the weeds were wrapped about my head./I went down to the bottoms of the mountains; the earth with her bars was about me for ever: yet hast thou brought up my life from corruption, O Lord my God. When my soul fainted within me I remembered the Lord. (2–7)

It is as if simply opening your mouth, giving utterance to your voice, releases something in you; as if finding words to express your total despair and the sense you feel of being shut up, unable to come forth, of having been rejected by the whole world, God included, makes the water return to the desert, makes life return to the one who was dead. The fact that the Psalm in Jonah is embedded in a narrative allows us to verify the truth of this, for no sooner has Jonah finished speaking than 'the Lord spake unto the fish, and it vomited out Jonah upon the dry land' (10). Of course it is important that Jonah and the 'I' of the other psalms on this topic cry out *to God*; but in a sense they only do so because God is the one who will always be prepared to listen. Simply giving voice, I would suggest, finding words for your anguish, is what in the first instance makes it possible to overcome that anguish.

But if that is the first step, that which returns you to the world of men and so to yourself, it is important to note that there is often a last step. Psalm 32, with which I began this discussion of the importance of utterance, opened, as you will remember, with the remark that 'When I kept silence, my bones waxed old through my roaring [better: *groaning*] all the day long' (Ps. 32:3). But it closes like this: 'Be glad in the Lord, and rejoice, ye right-eous: and shout for joy, all ye that are upright in heart'(11). And it is with those words, 'rejoice', *simchu*, and 'shout for joy', *harninu*, that I want to end. They are words we find used abun-dantly throughout the Psalms, and they are linked to words for singing and dancing and making music. This cluster is what distinguishes the Psalms from all the other books in the Bible, and if we grasp their significance we have, I think, grasped *the* essential element of the Psalms.

As with the notion of utterance, of calling out to God in despair, there is both an obvious and a deeper significance to this cluster. The obvious significance is that if we recognise that God is the Creator of the world and the force that guided Israel in her long and tortuous history, then of course we can do no other than praise him. The deeper significance can perhaps best be grasped by once again looking at Genesis 1, and then at a few other passages that reflect on that chapter.

The opening of the Hebrew Bible, as I said at the start, would have been a shock to someone used to the creation epics of other ancient Near Eastern cultures. In sober rhythmic prose the creation of the world by the single God is described, a creation which consists of division and separation and of putting bound-aries round things. But there are other places in the Bible where a rather different, more dynamic, more living view of the created universe is proposed. When, for example, at the end of Job, God speaks to Job out of the whirlwind, he says:

Where wast thou when I laid the foundations of the earth?

declare, if thou hast understanding./Who hath laid the measures thereof, if thou knowest? or who hath stretched the line upon it?/Whereupon are the foundations thereof fastened? or who laid the corner stone thereof;/When the morning stars sang together, and all the sons of God shouted for joy?/Or who shut up the sea with doors, when it brake forth, as if it had issued out of the womb?' (Job 38:4–8)

There was nothing in Genesis 1 about the morning stars singing for joy or the sea attempting to break out of its confines. Umberto Cassuto has argued that this is because the writers of the Torah, the first five books, were extremely conscious of the need to distance themselves from the creation epics of the surrounding nations, and they made sure than not a whiff of independent life was given to the elements of God's creation.[8] Be that as it may, the Bible often works like this, setting something down in one place and then qualifying or enriching it elsewhere, or even challenging it completely, as Job challenges Proverbs. I have suggested that in the Psalms of supplication we have evidence of anguished crying to the Lord which is rare in the other biblical books. But in the Psalms we also have, outside Job, the richest array of examples of a dynamic universe. 'The heavens declare the glory of God; and the firmament sheweth his handiwork./Day unto day uttereth speech, and night unto night sheweth knowledge' (19:1–2). In this Psalm, 19, God has set a tent for the sun, 'Which is as a bridegroom coming out of his chamber, and rejoiceth as a strong man to run a race' (5). In Psalm 66 we are told: 'All the earth shall worship thee, and shall sing unto thee; they shall sing to thy name' (4).

If the created universe is dynamic, this does not mean that it is chaotic. It is precisely because it is created by one God that

---

8 Cassuto, *passim*.

it unites in celebrating him. Even the roar of the sea is its own way of asserting its mighty power, vested in it by God, and therefore a testimony to God's own power, unimaginable to mortals like Job: 'Let the sea roar, and the fulness thereof; the world, and they that dwell therein./Let the floods clap their hands: let the hills be joyful together/Before the Lord; for he cometh to judge the earth' (98:7–9). Psalm 114 is perhaps the finest example of this motif, combined here with the parallel motif of God not only as Lord of creation, but as Lord of history: 'When Israel went out of Egypt, the house of Jacob from a people of strange language;/Judah was his sanctuary, and Israel His dominion./The sea saw it, and fled: Jordan was driven back. The mountains skipped like rams, and the little hills like lambs' (1–4). The sea fleeing is no doubt the Sea of Reeds at the exodus, and the Jordan turning backward is the sign of the entry of the Israelites into the promised land. But the hills skipping like rams is purely gratuitous; like the singing of the mountains and the morning stars, it is a sign of spontaneous joy.

But if the hills and the stars can break out into shouts of joy and song, into skipping and dancing, what of man? 'Make a joyful noise unto the Lord, all the earth,' says Psalm 98, 'make a loud noise, and rejoice, and sing praise./Sing unto the Lord with the harp; with the harp, and the voice of a psalm./With trumpets and sound of cornet make a joyful noise before the Lord, the King' (4–6). There is no divide between sea, mountains, and man. All must sing forth, and if the sea roars louder than men, men at least have timbrels and harps and cymbals and trumpets. And though of course such jubilation is good because it is a celebration of God's glory, it is also good *in itself*. The hills, like lambs, *need* to skip – it's in their legs, so to speak. And it's in the legs of men as well. Job is perhaps meant to be cowed by God's enumeration of His wonders, but the Psalms insist that man most fulfils himself when he moves beyond the sitting posture of study, beyond the careful use of language in its civic setting, to the expression of pure joy in the *ordered freedom* of song and dance:

> Praise ye the Lord [*hallelujah*]

> Praise God in his sanctuary:
>> Praise him in the firmament of His power.

> Praise him for his mighty acts:
>> Praise him according to his excellent greatness.

> Praise him with the sound of the trumpet:
>> Praise him with the psaltery and harp.

> Praise him with the timbrel and dance:
>> Praise him with stringed instruments and organs.

> Praise him upon the loud cymbals:
>> Praise him upon the high-sounding cymbals.

> Let every thing that hath breath praise the Lord
>> Praise ye the Lord. [*hallelujah*]

4. The Opinion of Pythagoras
for Tony Nuttall

CLOWN: What is the opinion of Pythagoras concerning wild fowl?
MALVOLIO : That the soul of our grandam might happily inhabit a bird.
CLOWN :   What think'st thou of his opinion?
MALVOLIO: I think nobly of the soul and no way approve his opinion.
CLOWN :   Fare thee well. Remain thou still in darkness.

(Twelfth Night, IV.ii.51–5)[1]

IT USED TO BE A QUARREL between philosophers and poets: Plato against Homer, St Augustine against Virgil and Ovid. But in recent times it has become a quarrel within philosophy itself: Kierkegaard against Hegel; Nietzsche against Plato; Nussbaum against Kant. What, in their different ways, Kierkegaard and the rest are saying is that there is an unbridgeable gap between life and thought, which philosophy has always refused to recognise, has even, in effect, conspired to hide. Works of art, though, can help us grasp the nature of that difference and so help us in our philosophical task of understanding ourselves and the world. To read Chapter 22 of Genesis, to listen to Mozart's *Don Giovanni,* to enter the world of Sophocles or Euripides, these philosophers say, is to understand something about our condition which philosophers have not simply failed to recognise, but have been instrumental in occluding.

Does Shakespeare have anything to offer this debate? I'd like to look, in the brief time at my disposal, at one play, *Twelfth*

---

1 All quotations are from the Signet Classic edition of *Twelfth Night,* edited by Herschel Baker, New York, 1965. This edition has the advantage of including the source of the play, discussed below.

Night. More perhaps than any other play of Shakespeare's, it shows up the difficulty discursive thought has when faced with a work of art. This is not an arcane subject. It is simply the result of the fact that we, as viewers or readers of the play, experience far more than our critical or philosophical vocabulary seems able to articulate. The problem, in other words, does not come with our immediate responses (the plural is important) to the play, but with our attempts, after the fact, to make sense of that experience to ourselves and others. The task of criticism, as I (and, I am sure, Tony Nuttall) see it, is to break down that critical response, to articulate better what we all feel as we watch or read.

One way to start is to see what Shakespeare made of his source, which here, as so often, is well-known and, at first sight, rather faithfully followed. Barnabe Rich's *Of Apolonius and Silla*, published in 1581, is itself distantly derived from *Gl'Inganni* (*The Deceived*), a Plautine comedy produced in Siena in 1531. Rich begins with a generalisation, that all love is folly, though there is such a thing as 'reasonable love', love, that is, which depends on 'desert' or reciprocity. To illustrate this he tells a tale which he carefully anchors in time and place: 'During the time that the famous city of Constantinople remained in the hands of the Christians, amongst many other noblemen that kept their abiding in that flourishing city there was one whose name was Apolonius...' This 'Duke', having led a valiant band against the Turk, and triumphed, is shipwrecked on the return voyage on the island of Cyprus, where he is welcomed by its ruler, who has twin children, Silvio, a son, and Silla, a daughter. Silla falls in love with Apolonius, who, more interested in arms that in women, ignores her. This only feeds her passion, and, when Apolonius sails for home she follows him, disguised as a serving maid and with her faithful servant as her brother. The captain of the ship takes a fancy to her; she manages to keep him at bay for a while, but then, as he is about to have his way with her (the Mills and Boon phrase is appropriate to the tone of this tale) a storm wrecks the ship and washes her up on dry land.

Disguising herself now as a man, and taking her brother's name, Silvio, she makes her way to Constantinople, where she manages to enter the service of her beloved Apolonius, who has in the meanwhile begun to pay court to a noble lady called Julina: 'So my Duke,' says Rich,

> who in the time that he remained in the Isle of Cyprus had no skill at all in the art of love, although it were more than half profferred to him, was now become a scholar in Love's school, and had already learned his first lesson, that is, to speak pitifully, to look ruthfully, to promise largely, to serve diligently, and to please carefully; now he was learning his second lesson, that is, to reward liberally, to give bountifully, to present willingly, and to write lovingly.

To this end he sends 'his man', Silvio, in whom he now 'reposed his only confidence', 'to go between him and his lady'.

The lady of course falls in love with the messenger. Meanwhile the real Silvio comes to Constantinople in search of his sister, happens upon Julina and willingly responds to her advances. Invited to her house for supper, he is easily persuaded to remain for the night: '[T]hey passed the night with such joy and contentation,' says Rich, and the laddish wink and nudge is typical, 'as might in the convenient time be wished for; but only that Julina, feeding too much of some one dish above the rest, received a surfeit, whereof she could not be cured in forty weeks after, a natural inclination in all women which are subject to longing and want the reason to use a moderation in their diet.'

The next day Silvio goes his way, leaving the city in search of his sister. Julina, however, tells the insistent Duke that she is now betrothed to someone else, none other, in fact, than his serving man. Confronted by the furious Duke Silla protests her innocence, utterly baffled by the accusation. In a scene worthy of Kleist, but of course rendered here wholly without the metaphysical anxiety characteristic of the German writer, Rich tells us that 'hearing an oath sworn so divinely that he had gotten a woman with child, [Silvio] was like to believe that it had been true in very deed; but remembering his own impediment, thought it impossible that he should commit such an act.' By now she has succeeded in turning both the Duke and Julina against her, and finally has no option but to prove the truth of her denial. Note how Rich manipulates the pronouns so as to gain maximum effect without any thought of their metaphysical implications: 'And herewithal loosing his garments down to his stomach, showed Julina his breasts and pretty teats, surmounting far the whiteness of snow itself, saying: "Lo, madam, behold here the party whom you have challenged to be the father of your child; see, I am a woman..."' The Duke, when apprised of this, and moved by Silla's subsequent story of her love and devotion to him, proposes to her and is accepted. The real Silvio, hearing of the strange events that have occurred in Constantinople, returns to find his sister, whereupon everything is made clear and he and Julina also marry. '[T]hus Silvio, having attained a noble wife, and Silla, his sister, her desired husband, they passed the residue of their days with such delight as those that have accomplished the perfection of their felicities.'

You will forgive me for spending so much time detailing the plot of this insignificant romance, but it is important to get the feel of it, so as to grasp both what Shakespeare saw in it and how vastly it differs from *Twelfth Night*. Rich is clearly interested solely in the confusion of the plot and in the titillation afforded by the false accusation. On the way he provides Shakespeare with the scaffolding for his play and a hint as to how he might treat the Duke. But it is important to recognise that Shakespeare has little interest in what is at the centre of Rich's story, the final revelation. It is also important to grasp that Shakespeare has not simply taken over the story and added a comic subplot. Already in *A Midsummer Night's Dream* he had hit on how to integrate main plot and subplot, nobles and commoners, but in that play the distance between the two was still retained. Here they are fused into a seamless whole. In fact, it is a mistake, in my opinion, even to speak of plot and subplot. The play, after all, is not called *Of Orsino and Viola* but *Twelfth Night or What you Will*. Critics have always been aware of the fact that this implies that we are dealing with a carnival play, a festive comedy, but even C.L. Barber, the author of a superlative book on Shakespeare's festive comedy, fails, when it comes to this play, to rise to the challenge of its title.

The key thing to note is how, as we watch or read, we find ourselves embarked on a roller-coaster ride whose effect is quite different from that of reading Rich's romance. In Rich there is a single narrative voice, ironic, titillating, omnipresent. By contrast in Shakespeare every new scene, and sometimes within a scene itself, the register changes abruptly. We might be tempted to say that this is simply the difference between a play and a work of prose fiction. But that is not so. A play by Racine or Ibsen affects us quite differently, and even Shakespeare's other plays, whether in the genres of comedy, tragedy or romance, do not change register quite as violently as does *Twelfth Night*.

In fact one way of approaching the characterisation within the play is to say that some characters, notably Orsino, Olivia, Sir Toby and Sir Andrew, have only one register, while others, notably Viola and Feste, seem protean – and that this is a clue to their characters and affects our response to them.

> 'I shall never believe he's guilty,' she said. 'Never.'
> Ronald thought: 'How that second, histrionic "never" diminishes her – how it debases this striking girl to a commonplace.'

This is from Muriel Spark's early novel, *The Bachelors*. It shows how we reveal ourselves in what we say — sometimes in the content, but more often in the manner of our saying. Barnabe Rich, who does not on the whole go in for dialogue, presents us with flat characters, characters who are given certain traits and then put through the hoops of the plot. In Rich the Duke and Silla are both equally examples of 'unreasonable love', a love which is hopeless since it is not based on reciprocity. In Shakespeare the gulf between Orsino and Viola is enormous. Orsino is the embodiment of self-love. 'If music be the food of love, play on,/ Give *me* excess of it' is his first sentence, and his last words are:

> Cesario, come —
> For so you shall be while you are a man,
> But when in other habits you are seen,
> *Orsino's* mistress and *his fancy's* queen.
>
> (v.i.387–90; my emphases)

Viola, by contrast, has little thought for herself. When we first meet her she is concerned only for her brother, and, later, though in love with Orsino, is constrained by her duty and her disguise, and can only speak her thoughts by indirection.

Orsino, locked in himself, will never surprise us or himself. Viola, by contrast, does both. And she does this because Shakespeare, like Mozart, has the resources to change gear suddenly. Listen:

> VIOLA : If I did love you in my master's flame,
> With such a suff'ring, such a deadly life,
> In your denial I would find no sense;
> I would not understand it.
> OLIVIA: Why, what would you?
> VIOLA: Make me a willow cabin at your gate
> And call upon my soul within the house;

Write loyal cantons of contemnèd love
And sing them loud even in the dead of night;
Hallo your name to the reverberate hills
And make the babbling gossip of the air
Cry out 'Olivia!' O, you should not rest
Between the elements of air and earth
But you should pity me.

(I.v.265–77)

This is quite as rhetorical as 'If music be the food of love...
Give me excess of it.' But it knows itself to be rhetoric, much
as Cherubino does when he sings *Voi che sapete*, while neither
Orsino nor the Count is in control of his words, since both
imagine they come 'from the heart'. Paradoxically, it is precisely
because both Viola and Cherubino consciously 'sing' that we
feel their sensibility vibrating in their words. The act of singing
liberates them, allows them to discover who they are. And Olivia
clearly picks this up as much as does the audience, for here surely
is the moment at which she falls in love with 'Cesario'.

But Shakespeare has not only got varieties of rhetoric at his
command. Everything Viola does and says conveys her character: we respond to her not as to a set of characteristics, but as
we respond to someone we meet and who makes a powerful
impression upon us. For, as Nuttall said long ago in a splendid
early essay,[2] to try and turn a Shakespeare play into a late story
by Henry James is to bark up the wrong tree. Her willingness
to trust to time ('O Time, thou must untangle this, not I' –
II.ii.40), in contrast to the desperation of Orsino, Olivia and
Malvolio to reach their different goals as soon as possible; her
feminine fear of physical danger; her refusal to allow her secret
love to interfere with her duty to her master – all this conveys
a sense of her quality, of a balanced recognition of the complex-

2 A.D. Nuttall, 'The Argument About Shakespeare's Characters', *Critical
   Quarterly* 7, 1965, pp.107–20.

ities of the world and of the fact that it rarely fits in with our desires, which give her a kind of wisdom and moral authority.

There is more. (With Shakespeare and Mozart there is always more.) Is it a coincidence that two of the most charged images of classical mythology employed in the play come in the first and second scenes? In the first Orsino dramatises himself as Actaeon, the hunter turned prey, allegorising the story in good Renaissance fashion to make it describe his inner state:

> O, when my eyes did see Olivia first,
> Methought she purged the air of pestilence,
> That instant was I turned into a hart,
> And my desires, like fell and cruel hounds,
> E'er since pursue me.
>
> (I.i.20–24)

In the second scene the captain describes to Viola how he saw her brother escape the shipwreck:

> When you, and those poor number saved with you,
> Hung on our driving boat, I saw your brother,
> Most provident in peril, bind himself
> (Courage and hope both teaching him the practice)
> To a strong mast that lived upon the sea;
> Where, like Arion on the dolphin's back,
> I saw him hold acquaintance with the waves
> So long as I could see.
>
> (I.ii.10–17)

This is Sebastian, not Viola, but in Shakespeare, as in Mozart, the music has the habit of migrating from character to character. The brother and sister, as alike as two peas and both miraculous survivors of the cruel sea, are in a sense one, and what holds for Sebastian will hold for Viola. Where Orsino is torn by his inner demons, the brother and sister have the spiritual and bodily agility to breast the seas, and both survive because they know how to 'hold acquaintance' with both inner and outer waves. With the image of Arion, as with that of Actaeon, Shakespeare gives us the tools, so to speak, to make sense of what we are witnessing, gives us a key to character. Of course it would not work if he then failed to provide us with characters to embody those traits, but neither Shakespeare nor Mozart fails us in such circumstances; their grasp of character is as sure as their grasp of verbal and musical form.

If scenes 1 and 2 present us with very different registers, then scene 3 continues the process. After 'If music be the food of love' (I.i.1) and 'What country, friends, is this?'(I.ii.1), we have: 'What a plague means my niece to take the death of her brother thus? I am sure care's an enemy to life' (I.iii.1–3). This is as great a leap in register as we find in the shocking transition from *Combray* to *Un Amour de Swann* in the first volume of *A la recherche*. Yet Toby and Andrew are as limited in their view of the festive spirit as Orsino is in his view of love; all three are blind to the springs of their own characters, are locked in a particular and limited view of who they are and what they want out of life.

But what of Feste? Talk of 'Shakespeare's clowns and fools' does us a disservice. We fail to see the particular kind of fool Feste is, why we respond to him with much more sympathy than we do, for instance, to Launce in *The Two Gentlemen of Verona* or Lancelot Gobbo in *The Merchant of Venice*. 'Well, God give them wisdom that have it, and those that are fools, let them use their talents' (I.v.14–15), he tells Maria, who is quite capable of sparring with him. Indeed, the exchanges between the two of them remind us of how the ideal conversation should perhaps be conducted. Georg Simmel, in his 1910 essay, 'Sociability', helps us out. 'Simmel', says Rosalind Krauss in an essay on Picasso's 1912–13 collages which stimulated much of the thought in this paper,

> wants to project a social space in which signs circulate
> endlessly as weightless fragments of repartee, stripped of

practical content – that of information, argument, business – taking as their content, instead, the functional play of conversation itself, conversation whose playfulness is expressed by the speed and lightness with which its object changes from moment to moment, giving its topics an interchangeable, accidental character.[3]

It is in this way, Simmel says, that conversation is 'the purest and most sublimated form of mutuality among all sociological phenomena', since conversation 'becomes the most adequate fulfilment of a relation which is, so to speak, nothing but relationship, in which even that which is otherwise the pure form of interaction is its own self-sufficient content.' Conversation of this kind is, in fact, a way of being Arion in a social setting, and it contrasts markedly with the attitude to dialogue of so many of the other characters. Olivia, for example has too great a sense of herself and her worth to show the suppleness required. Feste teases her: 'Wit, and't be thy will, put me into good fooling. Those wits that think they have thee do very oft prove fools, and I that am sure I lack thee may pass for a wise man. For what says Quinapalus? "Better a witty fool than a foolish wit." God bless thee, lady.' She tries half-heartedly to play the conversation game: 'Take the fool away.' 'Do you not hear, fellows? Take away the lady,' responds Feste, whereupon she tries to bring the conversation to a close by reasserting her authority, her social superiority: 'Go to, y'are a dry fool! I'll no more of you. Besides, you grow dishonest' (I.v.31–40).

Like Viola's, Feste's strength comes from the fact that he expects nothing from life. Hence he has the suppleness to respond, both verbally and physically, to any situation, whereas those who are always expecting life to give them what they want are helpless before its blows. Like Viola, too, he has a role, a

3 Rosalind Krauss, 'The Circulation of the Sign', in *The Picasso Papers*, New York, 1998, pp.25–85. The quotes are on pages 63–4.

mask, which helps him be himself. And, like Viola, he can change register. We will see in a moment how he does so in the song that concludes the play. But before that let us glance at a non-musical change of register. Here he is as the curate Sir Topas in catechetical mode testing Malvolio's sanity:

CLOWN: What is the opinion of Pythagoras
concerning wild fowl?
MALVOLIO: That the soul of our grandam might
happily inhabit a bird.
CLOWN: What think'st thou of his opinion?
MALVOLIO : I think nobly of the soul and no way
approve his opinion.
CLOWN : Fare thee well. Remain thou still in darkness.

(IV.ii.51–8)

At a first level this is a perfectly serious test and Malvolio comes out of it with flying colours: he not only knows the history of philosophy, he is also clear about where any good Christian should stand in relation to it: soul and body are one and the Pythagorean view that we can be a bird in one life and a human being in another is anathema. This of course fits in with the central theme of the play: that of the one and the many and the hybrid nature of human 'one-ness'. And, as the title reminds us, the play takes place on the day of Epiphany, the day on which the wise men recognised the child in the manger as the incarnate God. The message of the Incarnation is that we are fully ourselves not by remaining locked in the prison of our prejudices and preconceptions, not by trying to get what we want, but by giving ourselves to others and to the world. As Viola puts it to Olivia: 'What is yours to bestow is not yours to reserve' (I.v.186). Only in this way will we be true in our bodies to our immortal souls.[4]

4 I am indebted to Manfred Pfister for much in this paragraph.

Such talk, however, risks missing the tone of the play, which, we have seen, is crucial to its meaning. What makes the exchange so funny is of course the way the history of philosophy is translated into the demotic: the Clown does not ask Malvolio for his views on the transmigration of souls in general, but 'What is the opinion of Pythagoras concerning wild fowl?' And Malvolio rises to the challenge not just of meaning but of tone: 'That the soul of our grandam might happily [*haply*, possibly] inhabit a fowl.' (Indeed, for once it is Feste who abandons the spirit of play with a rather Olivia-like parting: 'Fare thee well. Remain thou still in darkness.') That is why Malvolio is such a troubling figure. Unlike Olivia and Orsino, Toby and Andrew, he can adapt (wants to, indeed, even if he only does so clumsily in his attempt to please Olivia), and he has a kind of integrity. And of course (like Shylock) he acquires, through his ordeal, a disquieting dignity.

But there is more. As we watch and listen to this little exchange in the theatre I don't believe we think in the realistic terms, in the terms of plausible characterisation I have so far employed. I think there is a point at which we cease to think: 'How clever is Malvolio to answer Feste so accurately!' and at which we rejoice in the fact that Shakespeare has left reality behind and entered a different world, *carrying us with him in the process.*

What world? Do you remember the scene in one of the Marx Brothers films in which Harpo is found by Chico leaning against a wall: 'What for you lean against this wall?' Chico says. Harpo widens his eyes and gestures furiously. 'You comalong a me,' Chico says, and takes his arm. Harpo shakes his head even more vigorously and tries to repulse him, but Chico is stronger than he is and drags him away. As they go off the wall collapses.

The wall plays no role in the plot. Once the gag is over we forget about it. So why is it there? Well, partly just because it is a gag, and a good one at that: it makes us laugh. But the laughter stems from the reminder that film, realistic as it appears, is in fact an illusion, and that the walls we see are not the walls of houses but the flimsy walls of a studio, erected to simulate reality. The gag makes us laugh, and our laughter is full and wholesome, precisely because it releases us from the constraint of having to believe that what we see is real when we know deep down that it is not. We laugh in relief and gratitude at the puncturing of what Barthes calls the *reality-effect*, on which the film, like all film, depends, but which, unbeknownst to us, is a heavy burden for us to carry.

I don't know if there is a term for this puncturing of illusion in the theory of drama. It has something to do with Brecht's alienation effect, but there is something a little too didactic about Brecht's theories, despite his remarks about the beneficial effects of laughter. But if there isn't a term there should be, and it should be applied to the little exchange about Pythagoras we have been examining. For a moment we are free of the constraints of reality. We sense that neither Feste nor Malvolio could ever speak quite as the two of them do here. And we laugh, we have a sense of release, we rejoice that we have left the constraints of plot and characterisation behind us. I would suggest that, having left them behind, we are engaging with Shakespeare in one of those ideal conversations Simmel described, 'the purest and most sublimated form of mutuality... the fulfilment of a relation which is, so to speak, nothing but relationship, in which even that which is otherwise the pure form of interaction is its own self-sufficient content.'

The effect is of course momentary, as is the effect in the Marx Brothers. It cannot, in the nature of things, be otherwise. But it forms part of the texture of the play and remains, perhaps, the ideal towards which it is always pointing.

As I have said, the *raison d'être* for Rich's narrative is the relation at the end, which sorts out the confusion and makes possible the happy endings. But *anagnorisis* in the great artists is rarely so simple. As Terence Cave points out at the start of his monumental study of the subject:

> In Aristotle's definition, anagnorisis brings about a shift from ignorance to knowledge; it is the moment at which the characters understand their predicament fully for the first time, the moment that resolves a sequence of unexplained and often implausible occurrences; it makes the world (and the text) intelligible. Yet it is also a shift into the implausible; the secret unfolded lies beyond the realm of common experience; the truth discovered is 'marvellous' (*thaumaston*, to use Aristotle's term), the truth of fabulous myth or legend. Anagnorisis links the recovery of knowledge with a disquieting sense, when the trap is sprung, that the commonly accepted co-ordinates of knowledge have gone awry.[5]

As Cave recognises, *Twelfth Night* fits well into his argument. When in Act V, Sebastian and Viola appear on stage together for the first time, Orsino speaks for all the characters when he says: 'One face, one voice, one habit and two persons – / A natural perspective that is and is not' (v.i.216–17). Although commentators are still arguing about the precise meaning of 'a natural perspective', everyone agrees that even in the most derivative plays, such as *A Comedy of Errors*, a supernatural *frisson* attaches to the moment of anagnorisis: we know that it is the result of plot manipulation, yet nevertheless it seems – Shakespeare makes it seem – the result of some supernatural force at work in the doings of men. But my own feeling is that

5 *Recognitions*, Oxford, 1978, pp.1–2.

we should not make too much of it here. Shakespeare, as so often in his work, is slipping in something that does not quite belong, that will only be fully developed in the later romances, especially *The Winter's Tale*, where very great care is taken to liken the final revelation to 'an old tale' in order to mine its mythic potential. It is significant that a similar phrase occurs in *Twelfth Night*, but buried in Act III, where it refers merely to the absurd figure Malvolio is cutting (III.iv.133–4). At the climax of *The Winter's Tale* recognition does not so much clarify the confusions of the plot as bring out into the open deep strands in the play which had lain buried for years; and it finally puts the burden of guilt to rest, for Leontes, under the gaze of his new-found wife (like Pericles under that of his new-found daughter in the sister-play of that name) can confess his errors and be forgiven. Perhaps, too, the fact that alongside the recognition that someone long thought dead is alive there exists the recognition that another is irretrievably lost, adds to the sense of awe and wonder with which this moment is invested. It is as if those dead can finally be laid to rest. In *Twelfth Night*, by contrast with all of this, little is made of Orsino's remark and the exchange between brother and sister leading to their certainty that they are who they are is treated as comedy, and perfunctory comedy at that. In fact, in this play, Shakespeare seems to be at pains to defuse the sense of climax and revelation, to show us that little of significance is resolved or crucially changed: Viola remains dressed in her man's attire till the end; Malvolio leaves the scene with his curse on the assembled company, profoundly hurt by the treatment he has received and in no mood to forgive and change; and we do not feel that Orsino and Olivia are altered in any deep way. In fact, every character remains much as he or she was at the start.

And how does the play end? Not with an image of decisive change but with an image of repetition and sameness: the rain it raineth every day:

When that I was and a little tiny boy,
　　With hey, ho, the wind and the rain,
A foolish thing was but a toy,
　　For the rain it raineth every day.

But when I came to man's estate,
　　With hey, ho, the wind and the rain,
'Gainst knaves and thieves men shut their gate,
　　For the rain it raineth every day...

A great while ago the world begun,
　　Hey, ho, the wind and the rain;
But that's all one, our play is done,
　　And we'll strive to please you every day.

How are we to explain this? Why does Shakespeare make use of a plot which seems to derive its sole *raison d'être* from its denouement if he is not only not concerned with denouement but seems to wish actively to subvert it? And how are we to explain the fact that the viewer and reader does in fact feel that he has been through something transformative, that, having paid attention, he is not quite the same person at the end as he was at the start, which is the opposite of what happens to the reader of Rich, who is only confirmed in his attitudes and prejudices?

I think that Shakespeare, by denying us the comfort of closure, has made us aware that we have, in fact, from the first moment, been not so much following a story as exploring a field, and that, when the field is completely covered, the space saturated, as it were, the play must end – but end in such a way that we are once more returned to the field.

By talking about 'field' I am trying to bring out the way this play, though it does not feel unresolved, somehow also feels open. I think that what Bakhtin has to say about Dostoevsky can be of help here. 'What unfolds in his works,' he says, 'is not a multitude of characters and fates in a single objective world, illuminated by a single authorial consciousness; rather, *a plurality of consciousnesses, with equal rights and each with its own world*, combine but are not merged in the unity of the event.'[6]

Bakhtin goes on to show that though sympathetic and sensitive critics of Dostoevsky recognise that his work is multivoiced and polychronic, they invariably grant this only to take it back again. Either they take the polyphony present in the novels as a reflection of the multivoicedness found in the real world and thus transfer explanations 'directly from the plane of the novel to the plane of reality'; or they 'remonologize Dostoevsky's dialogical invention by identifying it with an entity called a reflection of the dialogical progression of the idea.' Each novel, Bakhtin goes on, would then 'form a completed philosophical whole, structured according to the dialectical method. We would have in the best instance a philosophical novel, a novel with an idea...[or] in the worst instance we would have philosophy in the form of a novel.'

In reality, says Bakhtin, in Dostoevsky every thought 'senses itself to be from the very beginning a *rejoinder* in an unfinalized dialogue.' 'Such thought,' he goes on, 'is not impelled toward a well-rounded, finalized, systematically monologic whole. It lives a tense life on the borders of someone else's thought.' (Note that the critic himself has to fight for his insight, to find the words to express what he experiences as he reads his chosen author. Neither the thought nor the expression comes to him ready-made. With 'It lives a tense life on the borders of someone else's thought' Bakhtin triumphantly scores.)

In Feste's last song, which ends *Twelfth Night*, we are given

---

6 I am once more indebted to Rosalind Krauss's brilliant essay on Picasso's collages for reminding me how Bakhtin's insights can be applied to other artistic endeavours. The Bakhtin quotations come from her essay, *ibid.*, pp.43–8; the quote beginning 'remonologize Dostoevsky's dialogical invention' is Krauss's paraphrase.

access to the world as beyond the understanding of any single person, a world multiple yet unchanging, transformed, held in suspension by the voice, the rhythm, the music. Like a firework the song rises up into the sky and then spreads, as it falls, over the whole play we have just experienced.

There is one more thing. Shakespeare and Mozart convey in their mature stage works, and especially in *Twelfth Night* and *The Marriage of Figaro*, a joy quite alien to Dostoevsky, and, indeed, to almost any other art known to me. I think that joy has to do with the fact that the spectator or reader is led into areas of experience he or she has always known existed but could never, by themselves, have arrived at. It reminds me of what Virginia Woolf said about Proust: that, reading him, you become, for a while, more intelligent, more sensitive, more aware than you ever are in your normal life; that you do not feel as though you had been transformed but simply made to realise your possibilities, the possibilities of human life, more fully and with more intensity than ever before or after — till, that is, you start reading Proust — or Shakespeare — once again.

5. I Dream of Toys

IN 1964 JOHN BERRYMAN PUBLISHED a remarkable book of poems, called *77 Dream Songs*. Four years later he published a further 308 'dream songs' under the mysterious and haunting title *His Toy His Dream His Rest*. The terms come from Elizabethan music. Giles Farnaby, who was a joiner or carpenter, like Snug in *A Midsummer Night's Dream*, before becoming a musician, wrote two pieces for the virginals, one called 'His Toy' and the other, divided into two, called 'His Dream, His Rest'. By a brilliant piece of imaginative wit Berryman has elided the two and produced his marvellous title.

There are many wonderful titles to the keyboard music of the time: 'Barafostus's Dream', 'Pavan and Galliard for Mr Peter', 'The Flatt Pavan', 'Watkins Ale', 'The Fall of the Leaf', 'The Irish Dump', 'The Frog Galliard', etc., etc.[1] A toy, it seems, was usually an unpretentious piece for lute or virginals, simple in form and light in texture, and more than fifty examples survive in English sources from the period 1590–1660, with contributions from all the greatest and many minor composers of the period: Bull, Gibbons, Tomkins, Dowland, Farnaby, Cutting. Gibbons has a piece called, in different sources, 'Toy', 'Air', 'Maske', 'Alman'. Bull has 'The Duchess of Brunswick's Toy'; Tomkins has 'A Toy: Made at Poole Court', and so on.

---

1 This paragraph leans heavily on *The New Grove Dictionary of Music and Musicians,* ed. Stanley Sadie, London, 1980, Vol. 19, p.102.

Thomas Mace writes: '*Toys* or *Jiggs*, are *Light-Squibbish Things*, only fit for *Fantastical* and *Easie-Light-Headed People*; and in any sort of *Time*.'

A toy, in Elizabethan parlance, was a trifle; you 'toy' with someone, or 'toy with their affections', a phrase of course still in use today. Toys, hobby-horses, etc. come in the same semantic cluster, as in the Prologue to Ben Jonson's *Bartholomew Fair*:

> Your Majesty is welcome to a fair;
> Such place, such men, such language and such ware,
> You must expect; with these, the zealous noise
> Of our land's faction, scandalised at toys,
> As babies, hobby-horses, puppet plays,
> And such-like rage...
>
> $(1-6)^2$

and in the puppeteer Leatherhead's remarks later in the play:

> What do you lack? What do you buy, pretty mistress? A fine hobby-horse, to make your son a tilter? A drum, to make him a soldier? A fiddle, to make him a reveller? What is't you lack? Little dogs for your daughters, or babies, male or female. (III.ii.39–44)

Leatherhead is fully aware of how toys function for children: 'a drum to make him a soldier, a fiddle to make him a reveller...' As Walter Benjamin, the only critic known to me who has tried to talk seriously about toys, has said:

> Today we may perhaps hope that it will be possible to overcome the basic error – namely the assumption that the imaginative content of the child's toys is what determines

---

2 All quotes are from *Selected Plays of Ben Johnson*, Vol. 2, ed. Martin Butler, Cambridge, 1989.

his playing, whereas in reality the opposite is true. A child wants to pull something, so he becomes a horse; he wants to play with sand, and so he turns into a baker; he wants to hide, and so he turns into a robber or policeman... The more appealing toys are, in the ordinary sense of the term, the further they are from genuine playthings; the more they are based on imitation, the further away they lead us from the real, living play... Imitation is at home in the *playing*, not in the *plaything*.[3]

I want to talk to you today about toys, not games, because I feel it is too easy for the notion of game to be 'skied', to be turned into a universal concept which embraces all human activities, as happens in Huizinga's *Homo Ludens* (1949) and Roger Caillois' *Les Jeux et les hommes* (1958). This tendency has its roots in the German Romantic idea that all life is a dream or a game, the best example of which is Hermann Hesse's *The Glass Bead Game* (*Das Glasperlenspiel*, 1943). Toys, on the other hand, can't be 'recuperated' by metaphysics or high culture. The point about a toy is that it can be made out of anything, even the most rubbishy materials, as Benjamin understood: cardboard boxes can become trains or planes; a stick can become a horse (the hobby-horse, *das Steckenpferd* or stick horse, as one says in German). The child can invest the most banal and everyday elements – sticks, wire, string, cardboard boxes – with life, and enter a world of the imagination playing with these, and then as quickly let them go, so that they revert once more to being simply bits and pieces, the meaningless refuse of the world.

I want to argue that there are two radically distinct kinds of art: art as window and art as toy. Art as window is the art we are most familiar with, the art of the realist novel and realist

---

3 'The Cultural History of Toys', in *Selected Writings*, Vol. 2, 1927–34, Cambridge, MA, 1999, pp.115–16.

painting, the art of Ibsen and Shaw and most films. It asks us to open the book or greet the rise of the curtain as though we had opened a window and were looking out at the world. Art as toy, on the other hand, is art as the hobby-horse on which we can jump and which we can ride for as long as we like, and then discard as a mere stick; it is an art which seeks our active co-operation.

Of course an argument could be advanced that *all* art is art-as-toy, that both my kinds depend on conventions, and it is merely that the conventions are a little more hidden in the realist novel, painting or play. There is some truth in this, but not, it seems to me, enough to invalidate my distinction. In any case, I do not want to get entangled in larger issues of aesthetics but rather to focus on my heuristic distinction in the hope that it will raise questions that are not usually answered by aesthetics, no matter how sophisticated.

There is a Romantic notion of art which insists that art, like dream, leads one mysteriously to a higher sphere. The apotheosis of this view is to be found in the Wagnerian concept of the *Gesamtkunstwerk* and in the reverent and darkened space of the Bayreuth opera house. Opposed to that is the notion of art as toy – the simultaneous recognition of the validity of desire and imagination, and of the futility of the Romantic project. Here there is no mystery, no darkness; here all the evidence is before you: the wood, the stick, the sticking-plaster holding it all together. And every step taken by the artist is out in the open.

The notion of art as toy clearly fits a clutch of modern artists: Stravinsky, for example, in *Petroushka* and *L'Histoire du soldat*; Picasso in his immediate post-Cubist phase, in a work like *The Absinthe Glass*, for example; or in his later sculptures, such as the *Mother with Pushchair* of 1950 or the toy car/monkey *Mother and Child* of 1953; Duchamp right through his career; Schwitters – to name but a few of the most prominent.

We need to be clear, though, about what exactly is going on

here: part of the artistic impact of the work of these artists is due to our pleasure at moving between the rubbishy basic element or the line and the dot (Klee) and its transformation. This can take very different forms. Duchamp, for example, is content to take an object of everyday life – a urinal, say – and yank it out of context, so that we look at it afresh, and also respond to his wit in doing what he has done. In the Picasso *Mother and Child*, on the other hand, the artist is not content with the simple play of wit – the bonnet of the toy car suddenly seen as the monkey's large flat nose and the front windows as its eyes – but goes on to create a version of one of the central icons of European art and to extend the range of that icon by adding a baby monkey clinging to the huge chest of the mother. Duchamp, we could say, is interested only in the play of wit, Picasso in using that play to respond to something in the world: the relationship of mother and child.

In both artists we are first of all made to see what turning the ordinary, the everyday, the inappropriate, into art implies, and the effect of the art work lies in this see-sawing between the world around us and the work of art. Duchamp is happy with the initial transformative play of wit while Picasso wants to go further and actually work with the new material, but in both cases the 'work' is visible and unmysterious: anyone can do it, you don't need inspiration or an artistic temperament, let alone genius – only an alertness of spirit. Except that such alertness does not come easily to most of us – you've got to be aware both of the potential of the discarded and of how a sudden change of context can make all the difference. But of course that is precisely what children do unthinkingly all the time with their toys. (And when I speak of toys I do not have in mind the £6000 toy car, almost indistinguishable from the real thing, which was recently on sale in Hamleys, the great London toy shop, itself, ironically, now up for sale. As Benjamin understood, the more elaborate and realistic a toy is, the less a toy it is.)

I have talked about a powerful strand in twentieth-century art, but it would be wrong to see the notion of art as toy as a purely modern phenomenon. I want to look now at a group of Renaissance English works, spanning the years 1590–1760 (a broad definition of the Renaissance, you might say, but you will I hope see my point in so labelling them as I proceed). I want to look at several Elizabethan and Jacobean plays, contemporary with the lute and virginal music I began with, and at two prose works of the eighteenth century, Swift's *A Tale of a Tub* and Sterne's *Tristram Shandy*.

Let me start with a work I have had occasion to refer to already, Ben Jonson's *Bartholomew Fair* (1614). As has often been noted, Jonson builds the work on the analogy of fairs and plays. He wants to defend plays against the Puritan attacks made on them – that they are the work of the Devil, the focus of idolatry; that they are an abomination, for they show men dressed up as women; and so on. He wishes to assert the importance of both plays and fairs for the health of society, and he recognises that an attack on those who attack plays can also furnish the subject of a play which, by simply being what it is, will refute these attacks.

The climax, as you will remember, comes when, in the final act, a puppet play is put on which parodies the romantic drama of the time. The puppet master, Leatherhead, opens the proceedings:

> Gentles, that no longer your expectations may wander,
> Behold our chief actor, amorous Leander,
> With a great deal of cloth, lapped about him like a scarf,
> For he yet serves his father, a dyer, at Puddle Wharf,
> Which place we'll make bold with, to call it our Abydus,
> As the Bankside is our Sestos, and let it not be denied us.
> Now, as he is beating, to make the dye take the fuller,

Who chances to come by, but fair Hero in a sculler;
And seeing Leander's naked leg and goodly calf,
Cast at him, from the boat, a sheep's eye and a half.
Now she is landed, and the sculler come back;
By and by you shall see what Leander doth lack.

(v.iv.126–37)

If Marlowe discovered that the new theatres were places where
an audience would pay to dream, and that he had the linguistic
ability to fuel those dreams, Jonson, like Aristophanes before
him, discovered that the theatre was also a place where the puncturing of dreams could lead to a different kind of release, the
release of laughter. Behind the absurd fantasies of Sir Epicure
Mammon lie the equally absurd yet almost realised fantasies of
Tamburlaine; behind Leatherhead's puppet play lies not a play
of Marlowe's but his erotic epylion, *Hero and Leander*.

The puppet Leander addresses the bargeman:

PUPPET LEANDER   Here, Cole. What fairest of fairs
    Was that fare that thou landest but now at Trig stairs?...
PUPPET COLE   It is lovely Hero.
PUPPET LEANDER   Nero?
PUPPET COLE   No, Hero.
LEATHERHEAD   It is Hero
    Of the Bankside, he saith, to tell you truth without erring,
    Is come over into Fish Street to eat some fresh Herring.
    Leander says no more, but as fast as he can,
    Gets on all his best clothes, and will after to the Swan.

(147–56)

Eventually Hero and Leander meet up at the Swan Inn:

LEATHERHEAD   This while young Leander with fair Hero
                                is drinking,
    And Hero grown drunk, to any man's thinking!
    Yet was it not three pints of sherry could flaw her,

84

Till Cupid, distinguished like Jonas the dawer,
From under his apron,where his lechery lurks,
Put love in her sack.Now mark how it works.
PUPPET HERO   Leander, Leander, my dear, my dear Leander,
    I'll forever be thy goose, so thou'lt be my gander...
PUPPET LEANDER   And sweetest of geese, before I go to
                                                    bed,
    I'll swim o'er the Thames, my goose, thee to tread.

(273–86)

The clomping verse and terrible rhymes are part of what this
play within a play is about (as is the equivalent play of *Pyramus
and Thisbe* put on by the mechanicals in *A Midsummer Night's
Dream*), but what is so wonderful about Jonson is that the apparently cynical description of romantic love as a purely physical
desire to tread and be trodden manages at the same time to
remind us of all those medieval poems about the love of birds,
whose last incarnation is Shakespeare's 'The Phoenix and the
Turtle', described by one recent critic as ' both a great poem
and a toy'.[4]

The puppet play of Hero and Leander, and the comments
of the stage characters on the play is, however, but the first of
two climaxes to *Bartholomew Fair*. The second follows on from
it and involves the ultimate breakdown of illusion and the ultimate argument in favour of theatre, as one of the stage
characters bursts in on the play and proceeds to argue with the
puppets. This personage is none other than the appalling
Puritan divine, Zeal-of-the-Land Busy, whose fleshly lust for
roast chicken and female flesh is written everywhere upon his
body, from his chin dripping with chicken fat to his eyes and
voice. Breaking into the tent where the puppet play is being
performed, he does not mince his words:

4 Barbara Everett, 'Set Upon a Golden Bough to Sing', *The Times Literary
   Supplement*, Feb. 16, 2001, p.17.

BUSY   Down with Dagon, down with Dagon! 'Tis I will
no longer endure your profanations.

LEATHERHEAD   What mean you, sir?

BUSY   I will remove Dagon there, I say, that idol, that
heathenish idol, that remains, as I may say, a beam, a
very beam, not a beam of the sun, nor a beam of the
moon, not a beam of a balance, neither a house-beam,
nor a weaver's beam, but a beam in the eye, in the eye
of the brethren; a very great beam, an exceeding great
beam; such as are your stage-players, rhymers, and
morris-dancers, who have walked hand in hand, in
contempt of the brethren... (V.V.I–13)

Leatherhead protests that his play has been licensed by the
correct authority, the Master of the Revels, but this only serves
to set Busy off again:

The master of the Rebels' hand, thou hast – Satan's! Hold
thy peace, thy scurrility shut up thy mouth; thy profession
is damnable, and in pleading for it, thou dost plead for
Baal. I have long opened my mouth wide, and gaped, I have
gaped as the oyster for the tide, after thy destruction, but
cannot compass it by suit, or dispute; so that I look for a
bickering, ere long, and then a battle. (21–9)

The battle that then ensues, though, takes place not between
Leatherhead and Busy but between the Puritan and the Puppet
Dionysius. 'First, I say unto thee, idol, thou hast no calling',
begins Busy. 'You lie', answers the puppet, 'I am called
Dionysius.' One of the bystanders cheers at this, whereupon
Busy turns on him as well: 'Take not part with the wicked,
young gallant. He neigheth and hinnyeth, all is but hinnying
sophistry. I call him idol again. Yet, I say, his calling, his profession, is profane, it is profane, idol' (59–78).

Busy's sole means of arguing is to repeat his accusations, a
method developed by Puritan preachers and clearly effective

with their congregations, but not likely to persuade either the puppet or the audience. However, he presses on:

> Busy   Yes, and my main argument against you is, that you are an abomination for the male among you putteth on the apparel of the female, and the female of the male.
>
> Puppet Dionysius   You lie, you lie, you lie abominably... It is your old stale argument against the players, but it will not hold against the puppets; for we have neither male nor female amongst us. And that thou may'st see, if thou wilt, like a malicious purblind zeal as thou art! (112–24)

At which point, says the stage direction, 'the Puppet takes up his garment'. Busy's capitulation is as abrupt as was his entry: 'I am confused, the cause hath failed me.' Then, says the puppet, 'be converted, be converted'. 'Be converted,' takes up the puppet-master, 'I pray you, and let the play go on.' 'Let it go on,' answers Busy, 'for I am changed, and will become a beholder with you!' (125–37).

The puppet's crushing retort does not simply make the obvious point that puppets have no sex. He uses for his own ends one of the best known passages of St Paul: 'There is neither Jew nor Greek, there is neither bond nor free, there is neither male nor female: for ye are all one in Christ Jesus' (Galatians 3:28). But just as all are one in Christ Jesus, so on the stage they not only have no sex but are no longer Burbage or Shakespeare but Hamlet, Falstaff, Zeal-of-the-land Busy – figures in a play. Whether Busy has understood this or is merely too drunk and confused to argue further is not a question Jonson wants to raise; what is clear is that the audience has been given a lesson in the nature of theatre, not by means of a lecture but through the exploration of the very roots of theatre: Jonson, Leatherhead, Busy, Hero, Leander, Dionysius and we ourselves as we sit in the auditorium and 'become beholders' are subsumed into something new, which both widens our horizons and allows us to make distinctions which tend to be blurred in ordinary life. We have been made to see just how and out of what materials the hobby-horse is made, and what the pleasures involved in riding and then discarding it can be.

A much later play of Jonson's, *A Tale of a Tub*, gives us a variant on all this. A tale of a tub is a cock-and-bull story, a piece of nonsense. Jonson, tongue firmly in cheek, presents us with a play about a certain Squire Tub, his other, Lady Tub, and a romantic intrigue, farcically treated, leading to marriage and a play on stage to celebrate it. That play turns out itself to be called 'A Tale of a Tub', and it presents us with 'motions' or 'shows' dealing with elements of the very play we have just been watching, with comments on it by the stage audience. Other characters include a joiner who is said to be a satire on Jonson's one-time partner, Inigo Jones, and a clerk called Metaphor, who, when beaten, becomes 'Allegory', since in Renaissance poetics an allegory is an extended metaphor and the beating presumably extends him, just as a piece of meat is 'extended' by being beaten flat. There is of course a great deal about hobby-horses and toys, usually with an obscene innuendo.

Both these plays of Jonson's end with a play-within-a-play, and the theatrical audience is meant to understand its own responses to what it has been watching by listening to the comments of the stage audience and testing these against its own reactions. Much the best known version of this play of perspectives is of course to be found in *A Midsummer Night's Dream*.

At the climax of that play, as you will recall, the rather perfunctory plot has been wrapped up and the 'rude mechanicals' try to put on their play of Pyramus and Thisbe before the court. I say 'try' because their ludicrous efforts are constantly interrupted by the banter of the courtiers. The whole scene is a remarkable exploration of the nature of art, illusion and play as Shakespeare understands it.

The important thing, it seems to me, is that none of the remarks of the courtiers, not even those of Theseus, ever quite encapsulates what we, the other audience, experience, and the disparity between the two, their comments and our experience, makes us work to understand just what it is we feel.

Theseus starts the scene by commenting on the play so far. Hippolyta has remarked that what the lovers have just told them of their experiences in the wood is 'strange'. 'More strange than true', responds Theseus. 'I never may believe/These antique fables nor these fairy toys' (v.i.2–3). Here 'toys' clearly means trifles – these trifles about fairies. He goes on:

> Lovers and madmen have such seething brains,
> Such shaping fantasies, that apprehend
> More than cool reason ever comprehends.
> The lunatic, the lover and the poet
> Are of imagination all compact.
> One sees more devils than vast hell can hold...
>
> $(4-9)^5$

Reason is here clearly meant to be our guide, but, in a way typical of Shakespeare, the last lines of the speech turn the tables on reason even if they do not totally endorse the imagination:

> And as the imagination bodies forth
> The forms of things unknown, the poet's pen
> Turns them to shapes, and gives to airy nothing
> A local habitation and a name.
>
> $(14-17)$

His queen endorses this, and even strengthens it, suggesting that 'strangeness' may have a reality which reason cannot apprehend:

---

5   I quote from the Signet Classics edition, edited by Wolfgang Clemens, New York, 1963.

> But all the story of the night told over,
> And all their minds transfigured so together,
> More witnesseth than fancy's images,
> And grows to something of great constancy;
> But, howsoever, strange and admirable.
>
> (23–7)

However, what is granted to lovers may not so easily be granted to actors when they speak lines like the following:

> PYRAMUS:　Sweet Moon, I thank thee for thy sunny beams;
> I thank thee, Moon, for shining now so bright;
> For by thy gracious, golden, glittering gleams,
> I trust to take of truest Thisby sight.
> But stay, O spite!
> But mark, poor knight,
> What dreadful dole is here!
> Eyes, do you see?
> How can it be?
> O dainty duck, O dear!
> Thy mantle good,
> What, stained with blood!
> Approach,ye Furies fell!
> O Fates, come, come,
> Cut thread and thrum;
> Quail, crush, conclude, and quell!
>
> (273–88)

Theseus cannot help showing off to his bride with a witty barb at the expense of the mechanicals and their play: 'This passion, and the death of a dear friend, would go near to make a man look sad.' But she will not be party to this: 'Beshrew my heart, I pity the man' (289–91).

All the way through the scene, in fact, the Humanist courtier-king cannot but be condescending. When, a little earlier, Hippolyta had come out with: 'This is the silliest stuff that ever

I heard', he responds: 'The best in this kind are but shadows; and the worst are no worse, if imagination amend them' (211–13). *Our* imagination can improve *their* muddled efforts, can lift us above the bumbled words and ludicrous actions and allow us to grasp the ideal which poet and actors were after. This is good Remaissance Humanist Platonism, but we feel that there is something wrong with it. And what is wrong with it, I think, is that it tries to turn an *activity* (putting on a play) into a *spectacle*, while Shakespeare, for his part, puts all his effort into making us see that the activity is the important thing: the playwright writing, the actors acting, the spectators watching.

We might be tempted to say: our pleasure at the play within the play of Act v is the pleasure of having to reconstitute the Ovidian story out of the shambles the mechanicals make of it. But that is not quite right either. For the main effect of the mechanicals' butchering of the Ovidian tale is to make us laugh, and, with laughter, comes empathy with them, comes the sense that we too, and Shakespeare himself, are basically no different, that each of us struggles in vain to control language and the world around us, but none of us can wholly do so. Our pleasure then would lie not in our putting together again what has been shattered, but in recognising something about our human condition.

The mechanicals, and Bottom in particular, are really children playing and the words and props are their toys. Bottom, as W.D. Snodgrass has pointed out,[6] wants to play all the parts: 'An I may hide my face, let me play Thisby too, I'll speak in a monstrous little voice, "Thisne, Thisne!" "Ah, Pyramus, my lover dear!" "Thy Thisby dear, and lady dear!"'(1.ii.52–5). And: 'Let me play the lion too. I will roar, that I will do any man's heart good to hear me. I will roar, that I will make the Duke

6 'Moonshine and Sunny Beams: Ruminations on *A Midsummer Night's Dream*', in *In Radical Pursuit*, New York, 1975, pp.203–40.

say, "Let him roar again, let him roar again"' (71–4). Quince, however, is adamant: 'You can play no part but Pyramus' (85). He wants, too, to make words mean anything he wants them to mean, and his delightful habit of confusing the senses is less suggestive of an inadequate grasp of language than of the baby's polymorphous perversity, as Snodgrass notes. And Bottom, in his innocence, his childishness, grasps what Theseus and Oberon never manage to grasp, that the world lies forever beyond our understanding and will never be amenable to reason:

> I have had a most rare vision. I have had a dream, past the wit of man to say what dream it was. Man is but an ass, if he go about to expound this dream. Methought I was – there is no man can tell what. Methought I was – and methought I had – but man is but a patched fool if he will offer to say what methought I had. The eye of man hath not heard, the ear of man hath not seen, man's hand is not able to taste, his tongue to conceive, nor his heart to report, what my dream was. I will get Peter Quince to write a ballet [i.e. ballad] of this dream. It shall be called 'Bottom's Dream', because it hath no bottom. (IV.ii.207–22)

A larger portion of Shakespeare's audience than of any modern audience would have been aware of the echoes of St Paul here. But it is not enough to say that Bottom misquotes Paul. There is method in his confusions, even if he himself is not aware of it. 'Eye hath not seen, nor ear heard,' wrote St Paul, 'neither have entered into the heart of man, the things which God hath prepared for them that love him. But God hath revealed them unto us by his Spirit: for the Spirit searcheth all things, yea, the deep things of God' (1 Corinthians 2:9–10). St Paul knows the answers. They have been revealed to him on the road to Damascus, and if only men could be brought to see the truth as he has seen it they would be saved. Bottom, on the other hand, discovers that the dream is bottomless and that man is but an ass if he go about to expound it. And Shakespeare, in this play, shows us that men are changeable and inconstant, and yet that out of the web of interlocking lives something of great constancy can emerge.

In 1704 Jonathan Swift published – anonymously – his own *Tale of a Tub*. The author's preface gives us Swift's own tongue-in-cheek explanation of the phrase:

> [A]t a grand committee, some days ago, this important discovery was made by a certain curious and refined observer; that seamen have a custom when they meet a whale, to fling him out an empty tub, by way of amusement, to divert him from laying violent hands upon the ship. This parable was immediately mythologised: the whale was interpreted to be Hobbes' *Leviathan*, which tosses and plays with all other schemes of religion and government, wherof a great many are hollow, and dry, and empty, and noisy, and wooden, and given to rotation... The ship in danger, is easily understood to be its old antitype, the commonwealth. But, how to analyse the tub, was a matter of difficulty; when, after long enquiry and debate, the literal meaning was preserved: and it was decreed, that in order to prevent these leviathans from tossing and sporting with the commonwealth, which of itself is too apt to fluctuate, they should be diverted from that game by a *Tale of a Tub*. And my genius being conceived to lie not unhappily that way, I had the honour done me to be engaged in the performance.[7]

Like the child deciding at one time that the cardboard box will

7 Jonathan Swift, *A Tale of a Tub*, ed. Charles Guthkelch and David Nichol Smith, Oxford, 1958, p.16.

be a train, at another a house, Ben Jonson had taken a stock phrase, *a tale of a tub,* and written a burlesque play about Squire and Lady Tub, while Swift, with equal confidence, reads the phrase in quite a different way so as to fit in with *his* needs. The work that follows is the richest and most complex he ever wrote. Drawing on Rabelais and Cervantes, on Montaigne and the Church Fathers, he presents us with a Grub Street hack who is so pressed by time and the demands of the world that he can never get his own work going. Swift toys with the reader, tantalising us with the protean nature of his own toy, that extraordinary collection of ludicrous allegories, digressions on madness, on 'the mechanical operation of the spirit' and even on digressions. Gone is the order, the 'sweet constancy' that, in spite of everything, underlies the Elizabethan and Jacobean plays. Once in the saddle of this particular hobby-horse we can only cling on for dear life and hope for the best.

A similar experience awaits the reader of my last example, Sterne's *Tristram Shandy.* You all know the story. Tristram is determined to write the story of his life, but, since it takes him several months to write the account of a single day, he can only fall further and further behind. This turns out not to matter in the least, or rather, this uneasy relationship between living and narrating becomes itself the subject of the book. As Tristram points out, if this is not to our taste, we are free to turn to something else:

> But every man to his own taste. — Did not Dr Kunos-trokius, that great man, at his leisure hours, take the greatest delight imaginable in combing of asses tails, and plucking the dead hairs out with his teeth, though he had tweezers always in his pocket? Nay, if you come to that, Sir, have not the wisest of men in all ages, not excepting Solomon himself, — have they not had their HOBBY-HORSES; — their running horses, — their coins and their cockleshells, their drums and their trumpets, their fiddles, their

pallets, – their maggots and their butterflies? – and so long
as a man rides his HOBBY-HORSE peaceably and quietly
along the King's high-way, and neither compels you or me
to get up behind him, – pray, Sir, what have either you or
I to do with it?[8]

Sterne/Tristram wants to be left alone to ride his hobby-horse
along the King's highway. He recognises that his book is a
toy/hobby-horse, that it is both inert and ridable, and sees no
reason why it shouldn't amble alongside the horses of more
solemn riders. The trouble with those, though, is that they wish
to go straight from point A to point B, whereas Sterne/
Tristram wants to be free to zig-zag, twist and turn, as his fancy
takes him. They are Theseuses, as it were, whereas he is Bottom.

In the end the book's greatness and originality lies precisely
in this, that it shows up narratives that go from A to B as poor,
limited things, driven to their conclusions by forces outside
their control. Milan Kundera, himself no mean exponent of the
novel as hobby-horse, puts it well:

These novels are like a narrow street along which someone
drives his characters with a whip. Dramatic tension is the
real curse of the novel, because it transforms everything,
even the most beautiful pages, even the most surprising
scenes and observations merely into steps leading to the
final resolution, in which the meaning of everything that
preceded it is concentrated. The novel is consumed in the
fire of its own tension like a bale of straw.[9]

On the other hand, by the time we have finished *Tristram Shandy*
(or Kundera's own *Immortality*) we feel we have been exploring
a field, in the course of which we have learned not facts about

---

8 Laurence Sterne, *The Life and Opinions of Tristram Shandy, Gentleman*, ed.
  Melvin and Joan New, London, 1997, p.13.
9 Milan Kundera, *Immortality*, tr. Peter Kussi, London, 1991, p.266.

the world but a series of *practices*. Like Bottom, Tristram is poly-morphously perverse, a creature who stays close to his feelings and does not let reason drag him from them. Both Tristram and Toby, the book hints, have, through no fault of their own, suffered castration – one through the accident of the sash window, the other through an accident of war – but this only releases the child in them, freeing them from the purposeful-ness of genital sexuality, such as drives Tristram's father and Toby's would-be lover, the Widow Wadman. He who will never be able to have children of flesh and blood will create this toy instead. And Sterne, who recognises that a book is not natural, as a child is natural, willingly embraces his book as a toy.

There is of course a sense in which a book *is* like a child: something wholly new is brought into the world, and it is some-thing with a life of its own, which the father can only nurture and then watch as it leaves his orbit. Shakespeare, Jonson, Swift and Sterne have all created something new, a new personality, which has passed into the world and left their authors behind. Unlike a Romantic such as Norman O. Brown,[10] though, none of them sees this as a form of transcendence or imagines that it will lead to apocalyptic transformation. Indeed, for all of them both transcendence and positivism are recognised as profound errors: the error of imagining that we can leave the constraints of the world behind and of imagining that we can grasp it simply by describing it. Like Kierkegaard,[11] we could say, they recog-nise the need to keep the wound of the negative open, to set up forms of play, and to induct the viewer/reader in a set of prac-tices rather than attempting to reach conclusions or asking us to admire a perfect finished product.

10 *Life Against Death*, London, 1959.
11 See 'Kierkegaard and the Novel' and 'Borges and the Plain Sense of Things' in this volume.

I had thought, in this talk, to steer clear of psychoanalytic vocabulary when dealing with toys, but I find that both *A Midsummer Night's Dream* and *Tristram Shandy* have lured me in that direction. It would, I think, be possible, taking one's cue from D.W. Winnicott, to develop a psychoanalytic model of the role of toys in life and of the toylike nature of art.[12] I want to resist this, however. I prefer the Kierkegaardian and Sternean models precisely because the psychoanalytic, no matter how tactfully deployed, still tends to lead to closure, to a translation of the role of toys into some other, superior model. And then it seems we are back with the Romantic notion of art and of game and we have lost the sense of art as toy, the sense that here all the evidence is before us and every step taken by the artist is out in the open. We have lost the sense that, in the hands of a master like Shakespeare or Sterne or Picasso, something is made which none of us could make, and yet that there is not an unbridgeable gulf between what we can all of us make and the monkey *Mother and Child, A Midsummer Night's Dream* or *Tristram Shandy*. For we too, everyone of us, these works insist, can get going, start the process off; all we need is to be alert and childlike.

When I started writing seriously, in my late teens, I felt crushed by the weight of the European tradition – all those massive novels like *War and Peace* and *Middlemarch*, standing there like mountains, utterly self-confident, without a chink in their armour. How could one begin to emulate them? How, indeed, could one begin? For they seemed never to have been begun by anyone, only to have existed, like mountains, since the creation of the world. But then I read Eliot and Proust and was overwhelmed by their acknowledgement, within their works, of

---

12 See, among Winnicott's many books, *The Piggle*, Harmondsworth, 1971.

inevitable failure – 'On Margate sands/I can connect/Nothing with nothing./The broken fingernails of dirty hands...'; Proust/Marcel's *zut zut zut* as he fails to find the words to convey his feelings about a particular spring day. Reading this I suddenly felt released – it was possible, I realised, to start with failure, with words which refused to line up, plots which refused to develop. That was no cause for despair, I discovered, but, on the contrary, the necessary start of a process of exploration, the end of which would be, not the abolition or the denial of failure, but its incorporation into a larger whole. And then I began to read the classics and I realised that there was a whole tradition there, in the Elizabethan and Jacobean dramatists, in the work of Rabelais and his successors, which taught the same lesson, a lesson which seemed to have been occluded by the high seriousness of the nineteenth century.

So now I dream of a work as ordinary and extraordinary as a simple toy – not the Hamleys £6,000 toy car, but a cardboard box, a piece of wood, some string – that will be capable of being taken to pieces and then put back together again, by the use of the hands, eight fingers, two thumbs, my thoughts in abeyance, my life without direction, just playing with this little toy.

It's a dream – but one I can awake from and try, every day, to bring a little nearer to realisation.

6. In Time: Rembrandt's Self-Portraits

Tucked away in the first gallery of this impressive exhibition of Rembrandt's self-portraits is a remarkable little painting of 1629, now in Boston (see Plate 1). It shows a young painter in the far corner of his studio, brush and palette in hand, gazing intently at a canvas that dominates the painting. We cannot see the work in progress, but the easel, the floorboards, the cracked wall and the old door are all carefully depicted. The distance between the painter and his canvas is emphasised by the slanting light which brings out the rough nature of the floorboards and catches the right-hand edge of the panel on the easel, but leaves the painter in relative shadow.

There is no way of knowing if the young painter depicted here is in fact Rembrandt himself, for the face under the large black hat is not personalised, is only the setting, as it were, for the two black eyes which stare calmly at the painting. It might well be his first pupil, Gerrit Dou, and not Rembrandt at all. But the curators of the show were wise to include it, for it demonstrates one direction in which Rembrandt's work did not go: the direction of Vermeer's lifelong meditation on the relation between painting, painter and viewer, and on the mystery of painting itself – a practice which takes place in ordinary circumstances, which unfolds in time, which is subject to human decisions, and yet which has something magical, supernatural, about it, which makes the finished product something radically different from all the other material elements that make up the room and its furnishings: the wood of the floorboards and door, the easel, the palettes on the wall, the table behind the painter, the clothes he wears.

The next time we see the canvas as well as the artist in this exhibition is in a work from the end of Rembrandt's life, the Louvre *Portrait of the Artist at his Easel* of 1660 (see Plate 2). Here there is absolutely no doubt that the painter is Rembrandt himself, for his head fills the centre of the canvas and the easel is relegated to the status of a prop, barely intruding into the pictorial space along the right-hand margin. The artist here is not meditating on his work but staring out at us, as he does in nearly all these works, an ageing man who just happens to be an artist. It is as though he had early made the decision to paint the world and all it offered, and had from then on ceased to be overly concerned with the enigma of art itself.

And yet of course, as with Shakespeare, of whom much the same could be said, the enigma of art, since it is itself part of the great mystery that is the world, inevitably becomes one of his subjects, but tangentially, in the wake of other things.

It is our great good fortune that Rembrandt had a model he was able to return to throughout his working life, and whom we can thus see maturing and ageing before our eyes. In his early career he uses this most accommodating of models to try out the rhetorical effects of expression and costume, rendering him in drawings, prints and paintings in a variety of postures and guises: as a beggar, as an elegant young man, as the prodigal son, with a plumed beret, tousle-headed, wide-eyed, smiling, grimacing, in oriental attire, with a helmet. In one delightful etching he has reduced his model to a hat and a single eye, as assured of his audience's awareness of who he is and what he is up to as was Picasso when drawing himself as Priapus.

Does the fact that the model is himself make any difference? Of course our Romantic age has always thought so. For us, after all, the artist is the modern saint, his calling and dedication to

that calling as mysterious and uplifting as the calling and dedication of the saint or hermit once was to Christian Europe. For
if the artist has heard a voice telling him what has to be done,
is that not proof that such a voice does indeed speak to men?
If he has found a totally fulfilling way to live, is there not hope
that we too may one day find it? These pictures have thus been
scrutinised and meditated upon much as Protestant theologians
have meditated upon biblical episodes such as Jacob's wrestling
with the angel, the sacrifice of Isaac (what did Abraham feel?
What did Isaac feel?) and the Passion of Christ. The catalogue
here is at pains to destroy this way of approaching the work. It
points out that in his early work Rembrandt used his own face
as a way of exploring rhetorical effects, either human expressions or the fall of light; that in the seventeenth-century
likenesses of famous artists sold well; that in depicting himself
in sixteenth-century garb Rembrandt was making a statement
about his affinity with the great artists of that time, especially
the Northern school of Dürer, Rogier van der Weyden and Jan
van Eyck. There is thus, it argues, nothing unique about
Rembrandt's self-portraits, no attempt to 'understand' himself
or paint his autobiography.

This is all very salutary, but, as is the way with these
debunking exercises by historically orientated scholars, it raises
as many questions as it answers, and it closes off problems
which should really have been opened up by an exhibition of
this kind. Why do Rembrandt's self-portraits come in their
dozens, enough to fill four rooms at the National Gallery, while
from other artists we have at most five or six? Why does
Rembrandt, in his old age, return again and again to his own
features in a way unparalleled by any of his contemporaries, and
produce thereby some of his greatest works?

These paintings from the 1660s, the last decade of his life, are
the glory of the exhibition. In one or two instances we see a new
application of the rhetorical trope, for now – in the portraits

of the artist as Zeuxis, as St Paul – in the three-quarter length portrait from the Frick, with its glowing golden jerkin – and above all in the familiar large self-portrait from Kenwood House of the ageing artist with palette and maulstick in his left hand (see Plate 3) the question becomes, not what effect this or that expression makes on others, but a much more charged and serious one. As it was for Donne or the aged Yeats, rhetoric is here for Rembrandt far more than a term of art, it is a way of life. How, he asks in these pictures, do I face the world, in my fame, in my old age? As St Paul preaching the message of the risen Christ? As Zeuxis, the ancient Greek painter, laughing as he paints a gnarled old woman? As a demi-god to whom has been granted the power to create which sets him above ordinary mortals?

In the most moving paintings, in particular the two that flank the Kenwood self-portrait in this exhibition – his self-portrait from the National's own collection and the 1669 self-portrait from the Hague (see Plates 4 and 5) – even that Donne-like, that Yeatsian self-dramatisation has gone. Donne had himself sculpted in his shroud, an actor to the last, but in these paintings all acting has ceased. As a result we lose our bearings completely. The catalogue is right to insist that we should not read into these pictures our notions of what it means to be old (for by so doing we merely substitute psychological clichés for the troubling image before us). But it is silent on how we *should* read them.

The first thing that has to be said is that they depict the triumph of gravity. Not seriousness but the force that pulls all things down to earth. Rembrandt's way of working – the freedom of his brushstrokes, his refusal to cover over or smooth out – is in stark contrast to the great Italian portraits also shown here, which are said to have influenced him: Titian's *Portrait of a Young Man* and Raphael's *Portrait of Baldassare Castiglione*. The wonder of these early sixteenth-century works, as of those of

1   Rembrandt van Rijn, *Artist in his Studio*, c.1628. Photograph ©
2006, Museum of Fine Arts, Boston, MA

2   Rembrandt van Rijn, *Portrait of the Artist at his Easel*, 1660. Paris,
Musée du Louvre. Photo RMN / © Hervé Lewandowski

3 Rembrandt van Rijn, *Self-Portrait with Two Circles*, c.1665. Kenwood, The Iveagh Bequest © English Heritage Photographic Library

4   Rembrandt van Rijn, *Self-Portrait at the Age of Sixty-Three*, 1669. Photo © The National Gallery, London

5 Rembrandt van Rijn, *Self-Portrait*, 1669. By permission of the Royal Cabinet of Paintings, Mauritshuis, The Hague

the Northern artists of the time, is that they seem to give us the very essence of the sitter. What is so difficult about the Rembrandts is that there is no essence. The paint catches the light and brings out the way the skin sags on the bones, the way the eyelids droop, the bursting of innumerable little veins. This is the human face under the sway of time. We cannot grasp the essence of a person because there is no essence to grasp, only a process which began at birth and will not cease until the moment of death.

What, we might wonder, does the artist feel as he thus describes a moment of his own journey towards oblivion? But as soon as we ask it, in the face of those paintings, we are bound to see that it is the wrong kind of question: the artist does not feel or think anything over and above the task in hand, which is itself a process, the process of making. As that early painting of the artist in his studio showed, there will always be a gap between the act of painting and the consequences of that act. The early pictures say, in effect: don't try to bridge the gap, don't try to see what is on the canvas that rests on the easel. The late paintings dispense with the problem altogether as all is swept into process: the finished work is before us, but in a sense it is never finished. We move over and round it, follow this brushstroke and that, and we are kept moving from paint to flesh and from paint to hair, from the energy of the mark to the tiredness of the eye, and it is no longer a question of linking process to product, the artist's activity with the painting that has been transported and hung here for our delectation – for looking too is a process, never-ending, under the sway of time, and as we stand back and look we discover that we too are in the process of ageing, sinking a little further every instant into the earth, so that it is our face we see there on the wall and we marvel that someone who lived so long ago should be able to reveal it to us, now.

7. Escape Literature: Tristram Shandy's Journey Through France

for Peter France

VOLUME 7 OF *Tristram Shandy* is the account of Tristram's journey through France. It is a travel book like no other. Not because it is fantastical, for the fantastic is, after all, a typical ingredient of the genre, but because, poised as it is between allegory and realism, the world of pilgrimage and the world of tourism, the ancient and the modern, it raises questions about travel and the literature of travel which have lost none of their force in the intervening centuries. And it does so, as always with Sterne, in such a way that it is a joy to read and re-read.

The opening chapter of *Tristram Shandy* is rightly celebrated, but the start of Volume 7 is no less breathtaking in its speed and audacity:

> No – I think, I said, I would write two volumes every year, provided the vile cough which then tormented me, and which to this hour I dread worse than the devil, would but give me leave —— and in another place – (but where, I can't recollect now) speaking of my book as a *machine*, and laying my pen and ruler down cross-wise upon the table, in order to gain the greater credit to it – I swore it should be kept a going at that rate these forty years if it pleased but the fountain of life to bless me so long with health and good spirits.

What, we wonder, is that 'No' doing there? Who is it addressed to? For the moment we are in the dark and have to put such questions aside. We know what happened to Tristram's plan to write the story of his life: since writing about a single year seems to take many years, Tristram is doomed not only never to finish his story but to move further and further away from his goal the more he writes. But this, I think, is the first we have heard of his 'vile cough' and the threat it poses to his intention to write two volumes a year for the next forty years. Having mentioned it, though, he seems to forget about it, proceeding to tell us about his health and good spirits. ' In no one moment of my existence', he says, addressing his spirits,

> have ye once deserted me, or tinged the objects which came my way, either with sable, or with a sickly green; in dangers ye gilded my horizon with hope, and when DEATH himself knocked at my door – ye bad him come again; and in so gay a tone of careless indifference, did ye do it, that he doubted of his commission –
>
> 'There must certainly be some mistake in this matter', quoth he.

We have left the immediate present, it seems, for the reminiscence of some past experience, yet the eruption of dialogue into the narrative catapults us back into the present: what is now being recounted may have happened in the past, but it is this past moment the narrative settles into. And, we wonder, may not that opening 'No' belong to the scene now being described?

And what a strange scene it is! For we are here in the medieval world of Everyman, where Death is a man who knocks at your door when your time is up. Yet our response is to laugh, for how can Death with a capital D co-exist with the realism of the narrative, with Tristram's wholly secular and novelistic tone? We find ourselves sliding helplessly from the allegorical to the merely metaphorical, uncertain how to take what is being narrated. What follows does not help us to resolve these issues:

Now there is nothing in this world I abominate worse, than to be interrupted in a story – and I was that moment telling Eugenius a most tawdry one in my way, of a nun who fancied herself a shell-fish, and of a monk damn'd for eating a muscle, and was shewing him the grounds and justice of the procedure –

'– Did ever so grave a personage get into so vile a scrape?' quoth Death. Thou hast had a narrow escape, Tristram, said Eugenius, taking hold of my hand as I finish'd my story –

Are we in the medieval world of Everyman or has Tristram suffered some sort of stroke or heart attack, but recovered? Sterne's biographer, Arthur Cash,[1] informs us that Sterne lost his voice in the spring of 1762 – between publication, that is, of volumes 5 and 6, which came out in that year, and 7 and 8, which came out in 1765. But we cannot simply use this information as a key to the novel. For the real question remains: what is the effect, within the novel, of presenting death as a person who knocks on your door and then engages you in conversation?

It is not enough to say that Sterne is merely dramatising an illness which struck him down in 1762, just as he was starting to write Volume 7. For by choosing to tell his story as he does he implicitly condemns himself for the frivolousness of his response. Or is that very frivolousness not perhaps Tristram's best weapon, that which makes Death wonder whether he has come to the right door, 'proof', as Kafka was to put it a century and a half later, 'that inadequate, even childish measures may serve to rescue one from peril'?[2]

Sterne lets us draw our own conclusions as he develops his narrative:

1 *Laurence Sterne: The Later Years*, London, 1986.
2 'The Silence of the Sirens', in *Collected Stories*, ed. Gabriel Josipovici, London, 1993, p.398.

But there is no *living*, Eugenius, replied I, at this rate; for as this *son of a whore* has found out my lodgings –

– You call him rightly, said Eugenius – for by sin, we are told, he enter'd the world – I care not which way he enter'd, quoth I, provided he be not in such a hurry to take me out with him – for I have forty volumes to write, and forty thousand things to say and do, which no body in the world will say and do for me.

Taking Tristram's oath literally, Eugenius digs into his Christian learning and comes up with St Paul's remark in Romans: 'Wherefore, as by one man sin entered into the world, and death by sin; and so death passed upon all men, for that all have sinned ... For if through the offence of one many be dead, much more the grace of God, and the gift of grace, which is by one man, Jesus Christ, hath abounded unto many' (5:12–15). This is probably the central passage in all scripture for Protestants, as the title of Bunyan's spiritual autobiography attests. But Tristram does not seem to be aware of its import, for he brushes aside his friend's intervention and asserts the feeling of all men in a secular world that they can't die now, they have still too much to do which no one else can do for them.

Yet Sterne persists in his refusal to come down firmly on the side of either allegory or metaphor, as though to alert us to the implications of each. Since I have so much still to do, Tristram says, it is imperative, now that Death has found out where I live, that I flee for my life. That would be my advice as well, responds Eugenius. '[T]hen by heaven! I will lead [Death] a dance he little thinks of,' cries Tristram, 'for I will gallop ... without looking once behind me to the banks of the Garonne; and if I hear him clattering at my heels – I'll scamper away to mount Vesuvius – from thence to Joppa, and from Joppa to the world's end.'

But even as he speaks his words alert us to the futility of his flight. For Joppa, modern-day Jaffa, was the very spot from which Jonah sought to escape the burden of prophecy laid upon him by the Lord. As everyone knows (including Tristram – for why else would the name have popped into his head? – though he chooses to suppress such knowledge), Jonah boarded the first ship to Tarshish, Tartessos in Spain, the furthest limit of the then known world, but his attempt at flight was abortive. The modern Jonah, trying to escape his fate, determines to fly east, since he dwells in the west, but we sense that *his* flight will be just as ineffectual as Jonah's.

A question thus hangs over Tristram's journey through France. It is clearly not undertaken in a simple spirit of adventure or curiosity. But is it undertaken to shake off the effects of a sudden illness, in a spirit of defiance, or as a form of convalescence? Or is it a vain attempt to escape from the final reckoning? And if it is the latter, then might not all journeys and indeed all books, including accounts of journeys, be seen as a vain and foolish flight from the stark reality which faces us all, that of our own death? And a further question obtrudes itself: Jonah fled to escape his calling, but what is Tristram's calling? Tristram tells us that he fled abroad to save his life for the production of further volumes. The epigraph to Volume Seven tells us that what follows is not a digression but *opus ipsum*, the very work itself. But why should he be so concerned for his work? If he, as a writer, has not, like Jonah, been called by God to prophesy or witness, then is his work not merely a form of self-indulgence, another way of vainly keeping death at bay?

Tristram is in too much of a hurry to consider these questions: '['T]was a vile moment to bid adieu in; [Eugenius] led me to my chaise – *Allons!* said I; the post boy gave a crack with his whip – off I went like a cannon, and in half a dozen bounds got into Dover.' But that last phrase raises a whole host of new questions: how much space should the travel writer devote to each stage of his journey? Is he a writer first and a traveller second, or a traveller first and a writer second? A world in which we can only take metaphorically the notion of Death as a man who comes to call on individuals when their time is up, in which God no longer speaks to men as He spoke to Jonah, is a world reduced to facts devoid of meaning. But then what dictates which facts are worthy of attention?

All these questions are raised in the very next chapter. Shouldn't I have said something about the journey to Dover? Tristram wonders. After all, 'a man should know something of his own country too, before he goes abroad.' Yet,

> I never gave a peep into Rochester church, or took notice of the dock of Chatham, or visited St Thomas at Canterbury, though they all three laid in my way –
> – But mine, indeed, is a particular case –
> So, without arguing the matter further with Thomas o'Becket, or anyone else – I skip'd into the boat, and in five minutes we got under sail and scudded away like the wind.

Once upon a time people travelled in order to reach the shrine of a saint or holy man. They left their homes and set out on often hazardous journeys in order to enter the presence – *praesentia* is the word the early pilgrim narratives use – of the holy man.[3] Chaucer's last and greatest work depends on our recognition of the importance of Becket's shrine at Canterbury for the men and women of the late Middle Ages in England. But Tristram's attitude to St Thomas is just the same as his attitude to St Paul and Jonah: he mentions or alludes to them, but only to reveal their lack of significance for him. Now – and I mean the now of Tristram's journey as well as that of my writing this – pilgrimage has been replaced by tourism, *praesentia* by the

---

3 See Peter Brown, *The Cult of the Saints: Its Rise and Function in Latin Christianity*, Chicago, 1981; Gabriel Josipovici, *Touch*, New Haven and London, 1997, pp.58–78.

gawping gaze. But what is the point of our modern curiosity? And why do we need to say and show that we have been there?

Tristram, in good Protestant fashion, has nothing but contempt for relics, but what has replaced them? In Lyons, for example, he first of all wants to see the great clock, then the Jesuit library with the famous collection of Chinese books, and only 'when these curiosities are seen', "twill be no hurt if WE go to the church of St Ireneus, and see the pillar to which Christ was tied – and after that, the house where Pontius Pilate lived'. On learning that these last are actually in the next town, he replies that he is glad of it, 'for so much the sooner shall I be at the *Tomb of the two lovers*' (xxx). But if this is of more interest to the modern traveller than visiting holy sights, just what kind of interest does it elicit? What, to repeat the question, is the status of those objects which have replaced relics? Once again Sterne raises more questions than he answers. For, having expatiated at length on the story of the two lovers, and lamented their sad fate, when he finally comes to the place where their tomb should have been – 'there was no tomb to drop [my tear] upon' (XL).

Sentiment and empathy have replaced *praesentia*. We visit the tomb of the two lovers or Anne Hathaway's cottage because we have heard about them; once there, we try to imagine ourselves into the lives of the dead. But sentiment is a weak, subjective thing. The notion of *praesentia*, like God's call to Jonah, has a public, social dimension, but sentiment is only to be found in the recesses of our subjectivity. Sentiment is what is left when allegory no longer carries conviction; by the late eighteenth century it was everywhere filling the gap left by the departure of the gods. And Sterne's relation to it is as ambiguous as his relation to allegory: he plays with it, laughs at it, but also half accepts it.

Sentiment tends, in Sterne, to descend rapidly into sex. The famous episode of the donkey and the macaroons ends, significantly, with Tristram's breeches getting torn by the poor donkey's panier. And if Chapter 28, the account of the visit to Auxerre, can be read as a satire on relics, it can equally well be read as a satire on the sexual obsessions of the modern, sentimental traveller. Here Sterne muddies the waters even more than usual, for he suddenly switches to a reminiscence of a visit to Auxerre undertaken many years before in the company of his father and Uncle Toby. The party visits the abbey of St Germain, where his father, addressing the sacrist, says: '[O]ur curiosity has led us to see the bodies, of which monsieur Sequier has given the world so exact a description.' 'This tomb', says their guide, 'contains the bones of Saint Maxima, who came from Ravenna on purpose to touch the body — ' 'Of Saint Maximus', interrupts the father. 'Excuse me,' says their guide, ''twas to touch the bones of Saint Germain, the builder of the abbey'. 'And what did she get by it? said my uncle Toby — What does any woman get by it? said my father — MARTYRDOM; replied the young Benedictine, making a bow down to the ground.' Once more we are caught between two worlds, not just the Catholic and the Protestant, the ancient and the modern, but a world of clear indisputable meaning and a world where meaning is forever deferred and sexual innuendo tends to take its place.

Sterne teases the reader mercilessly in this volume as in the rest of the novel, forcing him to acknowledge that when it comes to curiosity, the sexual always trumps the intellectual. At one point he promises to draw Janatone, the innkeeper's daughter, 'in all her proportions, and with as determin'd a pencil, as if I had her in the wettest drapery', but then he quickly corrects himself: '— But your worships chuse rather that I give you the length, breadth, and perpendicular height of the great parish church.' Yet Sterne does not leave it at that. He goes on to argue that it might be better after all to provide Janatone's measurements, since the churches of Montreuil will not change in fifty years, whereas 'he who measures thee, Janatone, must do it now – thou carriest the principles of change within thy frame' (IX). So Janatone is not simply introduced as a tease: she represents life, that which cannot be fixed or reproduced in a picture or a book, that which is snuffed out when Death comes to call. She is thus, in a sense, the modern equivalent of the holy man; but how is the writer to catch her *praesentia*?

He will have, to begin with, to acknowledge his own body and its subjection to time and confusion, and, if he is a travel writer, the physical fact of both travelling and writing. 'I love the Pythagoreans (much more than I ever dare tell my dear Jenny) for their ... *"getting out of the body in order to think well."* No man thinks right whilst he is in it; blinded as he must be, with his congenial humours, and drawn differently aside ... with too lax or too tense a fibre' (XIII). But that of course is ironic, and Sterne, like Swift before him, is well aware of the fact that our first task is to acknowledge that we cannot get out of our bodies and will never be able to think well unless we do acknowledge that.

At the same time, recognising that writing is a physical activity just as much as travelling makes us realise that writing will have its own rhythms and need not be tied to those of the journey. Indeed, though travel writers are unwilling to acknowledge this, the two rhythms may be totally at odds, and the exigencies of producing a travel book may run counter to the deepest desires of both traveller and writer:

> 'Now before I quit Calais,' a travel-writer would say, 'it would not be amiss to give some account of it.' – Now I think it very much amiss – that a man cannot go quietly through a town, and let it alone, when it does not meddle with him, but that he must be turning about and drawing his pen at every kennel he crosses over, merely o'my conscience, for the sake of drawing it. (IV)

Most travel books, in fact, could be written without ever venturing from one's home.[4] Sterne shows how, in Chapter 5, where he simply copies out chunks of what he found in Jean Aimar Piganiol's *Nouveau voyage de France* (1724) concerning Calais. He follows this by assuring the reader that he is not going to subject him to this sort of thing for too long. A few chapters later, though, he is at it again, but for a different purpose: 'I wish I was at Abbeville, quoth I', and he forthwith provides us with a list of staging posts derived from the eighteenth-century equivalent of a bus timetable, the *Liste générale des postes de France*, published annually from 1708 to 1779:

> *de Montreuil a Nampont — poste et demi*
> *de Nampont* a Bernay — poste
> de Bernay a Nouvion — poste
> de Nouvion a ABBEVILLE poste (IX)

This admirably conveys the speed of the journey, and saves him having to describe the countryside he passes through. When he gets to Paris he uses lists for a different purpose:

> In the quarter called the *City* – there are fifty-three streets.
> In *St James* of the Shambles, fifty-five streets.
> In *St Oportune*, thirty-four streets.
> In... (XVIII)

This is copied straight out of Germain Brice's *Description de la ville de Paris* (1752), but the list, as in Rabelais, functions not as a conveyor of information but as a reminder of the discrepancy between whatever can be put down in a book and the teeming reality of the living city. And this particular chapter ends by drawing into his dance even the pompous Latin inscription on

4 All my factual information on eighteenth-century France comes from the invaluable Florida edition of *Tristram Shandy*, edited by Melvyn and Joan New, reprinted by Penguin, London, 1997.

the portico of the Louvre: 'Non Orbis gentem, non urbem gens habet ulam, /Urbsve Domum, Dominum nec Donus ulla parem', which Sterne cheekily renders:

Earth no such folks! – No folks e'er such a town
   As Paris is! – Sing Derry, Derry, Down. (XVIII)

As he does elsewhere in *Tristram Shandy*, Sterne is constantly forcing the reader to recognise that what he or she is reading is a written account of a journey: 'What a tract of country I have run! how many degrees nearer to the warm sun am I advanced, and how many fair and goodly cities have I seen, during the time you have been reading, and reflecting, Madam, upon this story!' (XXVI) In the chapter on Auxerre he draws attention to a writerly muddle he pretends to have got himself into:

– Now this is the most puzzled skein of all – for in this last chapter, as far at least as it has help'd me through *Auxerre*, I have been getting forwards in two different journies together, and with the same dash of the pen – for I have got entirely out of Auxerre in this journey which I am writing now, and I am got half way out of Auxerre in that which I shall write hereafter . . .; for I am this moment walking across the market-place of Auxerre with my father and uncle Toby, in our way back to dinner – and I am this moment also entering Lyons with my post-chaise broke into a thousand pieces – and I am moreover this moment in a handsome pavilion built by Pringello, upon the banks of the Garonne, which Mons. Sligniac has lent me, and where I now sit rhapsodizing all these affairs. (XXVIII)

The confusion, and the emphasis on the physicality of writing, reach their climax when he discovers that his notes for the journey, left behind in the carriage he has sold, have been used by the new owner's wife as hair-curlers: '– O Seignieur! cried I

– you have got all my remarks upon your head, Madam! – *J'en suis bien mortifiée*, said she' (XXXVIII).

And yet, such is Sterne's genius, all those elements which would seem to militate against what we might simply call good travel writing – the journey as flight, the frenetic staccato style, the constant reminder that what we are reading is something written and physical – actually combine to make this a far more convincing account of a journey – even if that is all we are interested in – than the linear forms and studiously unquestioning stance of most travel writers. Take the sea journey from Dover to Calais. 'Pray, captain, quoth I, as I was going down into the cabin, is a man never overtaken by *Death* in this passage?' There is not even time for a man to be sick replies the captain, and then in eight magnificent lines Sterne creates for us the very feel of a ship being tossed on rough seas and the effect of this on the passengers:

> – When shall we get to land? captain – they have hearts like stones – O I am deadly sick! – reach me that thing, boy – 'tis the most discomfiting sickness – I wish I was at the bottom – Madam! how is it with you? undone! Undone! un – O! undone! sir – What the first time? – No, 'tis the second, third, sixth, tenth time, sir – hey-day – what a trampling over head! hollo! cabin boy! what's the matter –
>
> The wind chopp'd about! s'Death! – then I shall meet him full in the face.
>
> What luck! – 'tis chopp'd about again, master – O the devil chop it –
>
> Captain, quoth she, for heaven's sake, let us get ashore. (II)

At the end, having, he feels, left Death well behind him, Tristram decides there is no more need for speed and he can ride his mule slowly over the rich plains of Languedoc:

There is nothing more pleasing to a traveller – or more terrible to travel-writers, than a large rich plain; especially if it is without great rivers or bridges, and presents nothing to the eye, but one unvaried picture of plenty; for after they have once told you that 'tis delicious! or delightful! (as the case happens) – that the soil was grateful, and that nature pours out all her abundance, etc... they have then a large plain upon their hands, which they know not what to do with... (XLII)

Two hundred years later Roland Barthes (who had not, I think, read Sterne, worse for him) was to write: 'Among the views elevated by the Blue Guide to aesthetic existence, we rarely find plains (redeemed only when they can be described as fertile), never plateaus.'[5] Barthes links this to the Protestant emphasis on the morality of effort and solitude; Sterne, less obsessed by morality than Barthes, seems closer to the mark when he argues that plains do not figure in travel writing because plains are – well, just plains. As novels have to have plots to hurry them along, so travelogues need mountains and valleys. 'This', says Tristram, 'is most terrible work; judge if I don't manage my plains better' (XLII). The way he does so is not to expatiate on the plains of Languedoc, but to bring his book to a surprising end with what he calls, in a deliberately terrible pun, his 'plain stories' – stories, that is, designed to pass the time while one is travelling across plains.

The tale that follows, which forms the final chapter of the volume, is typical of Sterne in that it is impossible to determine how one is meant to react to it: 'A sun-burnt daughter of Labour rose up from the groupe to meet me as I advanced towards them; her hair, which was a dark chesnut, approaching rather to a black, was tied up in a knot, all but a single tress.' She approaches, and draws him into their revels:

5 *Mythologies*, tr. Annette Laveers, London, 1993, p.74.

The sister of the youth who had stolen her voice from heaven, sung alternately with her brother — 'twas a Gascoigne roundelay.

> VIVA LA JOIA!
>
> FIDON LA TRISTESSA!

The nymphs join'd in unison, and their swains an octave below them —

This is outrageous, but it is not satire. Like Benjamin,[6] Sterne grasps that pastoral is the genre of timelessness. '*Viva la joia* was in her lips — *Viva la joia* was in her eyes... Why could I not live and end my days thus?... [W]hy could not a man sit down in the lap of content here — and dance, and sing, and say his prayers, and go to heaven with this nut-brown maid?'

The answer is, because man is a creature of time and time will not stand still:

> Then 'tis time to dance off, quoth I; so changing only part-ners and tunes I danced it away from Lunel to Montpellier — from thence to Pesçnas, Beziers — I danced it along through Narbonne, Carcasson and Castle Naudairy, till at last I danced myself into Perdrillo's pavilion [that is, back home in Yorkshire], where, pulling a paper of black lines, that I might go on straight forwards, without digression or parenthesis, in my uncle Toby's amours
> — I began thus —

In Chapter 1 Tristram had defiantly (and, one felt, rashly) promised to lead Death a dance; here, at the end of the book, we find both the journey and the story of the journey, which had so often threatened to disintegrate into chaos, transmuted into dance. Not the Dance of Death which had so haunted the

---

6 Walter Benjamin, *The Origins of German Tragic Drama*, tr. John Osborne, London, 1998, p.92.

late Middle Ages and denotes the triumph of death; and not the timeless pastoral dance of the nut-brown maid, which tries to ignore death; but a dance *with* death, a dance which accepts death, time and the body. Like those intelligent and resourceful victims of Parkinson's disease or Tourette's syndrome, about whom Oliver Sacks has so movingly written,[7] who have learned to turn their tics and lurchings into something human and arresting – a game of ping-pong, the playing of the drums – Sterne, by accepting death, time and the body, transmutes flight into dance and brings light into darkness.

7 *The Man Who Mistook his Wife for a Hat*, London, 1985.

8. Dejection

Ridiculous the waste sad time
Stretching before and after.

IT'S FUNNY HOW LINES OF POETRY, metrically correct, come into my mind in the weeks after I have finished an extended piece of work and the exhilaration of getting to the end has worn off. Then I am left with a blankness, an emptiness, which feels as if it will last for ever. Nothing seems to interest me. Time passes, that is all. But slowly.

> Tomorrow and tomorrow and tomorrow
> Creeps in this petty pace from day to day.

The lines drop into my mind and I know they correspond to my condition, but I do not feel them. Or perhaps they come into my mind because they are lines about non-feeling. Macbeth too had completed a piece of work which he imagined would transform his life, only to find, as in a fairy-tale, that though it had done just that, it was not in the way he had imagined. The fact that his work is murder, regicide even, and mine merely the writing of a novel, seems to make no difference. We are not here in the realm of ethics but of something darker, deeper, something which seems to inhabit a place where body and spirit interact. The Romantics called it Dejection:

> A grief without a pang, void, dark and drear,
> A stifled, drowsy, unimpassioned grief,
> Which finds no natural outlet, no relief,
> In word, or sigh, or tear —

Coleridge has spent the evening gazing at the western sky, and in the poem he describes 'its peculiar tint of yellow green', and the clouds and the stars and the crescent moon 'as fixed as if it grew/In its own cloudless, starless lake of blue.' But, he confesses,

> I see them all, so excellently fair,
> I see, not feel, how beautiful they are!

His skill at the poetic description of nature has not left him, but because it is now mere skill, because the night sky no longer seems to have the ability to rouse his heart to joy, it mocks rather than helps him.

A century and a half later Wallace Stevens was to write his own dejection poem:

> After the leaves have fallen, we return
> To a plain sense of things. It is as if
> We had come to an end of the imagination,
> Inanimate in an inert savoir.
>
> It is difficult even to choose the adjective
> For this blank cold, this sadness without cause.
> The great structure has become a minor house.
> No turban walks across the lessened floors.
>
> The greenhouse never so badly needed paint.
> The chimney is fifty years old and slants to one side.
> A fantastic effort has failed, a repetition
> In a repetitiousness of men and flies.

I say these last words over and over again to myself: 'A fantastic effort has failed.' 'A fantastic effort has failed.' 'A fantastic effort has failed.' It is some sort of comfort to know that someone else has been through this and even found words for it. A fantastic effort has failed. The effort to understand. To break through the barriers of confusion. To make something which will stand up by itself and give pleasure to others. All that has failed. It reveals itself now as merely a repetition of what has been done before, by myself and others, 'In a repetitiousness of men and flies.'

Occasionally people praise a book or play of mine and tell me how much it has meant to them. Of course this pleases me, but it also troubles me. Like Kafka at least in this, I am haunted by the thought that one day I will be found out and then the good boy at the head of the class will be sent to stand in the corner, accused not just of failure but of fraud. Even Borges' lines, in his little parable, 'Borges and I', seem too optimistic: 'It is no effort for me to confess,' Borges writes, 'that he has achieved some valid pages, but those pages cannot save me, perhaps because what is good belongs to no one, not even to him, but rather to the language and to tradition.' For me, in these moods, there are no valid pages, even written by another under my own name, and the notion of tradition remains empty.

At the start of his poetic career Stevens had written another dejection poem, called, typically for the poet of *Harmonium*, 'The Man Whose Pharynx Was Bad':

> The time of year has grown indifferent.
> Mildew of summer and the deepening snow
> Are both alike in the routine I know.
> I am too dumbly in my being pent...
>
> The malady of the quotidian...
> Perhaps, if winter once could penetrate
> Through all its purples to the final slate,
> Persisting bleakly in an icy haze,
>
> One might in turn become less diffident,
> Out of such mildew plucking neater mould
> And spouting new orations of the cold.
> One might. One might. But time will not relent.

As with Coleridge, there is the sense that somewhere, some time, it was different; once winter did 'penetrate / Through all its purples to the final slate'. Now though there is only blankness and the seconds ticking by. Whereas for the Eliot of the *Quartets* there is the feeling that grace may touch one at any moment and in any place, 'in the rose garden', 'in the arbour where the rain beat', 'in the draughty church at smokefall', for Coleridge, as he understands it, there is a clear chronological pattern to be discerned:

> There was a time when, though my path was rough,
>   This joy within me dallied with distress,
> And all misfortunes were but as the stuff
>   Whence Fancy made me dreams of happiness:
> For hope grew round me, like the twining vine,
> And fruits, and foliage, not my own, seemed mine.
> But now afflictions bow me down to earth:
> Nor care I that they rob me of my mirth:
>   But oh! each visitation
> Suspends what nature gave me at my birth,
>   My shaping spirit of Imagination.

It is a tragic history. Once, quite naturally, we had the power to feel joy at the beauty of the world. Nature itself had given us this faculty which, in retrospect, we can see was tied to the notion of hope. Now, however, hope has gone and 'afflictions bow me down to earth'. But these, Coleridge suggests in a final twist, he could put up with, if it was merely a matter of private loss; what is so terrible is that they seem to have put out a light in Nature, to have killed off something far more precious than personal pleasure. To have killed off the 'shaping spirit' of Imagination. Thus in a strange way Coleridge's despondency, the result of personal troubles which have come upon him in adult life, is made a thousand times worse by his feelings of guilt at somehow having done irreparable damage to the very fabric of the universe by his despondency.

These Romantic odes, however, are nothing if not dialectical. Though the theme of the poem is dejection, the poet's private state, it ends not with dejection but with joy, not with himself but with another. Already in the course of the poem he had exclaimed, mysteriously, 'O Lady! we receive but what we give'. Now, at the end, the act of thinking not of himself but of another, turns the poem round:

> 'Tis midnight, but small thoughts have I of sleep:
> Full seldom may my friend such vigils keep!
> Visit her, gentle Sleep! with wings of healing.
>   And may this storm be but a mountain-birth,
> May all the stars hang bright above her dwelling,
>   Silent as though they watched the sleeping Earth!
>   With light heart may she rise,
>   Gay fancy, cheerful eyes,
>   Joy lift her spirit, joy attune her voice:
> To her may all things live, from pole to pole,
> Their life the eddying of her living soul!
>   O simple spirit, guided from above,
> Dear Lady! friend devoutest of my choice,
> Thus mayest thou, ever, evermore rejoice.

The ability to pray for the wellbeing of another shows that, despite what the poet felt as he began the poem, his imagination is not quite dead. He may not be able to respond to nature as he once had, but the final stanza shows him responding, in some measure, to the world outside himself. His desire for her to rejoice reveals — to us if not to him — that he is not as dead inside as he had thought.

Nevertheless, despite these ambiguous hints and signs, the pattern of dejection is clear in both Coleridge and Wordsworth. Wordsworth is in no doubt at all at the start of his ode 'Intimations of Immortality':

There was a time when meadow, grove, and stream,
The earth, and every common sight,
    To me did seem
    Apparelled in celestial light,
The glory and the freshness of a dream.
It is not now as it hath been of yore; –
    Turn whereso'er I may,
    By night or day,
The things which I have seen I now can see no more.

But what if Wordsworth and Coleridge were wrong? What if they had imposed a temporal pattern on something which is in fact far more arbitrary and capricious than they imagine? That, at any rate, is what the Eliot of the *Quartets* and the Stevens of his second dejection poem seem to suggest.

Stevens, in fact, goes much further than this. As we begin his poem we do indeed seem to be entering the world of Dejection:

After the leaves have fallen, we return
To a plain sense of things. It is as if
We had come to an end of the imagination,
Inanimate in an inert savoir.

Not even an inert *knowledge*, but an inert *savoir*. The use of the French word dramatises the poet's distance from any fount of living speech: language itself is inanimate, inert:

It is difficult even to choose the adjective
For this blank cold, this sadness without cause.

There is merely the state of emptiness, sadness, and it is as though any attempt by the poet to explain it, to find adjectives to describe it, to give reasons for its existence, would transform it, would give it precisely the life that it lacks. And since the lack of life is what defines this state, to explain it would be to distort and deny it.

And yet, instead of suggesting, as Coleridge and Eliot do,

that the failure to respond to the world is a wholly negative thing, a cause for guilt even, Stevens, in this poem, keeps the paradox before us. The title should have been a warning. Not 'Dejection', not 'The Man Whose Pharynx Was Bad', but 'The Plain Sense of Things'. As if dejection here will lead us not away from the world but towards it. The earlier poem had ended bleakly: 'But time will not relent.' This one ends:

> Yet the absence of the imagination had
> Itself to be imagined. The great pond,
> The plain sense of it, without reflections, leaves,
> Mud, water like dirty glass, expressing silence
>
> Of a sort, silence of a rat come out to see,
> The great pond and its waste of the lilies, all this
> Had to be imagined as an inevitable knowledge,
> Required as a necessity requires.

The poem refuses the transformative vision of Eliot's *Burnt Norton*, where the empty pond is momentarily filled with water and with the lotus of redemption. Here there is only

> The great pond,
> The plain sense of it, without reflections, leaves,
> Mud, water like dirty glass, expressing silence
>
> Of a sort...

But it is not a celebration of the ordinary à la William Carlos Williams either. It is, rather, the refusal of the consolations of the imagination, and therefore of art. It is as though the world could only be discerned when all fictions had been banished and even the imagination had finally been laid to rest. Thus the final task of art and imagination in this hard school becomes the banishing of art, the grasping of a world bereft of imagination. Imagination dead imagine, as Beckett, another apt pupil of this school, puts it.

The Coleridgean psycho-drama has been reversed. The

shaping spirit of the imagination is here identified as the ultimate source of falsehood, that which keeps us from the world,
or rather, keeps the world from us. It must be rooted out if we
are to experience 'the plain sense of things' (and 'plain' here as
well as meaning unadorned, carries at least an echo of the French
plein, 'full'); if we are to enjoy what Stevens in another late poem
called 'An Ordinary Evening in New Haven'. The rage for
reality, the rage to experience the world in its otherness and
abundant variety, thus becomes a rage *against* imagination and
its close ally, art. But of course, if the poet is to make sense to
himself of 'the plain sense of things' and if he is to convey that
sense to others, he will have to do it through art and the imagination. Hence 'the absence of the imagination had/Itself to be
imagined.'

This paradox has been at the centre of the greatest art of our
century. Thus in Proust's *A la recherche* it is only when Marcel
learns that there is no 'great work' for him to write that he
discovers how and what to write; it is only when Yeats understands that he cannot simply write another poem celebrating
Irish mythology or politics that he at last finds his true theme:

> Those masterful images because complete
> Grew in pure mind, but out of what began?
> A mound of refuse or the sweepings of a street,
> Old kettles, old bottles, and a broken can,
> Old iron, old bones, old rags, that raving slut
> Who keeps the till. Now that my ladder's gone,
> I must lie down where all the ladders start,
> In the foul rag-and-bone shop of the heart.

It is impossible to read this closing stanza of 'The Circus
Animals' Desertion' without a note of triumph creeping into
the voice. 'The foul rag-and-bone shop of the heart' should be
an image of despair, but Yeats has managed to turn it into an
image of heroic affirmation. Just as Stevens, a great experiment

having failed, returns us to 'the plain sense of things', so Yeats is forced, by his failure to find a theme for art, to arrive at last at that which is the ground of art and of life itself: not the self, as our psychologically oriented age imagines, but that unspoken and unspeakable source of all our strivings, images and desires.

And yet. And yet. If the failure of imagination is transformed into the final triumph of imagination, if the refusal of the temptations of art becomes the final triumph of art, is there not the danger that another and more insidious myth has slipped in under the guise of unblemished truth? 'The plain sense of things' may no longer be that when it is set before us in the form of a poem called 'The Plain Sense of Things', and what has happened to the ordinary evening in New Haven by the time we have finished the poem of that name?

No one was more aware of the pressure of this question than Kafka. In a diary entry for 1917 he writes:

> Have never understood how it is possible for almost everyone who writes to objectify his sufferings in the very midst of undergoing them; thus I, for example, in the midst of my unhappiness, in all likelihood with my head still smarting from unhappiness, sit down and write to someone: I am unhappy. Yes, I can even go beyond that, and with as many flourishes as I have the talent for, all of which seems to have nothing to do with my unhappiness, ring simple, or contrapuntal, or a whole orchestration of changes on my theme. And it is not a lie, and it does not still my pain; it is simply a merciful surplus of strength at a moment when suffering has raked me to the bottom of my being and plainly exhausted all my strength. But then what kind of surplus is it?

Kafka makes no distinction between writing a poem or story and writing a diary entry or letter. In the midst of my unhappiness, he says, I can write to someone: 'I am unhappy', and then

I can elaborate this rhetorically in all sorts of ways. That does not mean I am lying. Nor does it still my pain. It does, however, seem to be a 'merciful surplus of strength' just at the very moment when suffering seemed to have 'exhausted all my strength'. So then 'what kind of surplus is it?' Is it, as Coleridge would no doubt have thought, a blessed surplus, evidence that even in this extremity God has not forgotten me, or is it, as Beckett often seems to suggest, a damned surplus, one more twist of the knife in the wound? Is it manna from heaven or the final temptation of the serpent?

Four years later Kafka returns to this theme and expresses it in a more enigmatic and compressed fashion. He writes:

> Undeniably, there is a certain joy in being able calmly to write down: 'Suffocation is inconceivably horrible.' Of course it is inconceivable – that is why I have written nothing down.

We are here at the end point of a journey which began when Dr Johnson, in his commonsensical way, berated Milton for couching *Lycidas*, his lament for Edward King, in the language of outdated mythology. For Johnson grief does not need such trappings. Indeed, it is positively mocked by them. For Kafka, though, to speak one's grief at all, even to write down the simple and unadorned words 'I am unhappy', is somehow to demean one's grief, and with it language and truth. There is, quite simply, no word for 'this blank cold, this sadness without cause', and to put down a word is to give the lie to the state.

If this is indeed the case might it not be better simply to shut up or else to treat literature merely as an amusing game with words which cannot, in the nature of things, tell us anything about ourselves and the world? Some post-Romantic artists, most notably Rimbaud, have of course taken the first option; and Postmodernism, so-called, could be said to have taken the second. But I don't think that those, like Kafka, Stevens and

Beckett, who have gone on struggling with the problem, have thereby played false with themselves or with us. Certainly, as we read them we do not experience them as either falsely consoling or falsely depressing. Rather, their works are themselves like acts of mercy in a cold world.

For the fact is that death, loss, the sense of failure, the sense of being unable to speak in a form adequate to one's condition – these are central human experiences. When Beckett says: 'I am only interested in failure', he is not asserting a credo of gloom and doom, only reiterating that a meaningful art is one that does not flinch from any aspect of the human condition, even the recognition of the essential duplicity of art. And this remark helps us to understand why it is we treasure those Romantic poems of dejection more than the poems of joy and apocalyptic vision. By contrast, any aesthetic theory that would rule this out of bounds, either by saying that artists should stop writing about 'their problems' and write about 'the real world' instead, or by saying that since art is always duplicity the artist should confine his role to the merely playful – any such theory will give us plenty of rich food, yet leave us perennially hungry.

I find now that having written this talk about dejection has brought me a certain amount of release, even of satisfaction. Instead of trying to avoid the sense that in some way I had ceased to respond and simply 'get on with it', I faced it head on. By so doing I found, for the first time for a long time, that I had the sense of moving forward, not merely endlessly repeating. At the same time Kafka's quiet, puzzled remarks, continue to haunt me. May this not simply be a further step into the mire rather than the first decisive step towards solid ground?

Except that Kafka does not quite say that. As always with him, he confronts an enigma, does not seek a solution. He asks simply: 'But then what kind of surplus is it?'

9. Kierkegaard and the Novel

MY INTENTION IS NOT HERE TO WRITE ABOUT KIERKEGAARD as novelist, though that would be an interesting subject. After all, each of his pseudonymous works is in a sense an attempt to extend the range of fiction as well as philosophy, and I can see no good reason why they should be dumped in a box marked 'Philosophy' while Sterne's *Tristram Shandy* or Dostoevsky's *Notes from Underground* are dumped in one marked 'Literature'.

However, to write about Kierkegaard as novelist implies that we know what a novel is, and one of the things Kierkegaard does in the course of his brief glittering career is to raise questions about that very issue. He does so by reminding us that we cannot begin to understand what novels are, what fiction is, until we recognise that how we think about fiction depends on how we think about ourselves and our lives. In other words, if the concept of fiction cannot be taken for granted it is because story-telling is intimately bound up with what we are, not in our essence but in our concrete social and historical reality.

A good place to start is Kierkegaard's introduction to *On Authority and Revelation*. The book turns on the question of authority: what authority do I have for what I say and write? What authority do authors have in general and in the present age in particular? Artists are fond of referring to their 'calling', but in what sense have they been called? In the same sense as the Apostles were called by Jesus? And, if not, are they justified in using such a term?

Kierkegaard begins his introduction in a typically offhand way, with a reference to the world of the barber-shop, where rumours and gossip fly and which acts in small communities at the time Kierkegaard was writing, the 1840s, as a kind of informal newspaper. Then, with no apparent change of gear, he plunges into the heart of the matter: '[I]t is not improbable that the lives of many men go on in such a way that they have indeed premises for living but reach no conclusions... For it is one thing that a life is over, and a different thing that a life is finished by reaching a conclusion.'[1] The ordinary man, he goes on, the one whose life has no conclusion, may, if he finds he has talent, decide to become an author. But, says Kierkegaard,

> he may have extraordinary talents and remarkable learning, but an author he is not, in spite of the fact that he produces books... No, in spite of the fact that the man writes, he is not essentially an author; he will be capable of writing the first... and also the second part, but he cannot write the third part – the last part he cannot write. If he goes ahead naïvely (led astray by the reflection that every book must have a last part) and so writes the last part, he will make it thoroughly clear by writing the last part that he makes a written renunciation to all claim to be an author. For though it is indeed by writing that one justifies the claim to be an author, it is also, strangely enough, by writing that one virtually renounces this claim. If he had been thoroughly aware of the inappropriateness of the third part – well, one may say, *si tacuisset, philosophus mansisset* [if he had kept quiet he would have remained a philosopher].

---

1 *On Authority and Revelation: The Book on Adler, or a Cycle of Ethico-Religious Essays*, tr. Walter Lowrie, Princeton, 1955. All the quotations that follow are from the Introduction.

And he concludes with a pregnant aphorism: 'To find the conclusion, it is necessary first of all to observe that it is lacking, and then in turn to feel quite vividly the lack of it.'

It is not too much to say that those who have felt the full force of Kierkegaard's argument here will be forever separated from those – the bulk of writers, readers and reviewers of fiction in Kierkgaard's day and our own – who have not. And I hasten to add that one does not need to have read Kierkegaard to feel it, only to be aware of the possibilities of art in the post-Romantic age. For Kierkegaard is merely articulating, with great humour and also great power and acumen, what has been felt and struggled with by Hölderlin and Mallarmé, Kafka and Proust, Rilke, Eliot and Wallace Stevens: that since the writer has no authority for what he is saying, to go on writing as if he had is the greatest sin, for it falsifies the way things are instead of helping to clarify it.[2]

The argument turns on the question of the difference between endings and conclusions: 'For it is one thing that a life is over and a different thing that a life is finished by reaching its conclusion.' In the first case a man goes through life and then dies. His life has not had any meaning, it has simply consisted of a series of actions and reactions, and his death does not have any meaning either. His life is like a line which goes along the page for a while and then stops. To say that the line goes from A to B implies that there is a shape to it, a certain kind of progression. But the line does not 'go' anywhere. It exists for a while and then stops. Clov and Hamm in Beckett's *Endgame* wind up an alarm clock and then listen to it ringing. When it stops Clov says: 'The end is terrific!' 'I prefer the middle,' replies Hamm. This is both funny and disturbing. Funny because

---

2   Erich Heller and Maurice Blanchot are the critics who have most fully understood the implications of the Romantic crisis of authority, and explored it in all their writings with consummate skill.

Hamm and Clov, by treating or pretending to treat the undif-
ferentiated sound of an alarm clock as they would a piece of
music, make fun of concert-goers. Disturbing because behind
the concert-goer stands the critic of art in general, and its prac-
titioners, and we ourselves, who insist on seeing meaning and
value in our lives when we know full well that in the end there
is none. As Kierkegaard puts it: all we ever have in life are gossip
and rumours; our world is the world of the newspaper and the
barber-shop, it is not the world of Jesus and his Apostles. A
person seduced by our culture's admiration for art into
becoming a writer embarks on a more dangerous enterprise than
he or she may realise. If they embark on a work of fiction they
imply that they have escaped the world of rumour, that instead
of living horizontally, as it were, they live vertically, in touch
with some transcendental source of authority. And we who read
them do so because we feel that this must indeed be the case.
But the closer they get to the end the clearer it becomes that
there is no vertical connection. And should they try to bring
their work to a close the contradiction between what it implies
and the truth of the matter will become quite obvious. The only
way for some semblance of truth and clarity to emerge is for
the author to recognise that the conclusion, that which would
finally give authority to the book, is lacking, to feel this quite
vividly and to make us feel it as well.

I have been moving indiscriminately between the terms
'fiction', 'the novel' and 'the writer', but it is time to try and
distinguish them. Kierkegaard himself does not do so explicitly, but it is clear that in the passage above he is thinking of
novels, and elsewhere he makes it clear that there is a historical
dimension to the problem, that earlier writers, such as the
authors of fairy-tales and the ancient Greek tragedians, were not
faced with the same problems as those who write in the age of
the barber-shop and the newspaper. It may be helpful, though,
to turn first to a writer who, out of the same concerns as

Kierkegaard, *has* attempted to define the difference between the storyteller and the novelist. That writer is Walter Benjamin.

In one of his finest essays, 'The Storyteller', Benjamin notes that

> The earliest symptom of a process whose end is the decline of storytelling is the rise of the novel at the beginning of modern times. What distinguishes the novel... from all other forms of prose literature – the fairy tale, the legend, even the novella – is that it neither comes from oral tradition nor goes into it... The storyteller takes what he tells from experience – his own or that reported by others. And he in turn makes it the experience of those who are listening to his tale. The novelist has isolated himself. The birthplace of the novel is the solitary individual, who is no longer able to express himself by giving examples of his most important concerns, is himself uncounseled, and cannot counsel others.[3]

Benjamin finds the authority of the storyteller to rest in death: 'Dying was once a public process in the life of the individual and a most exemplary one... In the course of modern times dying has been pushed further and further out of the perceptual world of the living.' As we live isolated and alone, so we die 'stowed away in sanatoria or hospitals'; but 'not only a man's knowledge or wisdom, but above all his real life – and this is the stuff that stories are made of – first assumes transmissible form at the moment of his death.'[4] A public death surrounded by traditional customs is what once gave 'that authority which even the poorest wretch in dying possesses for the living around him. This authority,' concludes Benjamin, 'is at the very source of the story.'

3 'The Storyteller', in *Illuminations*, ed. Hannah Arendt, tr. Harry Zohn, London, 1970, p.87.
4 *Ibid.*, pp.93–4.

There may be something romantic and mystical in Benjamin's formulation, but it is easy to see that he is on to something serious and substantial. The storyteller is part of a tradition: he acquires his wisdom from others and in turn passes it on to others. The novelist, by contrast, is isolated, 'is himself uncounseled and cannot counsel others'.

Kierkegaard, unfortunately, did not write about storytelling as opposed to novel-writing, but he did touch on the issue in a diary entry from 1837, before, that is, he had published any of his works. He is meditating on the telling of stories to children, and he puts forward the view that there are

> two recommended ways of telling children stories, but there are also a multitude of false paths in between. The *first* is the way unconsciously adopted by the nanny, and whoever can be included in that category. Here a whole fantasy world dawns for the child and the nannies are themselves deeply convinced the stories are true... which, however fantastic the content, can't help bestowing a beneficial calm on the child. Only when the child gets a hint of the fact that the person doesn't believe her own stories are there ill-effects – not from the content but because of the narrator's insincerity – from the lack of confidence and suspicion that gradually develops in the child.[5]

The second way, he goes on, 'is possible only for someone who with full transparency reproduces the life of childhood, knows what it demands, what is good for it, and from his higher standpoint offers the children a spiritual sustenance that is good for them – who knows how to be a child, whereas the nannies themselves basically are children'. And he concludes that 'false paths

---

5 Søren Kierkegaard, *Papers and Journals: A Selection*, tr. Alastair Hannay, London, 1996, p.73. The following quotations come from this section, pp.73–7.

crop up by coming beyond the nanny position but not staying the whole course and stopping half-way.'

The movement of thought here is typical of Kierkegaard. First we have an original, 'natural' situation; then a series of false intermediary positions, positions which fail to take account of the new situation; and, finally, a radical solution which takes the new situation fully into account. The storyteller in Benjamin's argument, we could say, is like the nanny who, deeply convinced of the truth of what she is saying, bestows a beneficial calm on the child. The novelist is like the nanny who can no longer quite believe what she is saying, and thus leaves the child uneasy and suspicious. The 'essential writer', the one who senses that a conclusion is lacking, feels quite vividly the lack and makes the reader feel it too; by so doing he, 'from his higher standpoint offers the children a spiritual sustenance that is good for them'. The 'essential writer' thus in a sense 'knows how to be a child, whereas the nannies themselves are basically children.'

The same pattern is to be found in an essay in the first part of *Either/Or*, 'The Tragic in Ancient Drama Reflected in the Tragic in Modern Drama'. Here it is drama, not fiction, that Kierkegaard is concerned with, but the parallels with Benjamin's essay are striking. In ancient Greek culture, says Kierkegaard, 'even if the individual moved freely, he nevertheless rested in the substantial categories of state, family, and destiny.'[6] Modern man, on the other hand, is alone, and takes all decisions for himself. Thus tragedy is alien to him, for by throwing 'his whole life upon his shoulders as being the result of his own acts', he turns 'tragic guilt into ethical guilt'; the tragic hero becomes merely the bad man, and badness and goodness have no aesthetic interest. Thus writers who persist in trying to write

6 *Either/Or*, Vol. 1, tr. D.F. and L.M. Swenson, revised by Howard A. Johnson, New York, 1959, pp.141–2.

tragedy today merely produce banality and confuse instead of clarifying our relation to the world. There is, however, he goes on, a truly modern kind of tragedy, but it cannot form the subject of drama because it does not belong to the realm of the aesthetic at all. This is a totally inward kind of tragedy, and its paradigm is Christ, who lived a life of absolute obedience without any outward evidence that he was doing so. The modern writer who wishes to write tragedy must do so then in a roundabout way, by showing us that tragedy is no longer possible and making us intuit what cannot be said. In other words, he must force us to recognise that the conclusion, that which would finally give authority to his play, is lacking, and making us feel vividly the lack of it. That is what Beckett does in *Endgame*. 'What's happening? What's happening?' Hamm asks at one point. 'Something is taking its course', replies Clov. Something, somewhere, is taking its course, which is quite a different thing from the ringing of the alarm clock, but it is also something that cannot be brought out into the open and given a clear beginning, middle and end.

But the sense of lack, of modern storytelling as false coinage, pseudo-nutrition, is to be found in all the great Modernists, and notably in Kafka, where it reaches its clearest expression in one of his last stories, 'A Hunger Artist', in which the fasting showman confesses, as he is dying, that he only fasted 'because I couldn't find the food I liked. If I had found it, believe me, I should have made no fuss and stuffed myself like you or anyone else.' It is already there in Kafka's outburst, in an early letter to his friend Oskar Pollack:

> I think we ought to read only the kind of books that wound and stab us. If the book we're reading doesn't wake us up with a blow on the head, what are we reading it for? So that it will make us happy, as you write? Good Lord, we would be happy precisely if we had no books, and the kind of books that make us happy are the kind we could

write ourselves if we had to. But we need the books that affect us like a disaster, that grieve us deeply, like the death of someone we loved more than ourselves, like being banished into forests far from everyone, like a suicide. A book must be the axe for the frozen sea inside us. That is my belief.[7]

To understand more fully what it was Kierkegaard had against the novel and modern tragedy we have to understand what it was Kierkegaard had against the greatest philosopher of the preceding generation, Hegel. 'I nurture what is for me at times a puzzling respect for Hegel,' he writes in his journal in 1845, for all the world like Nietzsche trying to come to terms with his own ambivalent feelings towards Wagner.

> I have learned much from him, and I know very well that I can still learn much more when I return to him again... His philosophical knowledge, his amazing learning, the insight of his genius, and everything else good that can be said of a philosopher, I am willing to acknowledge... But nevertheless, it is no less true that someone who is really tested in life, who in his need resorts to thought, will find Hegel comical despite all his greatness.[8]

What is it that is so comical about Hegel? It is, simply, that he forgets the one essential thing: that each of us has a single, unique life and each of us must die, and that this is not a mere contingent fact about us, but the most important thing. An 'objection must first be made to modern philosophy,' says Kierkegaard in the *Concluding Unscientific Postscript*, that massive work he thought would cap his pseudonymous production and lay the ghost of Hegel once and for all:

7 Franz Kafka, *Letters to Friends, Family and Editors*, tr. Richard and Clara Winston, London, 1978, p.16.
8 *Papers and Journals*, p.195.

Not that it has a mistaken presupposition, but that it has a comical presupposition, occasioned by its having forgotten, in a sort of world-historical absent-mindedness, what it means to be a human being. Not indeed, what it means to be a human being in general; for this is the sort of thing that one might even induce a speculative philosopher to agree to; but what it means that you and I and he are human beings, each one for himself.[9]

What Kierkegaard objects to in Hegel's system (leaving aside the question of how right his critique of Hegel may be and how far he is simply attacking Hegelianism, the dominant philosophy of the age) is this: that in asking us to think of history and of individual lives from the end, backwards, it misses what is central to life: that it is lived forwards.[10] As far as history is concerned this means that it will always be an account of the winners, never of the losers, since in world-historical terms it was necessary for the losers to lose. As far as the individual is concerned it leaves out of account the fact that for us there is no pattern, only the moment with its choices. For Kierkegaard, Hegel's system and the bland Hegelian Christianity trumpeted from pulpits every Sunday are not simply wrong on that score: in their insistence that a pattern is known to the speaker (that Abraham sacrifices his son as a prefiguration of Christ's sacrifice for us, for example) it falsifies both the past (ignoring Abraham's anguish as he went to Mount Moriah) and the

---

9 *Concluding Unscientific Postscript*, tr. David F. Swenson and Walter Lowrie, Princeton, 1968, p.109.

10 See IV A 164: 'It is quite true what philosophy says: that life must be understood backwards. But then one forgets the other principle: that it must be lived forwards. Which principle, the more one thinks it through, ends exactly with the thought that temporal life can never properly be understood precisely because I can at no instant find complete rest in which to adopt the position: backwards' (*Papers and Journals*, p.161).

present (since it treats its audience as though they were already dead and in heaven).

How to wake people up? How to bring them back to a sense that their own lives are infinitely precious? Not, at any rate, by presenting them with another system, for the whole point is that

> [a]n existential system cannot be formulated. Does this mean that no such system exists? By no means; nor is this implied in our assertion. Reality itself is a system – for God; but it cannot be a system for any existing spirit. System and finality correspond to one another, but existence is prcisely the opposite of finality... Existence separates, and holds the various moments of existence discretely apart; the systematic thought consists of the finality which brings them together.[11]

Kierkegaard has a model for his method, which depends not on what is said but on the tension between what is said and the person speaking, and that model is Socrates. In his earliest book, *The Concept of Irony*, he contrasts the irony of Socrates with the System of Hegel, and shows how little Hegel understands Socrates. Hegel does not understand, says Kierkegaard, that the 'self' of Socrates is not a plenum but only the marker of 'I know nothing'. Hegel sees Socrates as a part of his System, as the triumph of the individual and subjectivity over the Gods and external authority, whereas, says Kierkegaard in a wonderful image, Socrates 'placed individuals under his dialectical vacuum pump, pumped away the atmospheric air they were accustomed to breathing, and left them standing there.'[12] The discourse of Socrates, he says, 'does not have the powerful pathos of enthusiasm; his bearing does not have the absolute authority of personality; his indifference is not a blissful relaxation in his

---

11 *Concluding Unscientific Postscript*, p.107.
12 *The Concept of Irony*, tr. H.V. and E.H. Hong, Princeton, 1989, p.178.

own repletion... What bears him up is the negativity that still has engendered no positivity.'

Kierkegaard comes back to this point about negativity in the *Postscript*. As ever, he is aware of the traps that lie in wait for even the most rigorous thinker: 'The subjective existing thinker who has the infinite in his soul has it always, and for this reason his form is always negative,' he says. 'When it is the case that he actually reflects existentially the structure of existence in his own existence, he will always be precisely as negative as he is positive, for his positiveness consists in the continuous realization of the inwardness through which he becomes conscious of the negative.' He goes on to say that

> Among the so-called negative thinkers, there are some who, after having had a glimpse of the negative have elapsed into positiveness, and now go out into the world like town criers to advertise, prescribe, and offer for sale their beautific negative wisdom...These town criers of negativity are not much wiser than the positive thinkers, since they are essentially positive. They are not existing thinkers; once upon a time perhaps they were, until they found their result; from that moment they no longer existed as thinkers, but as town criers and auctioneers.[13]

We have seen many such in modern times. Indeed, the entire movement known as Postmodernism can be seen as a prime example of Kierkegaard's dictum. Instead of a struggle to 'hold apart' came a new system, which 'brings together', even if it was a system based on some theory of apartness. Kierkegaard, by contrast, remains aware that 'the genuine subjective thinker is always as negative as he is positive', and that 'he continues to be such as long as he exists, not once and for all in a chimerical

13 *Concluding Unscientific Postscript*, p.78.

mediation.' Such a thinker, he says, 'is conscious of the negativity of the infinite in existence, and he constantly keeps the
wound of the negative open, which in the bodily realm is some
times the condition for a cure.' The others let the wound heal
over and become positive; they cease to be learners and become
teachers.

How to stop oneself becoming a teacher? How to think
against thinking? For that is what it amounts to, since thinking,
even thinking that existence is always more and other than
thinking, is still always thinking. That is Kierkegaard's central
insight and central preoccupation, as the journals show, from
the beginning to the end of his writing life. Thus, in a series of
diary entries from 1837 (before, that is, he had written any of
his books) he notes that 'the humorist' can never become 'a
systematizer' since 'the systematizer believes he can say everything, and that whatever cannot be said is wrong and
unimportant', whereas the humorist 'lives in life's fullness and
so feels how much is always left over, even if he has expressed
himself in the most felicitous manner possible (hence this disin-
clination to write)'.[14] This leads him into a powerful meditation
on the difference between the indicative and the subjunctive,
between, that is, the mode of existence and the mode of possibility: 'The indicative thinks something as actual (the identity
of thinking and the actual). The subjunctive thinks something
as thinkable.' The writer sensitive to the difference between
thinking and living will reflect this distinction by choosing the
subjunctive, the mode of possibility, not the indicative, the
mode of actuality: 'One should be able to write a whole novel
in which the present tense subjunctive was the invisible soul, as
light is for painting.' The true writer, conscious of the precious
nature of the actual, will use the subjunctive precisely because

14 *Papers and Journals*, pp.90–1.

the indicative means so much to him: 'That is why one can truthfully say that the subjunctive, which enters as a glimpse of the individuality of the person in question, is a dramatic line whereby the narrator steps aside and makes the remark as being true of the character (poetically), not as factual, not even as if it might be fact; it is presented under the illumination of subjectivity.'

Kierkegaard is still struggling with the problem in 1850, five years after the publication of the *Postscript,* which was supposed to have settled it once and for all. '"Actuality" cannot be conceived,' he writes in his journal for that year:

> Johannes Climacus [in the *Postscript*] has already shown this correctly and very simply. To conceive something is to dissolve actuality into *possibility* – but then it is impossible to conceive it, because conceiving something is transforming it into possibility and so not holding on to its actuality. As far as actuality is concerned, conception is retrogressive, a step backward, not a progress. Not that 'actuality' contains no concepts, by no means; no, the concept which is come by through conceptually dissolving it into possibility is also inside actuality, but there is still a something more – that it is actuality. To go from possibility to actuality is a step forward (except in respect of evil): to go from actuality to possibility is a step backward. But there's this deplorable confusion in that modern times have incorporated 'actuality' into logic and then, in distraction, forgotten that 'actuality' in logic is still only a 'thought actuality', i.e. it is possibility.[15]

Everything would be fine if works like Hegel's *Phenomenology* presented their ideas as hypotheses, not actuality, but does this happen? No. And it is the same with history:

15 *Ibid.*, p.470.

But isn't history actual? Certainly. But what history? No doubt the six thousand years of the world's history are actuality, but one that is put behind us; it is and can exist for me only as thought actuality, i.e. as possibility. Whether or not the dead have actually realised existentially the tasks which were put before them in actuality has now been decided, has been concluded; there is no more existential actuality for them except in what has been put behind them, which again, for me, exists only as ideal actuality, as thought actuality, as possibility.[16]

In other words, I can think of history as actuality, but the very thinking of it robs it of its actuality.

This is so difficult to grasp precisely because 'to grasp' means 'to understand' and Kierkegaard is arguing here that there will always be a gap between understanding and lived actuality. We can get a purchase on his argument by turning to one of Beckett's finest stories, 'Dante and the Lobster'. There the protagonist, Belacqua Shua, a Dublin intellectual and layabout, having bought a lobster for dinner at his aunt's behest, is appalled when he discovers that the creature is alive and the aunt about to cook it by dropping it into boiling water. He tries to placate his feelings of guilt and horror with the cliché: 'It's a quick death, God help us all.' But the narrative will not let him get away with this: 'It is not,' the story ends. Here the distinction between the subjunctive and the indicative is a gulf which divides those – the aunt, Belacqua, the reader – who are only asked to imagine what it is to die by being plunged alive into boiling water, and the lobster, for whom this is actuality. Of course 'It is not' is still part of the story, and even the reader's recognition that 'it is not' a quick death is still only an imagi-

16 *Ibid.*, p.470.

native recognition, still, for us, one possibility among others. So Beckett will have to start again and, as he says elsewhere, fail again, fail better.

We can now begin to see why Kierkegaard said that the more an inessential writer writes the more he reveals that he is not a writer. For he writes as though system and existence were one, and, not noticing that anything is amiss with his method, he perpetuates confusion and misunderstanding. In *Fear and Trembling*, on the other hand, Kierkegaard brings out powerfully how impossible it is for narrative, and even for language to convey what the individual is going through as he faces the choices life puts before him. All the narrator, Johannes de Silentio, can say is: I understand only that I do not understand Abraham. Thus he can bring us to the point where we too understand that we do not understand, and then leave us there.

In *Either/Or* Kierkegaard sets two life-views against each other by means of collage, forcing us to make our choice between them and then to recognise that both are right and neither is, so that we go round and round, warming to the young man of the first part, with his wit and melancholy and vulnerability, then recognising that the older man is right when, in the second half, he criticises the young man for wallowing in his condition, for wanting all women, all futures, instead of committing himself to one. Yet we also come to see that the older man is a complacent and self-satisfied bore who has no inkling of the impossibility of choice for one who has begun to question the values of a bourgeois existence of marriage, children and getting on in life. Still, tiresome as he is, is the older man not perhaps right? Would things not perhaps change decisively for the young man were he to take the plunge and commit himself? Perhaps the older man has been through the same thing and simply found it in himself to make his choice.

Either/Or is a brilliant exploration of the possibilities open to human nature in the wake of the French Revolution; at the same time it is a powerful political critique both of a reliance on tradition and on the individual. In *Fear and Trembling* the question is no longer to set two life-views against each other but to ask how it is possible to become a Knight of Faith, like Abraham. The narrator can make us feel vividly that he – and we – cannot really understand Abraham, but the implication remains that so long as he goes on writing about Abraham he himself will never be a Knight of Faith. That is Kierkegaard's problem: you cannot live in both the subjunctive and the indicative at the same time. He cannot remain simply ironical, like his beloved Socrates. Times have changed. Christianity, with its new imperatives, has come into the world and, besides, there is no Plato to write down his words. He is committed to writing in order to make people see the lies they are telling themselves, but so long as he goes on writing he remains in the subjunctive mode and so cuts himself off from the life he most desires. He feels that if only he could make the leap he would himself become a Knight of Faith, quietly going about his tasks in the world, unknown to men but in a meaningful relationship to God and to himself. But what does it mean, to make the leap? To stop writing? To take Holy Orders? He has in a sense already made the leap by devoting himself to his vocation. But what is this vocation? Has God in fact called him? Is this what God really wanted of him? Did God not perhaps rather want him to marry Regine, and lead a quiet, unadventurous life, far from the temptations of authorship? There is, of course, no answer to these questions, yet they will not go away. If only, he thinks, he could quiet his intellect, put to sleep his febrile imagination, then perhaps he would, finally, be a kind of Abraham. But he cannot. This is the sort of person he is and the sort of person his upbringing has made him, and all he can do is go on writing about the difficulty, the impossibility, the desirability, of that leap.

The trouble is that Abraham does not need to make a leap.

He just is – Abraham. Kierkegaard understood this well, and seeks to explain the difference by arguing that since Christ's Incarnation matters have changed totally. To be natural is no longer enough, for what Christ teaches is that nature must be redeemed by faith:

> Voltaire is said to have remarked somewhere that he would refuse to believe in the hereditary nobility until there was historical proof of a child being born with spurs. Similarly I would say: I propose for the time being to keep to the old view that the Christian and the human, the humane, are qualitative opposites; I propose keeping to that until we are informed that a naturally, in other words innately, self-denying child has been born.[17]

As no child is born with spurs, so no child is born a Christian. And baptism is of course merely the Church's way of fitting spurs on to the child and pretending they are now a natural part of him. For Kierkegaard, radical Protestant that he is, the logic of his position is simply this: 'To love God is impossible... without hating what is human.'

At other times, though, he is less certain of his ground. Perhaps this Manichaean view is not the truth but only his own biased perspective on things:

> If I look at my personal life, am I a Christian or isn't this personal existence of mine a pure poetic existence with a dash of the demonic?... Is there not an element of despair in all this, starting a fire in a kind of betrayal, just to throw oneself into God's arms? Maybe, since it might turn out that I didn't become a Christian.[18]

---

17 *Ibid.*, p.525.
18 *Ibid.*, p.392.

Such torments can be replicated in the letters and diaries of Kafka and in the utterances of many of the great Modernist writers. They, however, seem to have been able to develop and grow through an innate trust in the act of writing itself, in their willingness to embrace confusion and uncertainty and to find a new voice in the process. But a very narrow line divides such trust from the bad faith of becoming a 'hawker' and so failing to keep 'the wound of negativity' open. One could say that Kierkegaard's personal tragedy lay in the fact that he was not enough of a writer to trust in the writing process itself (though he appears to have taken a great deal of pleasure in it) but too much of one ever to be a Knight of Faith. But then that too could perhaps be seen as the best way of defining all those modern writers whom, like Kierkegaard, we may call essential writers, to distinguish them from the scribblers, even the highly talented scribblers, who will always be with us.

10. Kafka's Children

'I HAVE ELEVEN SONS,' begins the story called 'Eleven Sons', and the entire piece consists of a description of these sons:

> The first is outwardly very plain, but serious and clever; yet, although I love him as I love all my children, I do not rate him very highly. His mental processes seem to me to be too simple. He looks neither to right nor to left, nor into the far distance; he runs around all the time, or rather revolves, within his own little circle of thoughts.
>
> The second is handsome, slim, well made; one draws one's breath with delight to watch him with a fencing foil. He is clever too, but has experience of the world as well; he has seen much, and therefore even our native country seems to yield more secrets to him than to the stay-at-home. Yet I am sure that this advantage is not only and not even essentially due to his travels, it is rather an attribute of his own inimitable nature, which is acknowledged for instance by everyone who has ever tried to copy him in, let us say, the fancy high dive he does into the water, somersaulting several times over, yet with almost violent self-control... [D]espite all this (I ought really to feel blessed with such a son) my attachment to him is not untroubled. His left eye is a little smaller than his right and blinks a good deal; only a small fault, certainly, and one which even lends more audacity to his face than it

would otherwise have... Of course, it is not the physical blemish that worries me, but a small irregularity of the spirit that somehow corresponds to it, a kind of stray poison in the blood, a kind of inability to develop to the full the potentialities of his nature which I alone can see. On the other hand, this is just what makes him again my own true son, for this fault of his is a fault of our whole family and in him it is only too apparent.

My third son...[1]

In a letter to Max Brod Kafka wrote: 'The eleven sons are quite simply eleven stories I am working on this very moment.' Inevitably, of course, critics have tried to relate each son to a specific story known to us. But this is misguided. Not because Kafka was having Brod on – it would be unlike him to do that – but because it implies that once we have matched the sons to the stories we have dealt with *this* story. Yet even if we knew – if Kafka had left us a list, say – which stories he was referring to with each description, that would only be the start rather than the end of our enquiry.

It is of course quite common for writers to talk about their books as their children, even to single one out as a favourite child, and we all know more or less what they mean. What is disconcerting about Kafka, here and everywhere else, is his literalism and his detail. It is already difficult enough to decide how to respond to these descriptions if we take them at face value – difficult because this ostensibly calm and scrupulous father-narrator seems to see so much more and more deeply than any

---

1 I have used the classic translations of the stories by Willa and Edwin Muir throughout. Occasionally I have altered their version in the interests of accuracy, making it clear where I do so. Elsewhere I have used the standard English translations. All the stories mentioned here can be found in *Franz Kafka, Collected Stories*, ed. and introduced by Gabriel Josipovici, London, 1993.

of us is likely to be able to do even where those closest to us are concerned; and because the physical and mental qualities of the sons seem to be so bafflingly intertwined ('He looks neither to right nor to left, nor into the far distance; he runs around all the time, or rather revolves, within his own little circle of thoughts.'). But our bafflement increases a hundredfold if we try to think of these sons as stories. Can stories really be imagined in this way? What can it mean to say that a story executes a fancy high dive so perfectly that it cannot be imitated, yet has a weakness in its left eye which seems to correspond to a deeper, a moral blemish, 'a kind of inability to develop the full potentialities of [its] nature'? What led Kafka to think of his fiction in this way, and what does it tell us about the fiction itself?

Throughout his life Kafka commented, in his diary and in letters to friends, on his own work and on that of writers he happened to be reading. These remarks suggest that though Kafka, unlike Proust, Eliot or Virginia Woolf, wrote no critical essays, he was anything but a naïve untutored genius. Like them he had obviously thought long and hard about his craft, and his comments on literature, like theirs, carry an authority denied most critics because it clearly matters so profoundly to him.

We have also got so used to thinking of him as a morbid and even masochistic individual that it is worth stressing that many of his observations are as punchy and self-confident as Eliot's. Thus on 8 October 1917 he noted in his diary that 'The Stoker' (which he had written in the great creative outburst of September–October 1912 and which later became the first chapter of his unfinished novel, *America*) was 'a sheer imitation of Dickens'. He goes on, however, forsaking syntax in his eagerness to get his thoughts down on paper:

Dickens's opulence and great, careless prodigality, but in consequence passages of awful insipidity in which he wearily works over effects he has already achieved. Gives one a barbaric impression because the whole does not make sense, a barbarism that I, it is true, thanks to my weakness and wiser for my epigonism, have been able to avoid. There is a heartlessness behind his sentimentally overflowing style. These rude characterisations which are artificially stamped on everyone and without which Dickens would not be able to get on with his story even for a moment.[2]

And he adds that Robert Walser (and this may surprise those who have tried to compare Kafka to Walser) 'resembles [Dickens] in his use of vague, abstract metaphors'.

This kind of balanced, even self-confident judgement, should make us wary of taking Kafka's frequent self-criticism as nothing but self-torment, based on his perennially poor view of himself. May it not be that Kafka knows better? Of course, like every writer, he has a tendency to think of his own work as both better and worse than it in fact is – but what does 'in fact is' mean here? We may rate his work very highly, but perhaps our standards are simply not high enough.

'Great antipathy to "Metamorphosis"', he writes in his diary on 19 January 1914. 'Unreadable ending. Imperfect almost to its very marrow.' 'Just now read the beginning [of 'Blumfeld, An Elderly Bachelor']', he notes on 9 February 1915. 'It is ugly and gives me a headache. In spite of all its truth it is wicked, pedantic, mechanical, a fish barely breathing on a sandbank.' A few days before (18 January) he had started his diary in typical

---

2 *The Diaries of Franz Kafka*, ed. Max Brod. Originally in two volumes, Vol. I (1910–13), tr. Joseph Kresh; Vol. II (1914–23), tr. Martin Greenberg with the cooperation of Hannah Arendt, Harmondsworth, 1964. All subsequent quotes are from this edition, which has been reprinted many times.

vein: 'Headache, slept badly. Incapable of sustained, concentrated work.' But then: 'In spite of that began a new story; I was afraid I should spoil the old ones. Four or five stories now stand on their hindlegs in front of me like the horses in front of Schumann, the circus ringmaster, at the beginning of the performance.'

How are we to take this? These horses can perform amazing, quite unhorsey feats, such as standing on their hind legs in front of their master, Kafka, ready to obey him. On the other hand they clearly have less natural life in them than their brethren who run on the open plain. Perhaps, though, it is the best that can be expected of story-horses: at least they are alive, not mechanical monsters or fish expiring on the river bank.

But what leads Kafka to describe stories in this way?

First of all we have to realise that words themselves are alive for him to an uncanny degree. In only the second sentence of the diary he jots down a phrase that he has overheard and comments on it: '"If he should forever ahsk me." The *ah*, released from the sentence, flew off like a ball on the meadow.' ['"Wenn er mich immer frägt." Das ä losgelöst vom Satz flog dahin wie ein Ball auf der Wiese.'] Words for him are always flying free of the sentences that contain them or lying in wait to trip up the speaker, as when he describes himself dictating a report in the insurance office in which he worked, and

> towards the end, where a climax was intended, I got stuck and could no nothing but look at K., the typist, who, in her usual way, became especially lively, moved her chair about, coughed, tapped on the table... Finally I have the word 'stigmatise' and the appropriate sentence, but still hold it all in my mouth with disgust and a sense of shame as though it were raw meat, cut out of me... (3 October 1911)

Words not only lie in wait to trip you up, they can warp even so natural a thing as filial love. On 24 October 1911 he notes that perhaps he has not always loved his mother as she deserved 'only because the German language prevented it'. The word *Mutter*, he goes on:

> is peculiarly German for the Jew, it unconsciously contains, together with the Christian splendour Christian coldness also, the Jewish woman who is called 'Mutter' therefore becomes not only comic but strange. Mama would be a better name if one didn't imagine 'Mutter' behind it.

At the same time the mere names of people he was attached to were capable of unleashing extraordinary torrents of feeling and prose, as in this passage from a letter to Milena:

> Milena (what a rich heavy name, almost too full to be lifted, and in the beginning I didn't like it much, it seemed to me a Greek or Roman gone astray in Bohemia, violated by Czech, cheated of its accent, and yet in colour and form it is marvellously a woman, a woman whom one carries in one's arms out of the world, out of the fire, I don't know which, and she presses herself willingly and trustingly into your arms, only the strong accent on the 'i' is bad, doesn't the name keep leaping away from you? Or is it perhaps only the lucky leap which you yourself make with your burden?)[3]

What must be noted about all these remarks is that they have nothing of the virtuoso quality Nabokov displays in his evocation of the beloved's name at the start of *Lolita*. What is disturbing about them is that we are never quite sure – as with the eleven sons – how much is being read into a word or name and how much is being drawn out of it. As always with Kafka,

3   *Letters to Milena*, ed. Willy Haas, tr. Tania and James Stern, London, n.d., p.46.

surface and depth, the literal and the metaphorical, mingle alarmingly.

Words threaten to make the sentences in which they appear fly apart; they conceal and reveal, acting as conduits to the depths of character and of life itself, or as obstacles on the way to such depths. What is at issue is never the beauty of the word but something far more mysterious and difficult to articulate. What he is after in his writing, he notes on 19 January 1911, is 'a description in which every word would be linked to my life, which I would draw to my heart, and which would transport me out of myself.' But that, unfortunately, is an ideal which is, he feels, for most of the time beyond his reach. 'Wrote badly', he confides to his diary on 20 October 1911, 'without really arriving at that freedom of true description which releases one's foot from the experienced.' On 5 November he records his bitterness and sense of isolation as Max Brod read out to a group of friends 'my little motor-car story':

> The disordered sentences of this story with holes into which one could stick both hands; one sentence sounds high, one sentence sounds low, as the case may be, one sentence rubs against another like the tongue against a hollow or false tooth; one sentence comes marching up with so rough a start that the entire story falls into sulky amazement...

He dreams then of being able one day to write something 'large and whole, well shaped from beginning to end', feeling that the story would then be able to detach itself from him 'and it would be possible for me calmly and with open eyes, as a blood relation of a healthy story, to hear it read.' As things stand though, he ends sadly, 'every little piece of the story runs around homeless and drives me away from it in the opposite direction'.

Unfortunately we don't know what the 'little motor-car story' was, but there are quite a few examples in the diaries of fragments of narrative followed by Kafka's caustic comments on them. 'Only the billowing overcoat remains,' he writes on 12 March 1912, 'everything else is made up.' But what does 'made up' mean here? Is not the whole fragment 'made up' by Kafka?

Two days earlier he had tried out a slightly longer story:

He seduced a girl in a small place in the Iser mountains where he spent a summer to restore his delicate lungs. After a brief effort to persuade her, incomprehensibly, the way lung cases sometimes act, he threw the girl – his landlord's daughter, who liked to walk with him in the evening after work – down in the grass on the river bank and took her as she lay there unconscious with fright. Later he had to carry water from the river in his cupped hands and pour it over the girl's face to restore her. 'Julie, but Julie,' he said countless times, bending over her. He was ready to accept complete responsibility for his offence and was only making an effort to make himself realise how serious his situation was... The simple girl who lay before him, now breathing regularly again, her eyes still closed because of fear and embarrassment, could make no difficulty for him; with the tip of his toe, he, the great, strong person, could push the girl aside. She was weak and plain, could what had happened to her have any significance that would last even until tomorrow? Would not anyone who compared the two of them have to come to this conclusion? The river stretched calmly between the meadows and fields to the distant hills. There was still sunshine only on the slope of the opposite shore. The last clouds were drifting out of that clear evening sky.

Here too his comment follows immediately:

Nothing, nothing. This is the way I raise up ghosts before me. I was involved, even if only superficially, only in the passage, 'Later he had...' Mostly in the 'pour'. For a moment I thought I saw something real in the description of the landscape.

This is very revealing. Here is Kafka trying to write a conventional 'realist' narrative, and his heart isn't in it. The act does not involve him, only its aftermath. But note that the sentence and especially the word he picks out, 'pour' (*schütten*) is no more beautiful or interesting in itself than the words 'threw' (*warf*) and 'took' (*nahm*). It is just that it seems to touch on a truth the rest of the story lacks. I myself would have added the word 'embarrassment', and I would agree that there was just the glimpse of 'something real' in the closing description of the landscape, calm and unaffected by the human drama which has just occurred within it.

And yet there are other moods when he can write: 'The firmness… which the most insignificant writing brings about in me is beyond doubt and wonderful' (27 November 1913). It is even the case that, at times, he feels that his writing gives him a quite magical power: 'When I arbitrarily write down a single sentence, for instance, "He looked out of the window", it already has perfection' (19 February 1911). Those early stories or gropings towards novels, the 'Description of a Struggle' and 'Wedding Preparations in the Country', on which he pinned all his hopes in his early twenties, are clearly written in an effort to maintain just this mood. Here what happens is governed not by the conventions of fin-de-siècle story-telling but simply by the feelings of the protagonist: 'Because I love pinewoods I went through woods of this kind, and since I like gazing silently up at the stars, the stars appeared slowly in the sky.' Here mosquitoes can fly through the belly of a fat man and the moon ceases to be a moon when given another name. As for the narrator, since the world immediately submits to his whims, it is difficult for him to retain any sense of himself as a person. At moments he is an all-powerful human being, at the next he is only an avalanche rolling down a mountainside.

Writing of this kind may initially feel promising, but it soon palls. If I have simply to write something down to summon it into being, if everything depends entirely on my mood as I write, then what is the point of writing anything at all? No wonder these early efforts got nowhere and were eventually abandoned by Kafka.

There is another theme running through his early letters and diaries, a theme which at the time he does not seem to know how to explain or exploit, but which is going to play a major part in his mature fiction. In a letter to Brod on 28 August 1904 he writes:

> It is so easy to be cheerful at the beginning of summer. One has a lively heart, a reasonably brisk gait, and can face the future with a certain hope. One expects something out of the Arabian Nights, while disclaiming any such hope with a comic bow and bumbling speech... And when people ask us about the life we intend to live, we form the habit, in spring, of answering with an expansive wave of the hand, which goes limp after a while, as if to say that it was ridiculously unnecessary to conjure up sure things.[4]

This is the world of Kafka's febrile drawings, which show ludicrously tall or squat people stretching, twisting, leaning towards or away from one another in what would be grotesque if it was an attempt at realism, but which instead conveys perfectly how we sometimes feel, both constrained in our bodies and lunging free, both playing a game and close to desperation. The early diaries are full of detailed descriptions of gesturing, which seems to be a sign of frustration when it is he himself who is doing the gesturing, but is clearly also as much a part of his extreme sensitivity to the world that surrounds him as his response to

4 *Letters to Friends, Family and Editors*, tr. Richard and Clara Winston, London, 1978, p.16.

words. These gestures are in fact the visual and physical equivalent of those words which suddenly take on a life of their own and burst free of the sentence in which normal, well-behaved words should quietly lie.

In a late diary entry (24 January 1922) Kafka, looking back at his life, specifically linked his writing with such gesturing:

> Childish games (though I was well aware that they were so) marked the beginning of my intellectual decline. I deliberately cultivated a facial tic, for instance, or would walk across the Graben with arms crossed behind my head. A repulsively childish but successful game. (My writing began in the same way...)

By this stage in his life Kafka had begun to think of writing not as a form of salvation but on the contrary as 'wages earned in the service of evil', as he put it in a terrible letter to Brod. But whether one accepts his judgement or not, it does not affect the clear link he makes here between writing and gesticulating. Just as excessive gestures were a way of escaping, even if only momentarily, the confines of his body and the behaviour required by society, so it was with his writing. The obverse of both is the image of the body turned to stone, the head sinking on to the chest, which recurs so often in the diary at moments of depression.

However, to grasp precisely what are the links between writing and gesturing we have to turn to a diary entry for 30 September 1911. There Kafka, after commenting on two well-known artists with whom he has obviously come into contact that day, Kubin the painter and Tucholsky the writer, focuses on a third figure:

> Szafranski, a disciple of Bernhardt's, grimaces while he observes and draws in a way that resembles what is drawn. Reminds me that I too have a pronounced talent for metamorphosing myself, which no one notices. How often I

must have imitated Max. Yesterday evening, on the way home, if I had observed myself from the outside I should have taken myself for Tucholsky.

But this talent for entering into and becoming another is not an actor's gift. 'My urge to imitate has nothing of the actor in it,' he writes on 30 December. A good actor, he goes on, homes in on the essential details of the person he is impersonating, while the sign of the poor actor is precisely that he is overwhelmed by the peripheral detail. Yet it is just such peripheral detail – 'the way certain people manipulate walking-sticks, the way they hold their hands, the movements of their fingers' – that he himself finds he can imitate with such ease.

And that fascination with peripheral detail, that ability to enter into the detail and live it, so to speak, is what immediately strikes us about even his earliest and most hesitant writing. The very first sentence of the diary, for example, runs: 'The onlookers go rigid when the train goes past' (the German avoids the repetition of 'go' and takes up only seven words: 'Die Zuschauer erstarren, wenn der Zug vorbeifahrt.') Is this the jotting down of something seen that day or the start of a story? As usual with Kafka, we cannot tell, and indeed the writing forces us to abandon such apparently well-founded distinctions. Though seemingly just a note to remind himself of an incident he has witnessed, the sentence actually catches and conveys an event. The diarist has not just looked hard, he has empathised instinctively not with this or that person on the station platform but with the entire episode of onlookers-at-a-station-platform-as-the-train-rushes-past.

Nevertheless, it was to be some time before Kafka discovered what to do with this gift of his for empathy and metamorphosis. In 1912, when Brod urged him to put together a volume of short stories for publication, he knew only that he must avoid the realism of the rape fragment and the expressionism of the long unfinished stories. Better to choose modest and even rather muted pieces which felt 'true' all the way through than fill a volume with excessive noise and falsehood. Thus, like Eliot's early 'Preludes' and 'Rhapsody on a Windy Night', or the quieter pieces Schoenberg and Webern were producing at roughly the same time, the 'stories' which make up Kafka's first published collection, *Meditation* (*Betrachtung*) are moving and disturbing precisely because they refuse to engage in narrative and yet are clearly more than simple descriptions. 'Absent-Minded Window-Gazing', for example, begins:

> What are we to do with these Spring days that are now fast coming on? Early this morning the sky was gray, but if you go to the window now you are surprised and lean your cheek against the latch of the casement.

A drama is being enacted here, but it is secret, muffled, hardly aware of itself, as in Joyce's 'Eveline'. Elsewhere he retrieves a fragment from the diary entry for 5 January 1912 about suddenly deciding to go out for a walk and in another piece tells how, to lift himself from his miserable mood, 'I force myself out of my chair, stride around the table, exercise my head and neck, make my eyes sparkle, tighten the muscles around them.' In 'The Wish to be a Red Indian' the whole piece consists of a single sentence, poised between mundane reality and impossible desire:

> If one were only an Indian, instantly alert, and on a racing horse, leaning against the wind, kept on quivering jerkily over the quivering ground, until one shed one's spurs, for there needed no spurs, threw away the reins, for there needed no reins, and hardly saw that the land before one was smoothly shorn heath when the horse's neck and head would be already gone.

Yet, interesting and original as these pieces are, they could clearly not satisfy someone who felt, like Kafka, that a thousand worlds were waiting to burst out of his head. If he was to let them out he would have, sooner or later, to solve the problem of how to write narrative without falling into the traps of either expressionism or realism, of a dependence on subjective whim which was self-defeating and a dependence on the themes and styles of his contemporaries which only struck him as unbearably hollow and false.

I have been talking so far as though Kafka were alone with his demons, though I did give a glimpse of him with Brod and his other friends as 'the little motor-car story' was read aloud. Much more important, of course, was the attitude of his family. Kafka has left us plenty of evidence about what his father thought of his work, but the main actor in what is perhaps the key episode in his development as a writer was not his father but an unnamed uncle. Kafka recounts it in his diary on 19 January 1911:

> Once I projected a novel in which two brothers fought each other, one of whom went to America while the other remained in a European prison. I only now and then began to write a few lines, for it tired me at once. So once I wrote down something about my prison on a Sunday afternoon when we were visiting my grandparents and had eaten an especially soft kind of bread, spread with butter, that was customary there. It is of course possible that I did it mostly out of vanity, and by shifting the paper about on the table-cloth, tapping with my pencil, looking around under the lamp, wanted to tempt someone to take what I had written from me, look at it, and admire me. It was chiefly the corridor of the prison that was described in the few lines, above all its silence and coldness... Perhaps I had a momentary feeling of the worthlessness of my description, but before that afternoon I never paid much attention to such feelings when among relatives to whom I was accus-

tomed (my timidity was so great that the accustomed was enough to make me half-way happy), I sat at the round table in the familiar room and could not forget that I was young and called to great things out of this present tranquillity. An uncle who liked to make fun of people finally took the page that I was holding only weakly, looked at it briefly, handed it back to me, even without laughing, and only said to the others who were following him with their eyes, 'The usual stuff', to me he said nothing. To be sure, I remained seated and bent as before over the now useless page of mine, but with one thrust I had been banished from society, the judgement of my uncle repeated itself in me with what amounted almost to real significance, and even within the feeling of belonging to a family I got an insight into the cold space of our world which I had to warm with a fire that first I wanted to seek out.

This stands, with the equivalent episode of Monsieur de Norpois' rejection of the young Marcel's literary efforts, as one of the key moments in modern literature. It is not an episode of which Chaucer or Milton or Goethe would have made much sense, I suspect, for in their day it would have been pretty obvious if a young man was gifted or not, and 'the usual stuff' would have been less of a put-down than 'unusual stuff'. In our world, though — and in this respect Proust and Kafka inhabit our world — matters are different: few can spot what is truly original when it first appears, and the burden on the artist is for that reason much greater: should he trust his instinct, which has so often let him down, or the judgement of others, which seems so massively authoritative and yet is so often at odds with his own?

Of course what makes this moment so important in both Kafka and Proust is not only that they had the ability to describe it for us, but that they had the resources of character to react to it, not by simply dismissing the judgement out of hand, but by incorporating it into their work, thus at the same time accepting and reversing it.

Two and a half years after that terrible Sunday afternoon, on 24 May 1913, Kafka noted in his diary: 'In high spirits because I consider "The Stoker" so good. This evening I read it to my parents, there is no better critic than I when I read to my father, who listens with the most extreme reluctance. Many shallow passages followed by unfathomable depths.'

'The Stoker' is also a story about a young man going to America. But this time Kafka does not wait for someone to wrench the page from him. He has grown in confidence to such an extent that he actually reads it out loud to the sternest judge of all, his father. And though he notes that his father listened 'with the most extreme reluctance', he himself is not in the least put out by this. As he reads he sees clearly that 'there are many shallow passages' in the story, but also that these are 'followed by unfathomable depths'.

What has happened to alter things in this way?

Put briefly, what has happened is the experience of the night of 22–23 September 1912. Under the date 23 September he transcribes the whole of a long short story and then comments on it:

> This story, 'The Judgement', I wrote at one sitting during the night of 22–23rd, from ten o'clock at night to six o'clock in the morning. I was hardly able to pull my legs out from under the desk, they had got so stiff from sitting. The fearful strain and joy, how the story developed before me, as if I were advancing over water. Several times during this night I heaved my own weight on my back. How everything can be said, how for everything, for the strangest fancies, there waits a great fire in which they perish and rise up again. How it turned blue outside the window. A wagon rolled by. Two men walked across the bridge... The appearance of the undisturbed bed, as

though it had just been brought in. The conviction veri-
fied that with my novel-writing I am in the shameful
lowlands of writing. Only *in this way* can writing be done,
only with such coherence, with such a complete opening
out of the body and the soul.

All his life Kafka was to look back to this night as the fulfilment of his dream of writing. Never again was he to feel such
total satisfaction, such a sense that at last he was doing what he
had long obscurely felt he had been put on earth to do.

'The Judgement' opens with Georg Bendemann sitting at an
open window from which, as from Kafka's window, a bridge
can be seen, daydreaming and writing a letter to a friend in far-
off Russia. 'Absent-Minded Window-Gazing' had stopped
there. Kafka perhaps sensed that the scene was a kind of
metaphor not just for modern life but also for the work of the
writer, daydreaming at his desk. Now, by bringing writing and
window-gazing into the same orbit, he discovers the way to
move forward. Just as Kafka's story of the two brothers had
been dismissed in a single sentence under the judgement of his
uncle, so now both letter and daydreams are banished by
Georg's father. The aged, enfeebled man suddenly rears up in
bed where Georg had solicitously – as he no doubt put it to
himself – tried to cover him up, and issues a judgement on the
writer and dreamer: 'An innocent child, yes, that you were, truly,
but still more truly have you been a devilish human being! –
And therefore take note: I sentence you now to death by
drowning!'

The terrible sentence is a strange kind of release for both
Georg and the narrative: 'Georg felt himself urged from the
room, the crash with which his father fell on the bed behind
him was still in his ears as he fled... Out of the front door he
rushed, across the roadway, driven toward the water.' The force
which drives him on makes all hesitation, all dreaming on his
part, a thing of the past. He swings himself over the side of the

bridge, 'like the distinguished gymnast he had once been in his youth, to his parents' pride,' and then lets himself drop. 'At this moment an unending stream of traffic was just going over the bridge.'

The indifferent landscape of the fragment about the rape has turned into an image of the world going its way as Georg's individual life of dream, desire, frustration and compromise comes to an end. In the earlier rape fragment the narrator had been guilty, but seemed unwilling to recognise his guilt; here he is guilty of no single evil act yet accepts his father's judgement, and so brings his own life and the story to its end. But it is as though the acceptance of that judgement had allowed a new kind of writing to be born.

Two days later 'The Stoker' was written. Karl Rossmann, as the rich long first sentence tells us, has been packed off to America by his parents for having got a serving girl with child, and the ship he is on has now entered New York Harbour. But if America stands — as it has for so many immigrants and writers — for freedom, for the chance to forge one's own life, one's own narrative, in the wide open spaces and bustling cities, then the story promptly turns its back on it. Realising suddenly that he has left his umbrella 'down below', Karl turns back and, descending into the bowels of the ship, finds, in those constraining corridors and boiler-rooms, the space where Kafka's narrative can function. From now on Kafka too will turn his back on the temptations of the free-floating novel (whether realist or expressionist) and concentrate on the stokers down below.

Yet free-floating narrative will always exert its pull (Kafka does after all go on trying to write his American novel), and it is precisely in the tension between the temptation and its denial, between the letter-writing by the open window and the self-immolation demanded by the tyrannical father, that Kafka will discover the ever renewable springs of his narrative powers.

Just as the narrative of 'The Judgement' emerges in all its force and inevitability out of the redirection of an energy that had earlier been spent half combating and half agreeing with the judgements of his family, so the arbitrary bodily movement described in the early letters and diaries and taken up in *Meditation* here gives way to Georg's rediscovery of his earlier gymnastic ability, once the pride of his parents, now the means of his self-destruction. Two months after writing 'The Judgement' and 'The Stoker' Kafka completed the greatest of his early works, 'Metamorphosis'. As he wakes from uneasy sleep Gregor Samsa finds himself transformed into a gigantic insect and thus having to come to terms with a body he cannot imagine and yet which is indubitably his (or should we say 'indubitably him'?) Forced to lie on his back, he can only glimpse his dome-like brown belly, while 'his numerous legs, which were pitifully thin compared to the rest of his bulk, waved helplessly before his eyes'. This is no erstwhile gymnast; on the contrary, it is someone who has for too long tried to live without listening to his body, which now exacts its dreadful revenge.

The long dense story which follows charts with dreadful precision the way in which Gregor is gradually forced to learn about what Donne, in a very different context, called 'my new found land'. And, as with Georg Bendemann, understanding arrives for Gregor, and a kind of peace, only with the recognition that he must accede to the wishes of his family, even — perhaps especially — if those wishes concern his own disappearance. And, like the early rape fragment and 'The Judgement', this story ends with the world going on its way regardless of the wishes of the protagonist. Here, though, this archetypal story of the body has to end with a celebration of the body as, having taken a tram out into the country, the parents gaze fondly at their sole remaining child, the sister Gregor had so wanted to help. 'And it was like a confirmation of their new dreams and excellent intentions that at the end of their journey their daughter sprang to her feet first and stretched her young body.'

In 'Reading Kafka' Maurice Blanchot has argued persuasively that that last sentence is the most terrible in the entire story.[5] At the same time every reader has recognised, however obscurely, that our reactions to this, as to all Kafka's mature stories, are profoundly ambivalent. We experience horror at what happens to Gregor, but at the same time a kind of joy at the fact that the story exists and lets itself be read. And if the reaction of the parents and sister mime out in the fiction our own inability to give meaning to Gregor's ordeal and death, then that too is part of the meaning of the whole. And if Gregor finds himself constrained more and more by his horrible body, till death comes as a merciful release, then for Kafka the writing of the story was a release from the frustration of years (even if he later had doubts about its ending) and a renewal of the sense that 'everything can be said, how for everything, for the strangest fancies, there waits a great fire in which they perish and rise up again.' For now at last the excess of gesture, the arbitrary jerking of arms and legs, has been made the subject not just of observation but of narrative; now at last his 'profound talent for metamorphosing myself, which no one notices', has found an outlet. Other writers have had this ability to empathise with a wide range of human beings; Kafka has now discovered in himself the unique gift of empathy with everything in the world, even a gigantic insect. It is a gift of which he will make full use in the years that follow.

But before that happens there is one story in the vein of 'The Judgement' that still needs to be written, though that does not

5   'La Lecture de Kafka', in *La Part du feu*, Paris, 1949, pp.9–19; translated as 'Reading Kafka' in *The Sirens' Song: Selected Essays of Maurice Blanchot*, ed. and introduced by Gabriel Josipovici, tr. Sacha Rabinovitch, Brighton, 1982, pp.21–9.

happen till almost two years later, in October 1914. 'In the Penal Colony' is the most repulsive story Kafka ever wrote, for while there is a kind of serenity in the way in which Georg and Gregor meet their deaths, and a deep sympathy with their bewilderment and despair, this story is glacial throughout. The peculiar horror of the two earlier stories lies in the combination of classic purity in the unfolding of the narrative and the almost unbearable subject-matter; that of 'In the Penal Colony' in the sense that not only is the subject-matter foul but the story itself, replicating the narrative, seems to have become a sort of malfunctioning machine:

> The explorer… felt greatly troubled; the machine was obviously going to pieces; its silent working was a delusion… The Harrow was not writing, it was only jabbing, and the Bed was not turning the body over but only bringing it up quivering against the needles.

Though in death the officer's look is 'calm and convinced', this is the result not of understanding but of madness, for there is no visible sign of 'the promised redemption', while 'through the forehead went the point of the great iron spike'.

The reason for this may lie in the fact that though Kafka was always to look back to his breakthrough as a wonder, a form of grace, he was also perhaps beginning to feel uneasy with the form it had taken. The narratives he had suddenly found it in himself to write and which had, for the first time, given him the kind of satisfaction he had always hoped for from his writing, may have struck him as too extreme, too full of anguish and pathos. It is as though he feels that the ambition of these early stories is too Utopian, too Romantic. 'In the Penal Colony' dramatises the painful discovery that Truth cannot be written, not even on the body.

Other factors were perhaps also involved in the change of direction that now began to manifest itself, chief among them

the growing realisation of the ambivalence of his desire for
marriage, and the coming of the war. Perhaps, he must have
begun to think, it was not his job or his bachelorhood or his
ill-health which were preventing the full flowering of his talents,
but something else, something which had to do with what man
is and what art can achieve. And if he suffered as a consequence,
what was his suffering compared to that which those at the front
were experiencing?

Be that as it may, the work he did in the years 1914–17, much
of which is included in the 1919 volume *A Country Doctor*, shows
a marked and significant shift of emphasis.

Kafka put together this volume of fourteen stories with the care
of a Yeats or a Wallace Stevens planning a new book of poems.
'The Bucket Rider', for example, which he had thought of
including, he dropped at the last moment, presumably because
it did not fit in with the rest of the volume. As it now stands,
the first and last stories call out to each other across the intervening gap and each story (including 'Eleven Sons') adds a new
twist to the central theme.

'We have a new advocate, Dr Bucephalus', the first story
begins. 'There is little in his appearance to remind you that he
was once Alexander of Macedon's battle charger. Of course, if
you know his story, you are aware of something.' But even the
usher at the law courts, who presumably does not know his
story, though he is, it is true, 'a man with the professional
appraisal of the regular small bettor at a racecourse', even he
finds himself 'running an admiring eye over the advocate as he
mounted the marble steps with a high action that made them
ring beneath his feet.'

However, this high-stepping urge is now kept well under
control, for '[n]owadays... there is no Alexander the Great'. Of
course, even in Alexander's day 'the gates of India were beyond

reach, yet the King's sword pointed the way to them'. Today, however, no one even points the way – for in which direction would he point? Many, it is true, still carry swords, 'but only to brandish them, and the eye that tries to follow them is confused'. So, 'perhaps it is really best to do as Bucephalus has done and absorb oneself in law books. In the quiet lamplight, his flanks unhampered by the thighs of a rider, free and far from the clamour of battle, he reads and turns the pages of our ancient tomes.'

A loss has been incurred, yet the last little paragraph is neither pathetic nor anguished, but merely resigned: 'Perhaps it is really best to do as Bucephalus has done.' His flanks are at least unhampered by the thighs of any rider – yet we recall the high action of his legs as he strides up the marble staircase and we feel the waste: a rider pressing into those flanks would at least have given him a goal, a sense of direction, something glorious to aim at. Instead, he consoles himself by poring over ancient law books, though whether he does this out of a sense of duty or desire or merely to pass the time, the story does not say.

Resignation and its cost is also the theme of the last piece in the collection, 'A Report to an Academy'. In what is probably the funniest story this great comic writer ever produced, an ape addresses a distinguished gathering, recounting how he dragged himself by sheer will-power out of his simian condition and up to his present position. The reason he has done this, he explains, is not from any innate desire on the part of apes to achieve the level of men, but rather that, having been captured and stuck in a tiny cage, he understood that his only chance of escape lay in imitating the men he could see walking about unconstrained before him.

He cannot, he explains, really comply with the wishes of the academy and speak about his life as an ape; that closed behind him when he was captured and lost to sight for ever when he decided to transform himself. He can only recount the stages of his transformation: 'I could never have achieved what I have done had I been stubbornly set on clinging to my origins, to the remembrances of my youth,' he explains, unconsciously echoing the tone of countless self-made men, Kafka's father among them. 'In revenge, however, my memory of the past has closed the door against me more and more.' As he grew increasingly at ease in the world of men, 'the strong wind that blew after me out of my past began to slacken; today it is a gentle puff of air that plays around my heels.' 'To put it plainly,' he tells the gentlemen of the academy, 'your life as apes... insofar as something of that kind lies behind you, cannot be further removed from you than mine is from me.' And yet, 'everyone on earth feels a tickling at the heels; the small chimpanzee and the great Achilles alike.'

He has transformed himself, he explains, because he had no option. Not in order to find freedom, that is too large a word, associated perhaps with his early life in the forests of Africa, but simply in order to find a way out of his horrible predicament. It is solely for that reason that he has learned to imitate the ways of men – smoking, spitting, drinking, talking. As a result of this single-minded effort he is now able to command the best hotel suites and address such august assemblies as this. 'And when I come home late at night from banquets, from scientific receptions, from social gatherings, there sits waiting for me a half-trained little chimpanzee and I take comfort from her as apes do.' And yet 'By day I cannot bear to see her, for she has the insane look of the bewildered, half-broken animal in her eye; no one else sees it, but I do, and I cannot bear it.'

So, like Bucephalus, he has managed to accommodate to new conditions without nostalgia and without recrimination. It is a decent enough life, even, perhaps, in the eyes of some (the animal in the zoo, the soldier at the front) an enviable one, but it entails a hardening of oneself, a willed denial of the breeze licking about one's heels, of the look in the eyes of the half-broken animal.

Nevertheless, this new-found balance testified to a second great creative period in Kafka's life. This is the period of the parables, the aphorisms, the re-telling of the myths of Poseidon and Prometheus, the meditations on Ulysses and the sirens and on Don Quixote and Sancho Panza, and of the innumerable perfect, tiny, yet ultimately mysterious stories that are as much a part of Kafka's legacy as the terrible stories of 1912–14. This is the period of the great flowering of his gift for impersonation, and no writer has ever managed to empathise with such a diversity not just of living creatures, but even of bridges and balls in wooden board games. ('If the ball was unemployed, it spent most of the time strolling to and fro, its hands clasped behind its back, on the plateau, avoiding the paths... It had a rather straddling gait and maintained that it was not made for those narrow paths.')

No story of those years shows more clearly how far Kafka has travelled from those earlier concerns and practices than the one called 'The Cares of a Family Man' (a clear but not quite adequate rendering of 'Die Sorge des Hausvaters'). It tells of Odradek, not exactly an object and not quite a creature, with a name which is not precisely Slav and not exactly German:

> At first glance it looks like a flat star-shaped spool for thread, and indeed it does seem to have thread wound upon it; to be sure, they are only old, broken-off bits of thread, knotted and tangled together, of the most varied sorts and colors. But it is not only a spool, for a small wooden crossbar sticks out of the middle of the star, and another small rod is joined to that at a right angle. By means of this latter rod on one side and one of the points of the star on the other, the whole thing can stand upright as if on two legs.

It's not that Odradek once had some sort of intelligible shape and is now only 'a broken-down remnant'; it has always been like that and though 'the whole thing looks senseless enough', it is, in its own way, 'perfectly finished'. In any case close scrutiny is impossible, for Odradek will never let himself be caught. He lurks in stairs and garrets and disappears for months on end, but always returns to 'our house'. When you ask him his name he squeaks 'Odradek', and when you ask where he lives he squeaks 'no fixed abode' and laughs – 'but it is only the kind of laughter that has no lungs behind it. It sounds rather like the rustling of fallen leaves.'

Not surprisingly he gets on the nerves of the narrator, the *Hausvater* of the title. What is going to happen to Odradek? he wonders. Can he possibly die? But only that which is living can die, and 'that does not apply to Odradek'. Is he then always going to be rolling down the stairs 'before the feet of my children, and my children's children'? And though he does no harm as far as one can see, 'the idea that he is likely to survive me I find almost painful.'

Kafka has come a long way from that early reading by Max Brod of the 'little motor-car story', when he confided to his diary that despite his desire for 'something large and whole and well-shaped from beginning to end', 'every little piece of my story runs around homeless and drives me away from it'. He now finds it possible to write with a free conscience a story about a creature who is neither large nor whole and who revels in the fact that he/it has no fixed abode and is likely to drive the *Hausvater* from his own house.

As long as Kafka imagined that art would help him enter a more meaningful realm than the one he inhabited in his daily life, as long as he imagined that the test of the quality of his art lay in the unbroken nature of the work he put into it, then it was inevitable that he would turn on himself and his surroundings in bitterness and frustration: he was lazy, he was weak, he was unhealthy, his family was suffocating him, his bachelorhood was crippling him, the office was destroying him, marriage would be the end of him. But now it is as though he comes to accept the romantic folly of such dreams and such despair. An art that respects the truth, he now comes to see, can only express its own and our human limitations, show that we become immortal only to the extent that we cease to be human and alive, only to the extent that we renounce our dreams of wholeness and belonging.

Odradek is nobody's son and nobody's father. He does not know the cares of a *Hausvater* and is not graspable in his essence, only in his movement. Odradek does not mean anything: he moves, gets in the way, disturbs. Accepting that writing stories means bringing Odradeks into being gives Kafka back the sense that there need be no end to the writing of stories and that the freedom from human cares lies precisely in such writing. As for us, we should cease to ask of them what they mean and ask instead how they move – both how they move in their own space and how they move *us*.

Here, for example, is a little piece that Max Brod did not even consider worthy of inclusion in any collection of Kafka's stories. Yet if it was all we had of Kafka it would immediately strike us as unique and irreplaceable. Though it is barely six lines long it is not a fragment in the sense that the rape piece was a fragment. It is only a fragment in the way an aphorism is a fragment, that is, as a questioning of the very notion of wholeness:

> I ran past the first watchman. Then I was horrified, ran back again and said to the watchman: 'I ran through here while you were looking the other way.' The watchman gazed ahead of him and said nothing. 'I suppose I really oughtn't to have done it,' I said. The watchman still said nothing. 'Does your silence indicate permission to pass?'

The German is considerably denser than the English. 'Ran past' misses the sense of 'overran' in *überlief*; 'then' hardly does justice to *Nachträglich*, which means 'retrospectively' or 'retroactively'; and 'you' of course fails to convey the fact that the German uses the familiar *du*, with its suggestion that the Watchman is both a figure of authority and one to whom the speaker is very close. But even in English this is a piece of writing which demands to be read at least twice; indeed, as so often in Kafka, the narrative mimics the way we need to read it.

A story which told how I ran past the first watchman, hid myself from the second, overcame the third and finally entered the castle or escaped from it might be exciting to read, but, once read, it would lose all interest for us. Its fire would burn, but only so long as the end had not been reached, and we would feel, in reading, as we do in our lives, that everything had gone by too fast, that the experience was, somehow, *thin* – but we would not have any idea how to slow things down, how to thicken and deepen the experience. Kafka has managed to do that. But he has done it by dramatising the fact that we always *run past* and so are always *looking back*. Thinness of experience is what we are condemned to. (We would, of course, destroy the story, make it thin again, if we were to substitute for it some generalising comment, such as 'to hesitate is to be lost' or 'human self-awareness will not allow us to act naturally'.)

This little story is almost totally free of the anguish and pain characteristic of 'The Judgement' and the stories that immediately followed. It opens a space and lives in it, a space which we too can enter and in which we too can live, though without Kafka we would never have been able to do so. Just as Ulysses escaped the silence of the sirens by a mixture of luck, innocence and cunning, so it is with Kafka and these stories of his middle period: he sails unscathed across the sea of narrative and takes his readers with him.

But it was not to last. For Kafka this rich creative period was only a moment on a fateful journey, only a point on the circumference of his dreams and desires. In 1917 he was found to be suffering from tuberculosis, and broke off finally with Felice. The precarious balance of these years was disturbed by the intrusion of his body and the stench of mortality. In his last stories the pain of 'The Judgement' and 'Metamorphosis' returns, but displaced, so to speak, no longer at the heart of the narrative but ever-present at the periphery. I am not sure it is not the more painful for that.

'A Hunger Artist', the title story of the little collection whose proofs he was correcting as he lay dying in Kierling Sanatorium in the spring of 1924, is the fullest expression of the change. 'I always wanted you to admire my fasting,' says the Hunger Artist. 'We do admire it,' says the overseer of the circus which employs him. 'But you shouldn't admire it,' says the Hunger Artist. 'Well then we don't admire it,' says the overseer. 'But why shouldn't we admire it?' 'Because I have to fast, I can't help it.' 'What a fellow you are,' says the other 'and why can't you help it?' 'Because I couldn't find the food I liked. If I had found it, believe me, I should have made no fuss and stuffed myself like you or anyone else.'

Like Bucephalus and the ape who lectures to the academy, the Hunger Artist has simply done what had to be done. In his case, however, it is not enough, for fasting, unlike the reading of old books or lectures to academies, kills.

> 'Well, clear this out now!' said the overseer, and they buried the hunger artist, straw and all. Into the cage they put a young panther. Even the most insensitive felt it refreshing to see this wild creature leaping around the cage that had so long been dreary.

This is only a variant of the endings Kafka had favoured since that little rape fragment, and which had provided such a terrifying closure to 'Metamorphosis'. But it is perhaps, for that very reason, still too close to pathos for him. 'Josephine the Singer, or the Mouse Folk', probably the last story he wrote, takes matters one step further. Josephine's art, of which she has been so proud, is perhaps not even art, her singing no different from the cheeping of all the other mice when properly listened to. Her people will not miss her when she is gone, and, 'since we are no historians', says the narrator, she will soon be forgotten, 'like all her brothers'.

Many years before, Kafka's uncle had taken the manuscript from his hands and declared to the assembled family that it contained only 'the usual stuff'. In this story Kafka sends a final answer to that uncle. For it recognises the human desire for song, for art, that will give meaning to our world and bring the singer recognition. But it accepts at the same time that such desires are, from another perspective, absurd, childish and unwarranted.

We are far, in this story, from the young Kafka's mixture of self-confidence ('I... could not forget that I was called to great things...') and self-doubt ('with one thrust I had been banished from society'). We are, rather, in the hands of a master who must have taken pride and pleasure in what he could do and yet who could also recognise its complete insignificance, and who had the skill and imagination to convey this double perspective without self-pity and without denying the total validity of either.

The paradox is that, because he gives us the food we need, Kafka himself will not be forgotten as long as there are books to read and human beings to read them. He lives for us in his fragmentary and living children more than he ever lived for himself in the bosom of his family, the Kafkas, and his city, Prague.

11. The Wooden Stair

BOOKS NEED TITLES as much as human beings need names, but the little pieces brought together here[1] are not precisely aphorisms, maxims, parables, reflections (the title Max Brod gave the first sequence), or tiny stories, though at one point or another they will remind the reader of all these. They were written by Kafka in two short bursts between October 1917 and February 1920, at a time of great inner torment, when he first learned that he had tuberculosis, broke off his long-standing intermittent engagement to Felice Bauer, took extended sick-leave from the Workers' Accident Insurance Institute, and accepted that he would never give his parents the pleasure of seeing their only son married or even recognised as a writer of consequence. The care he took with them shows that they were more than stray thoughts, that in his mind they formed clear sequences, and that he may even have planned to publish them. However, like so many of the projects of his last years, nothing came of it, and they remain, untitled, half-way between random jottings and finished works. As such, though, they form Kafka's most sustained meditation on life and death, good and evil, and the role of art in human life.

'Aphorism', like 'maxim', implies authority and control, an author's sense that he has encapsulated in lapidary form what

---

1   Franz Kafka, *The Collected Aphorisms*, tr. Malcolm Pasley, preface by Gabriel Josipovici, London, 1994.

everyone knows but few have been clear-sighted and skilful enough to express. They are thus the civilised and literate descendants of folk sayings, those pearls of wisdom polished by generations and passed on for the comfort and enlightenment of those to come. Clearly these little pieces of Kafka's do not fall into this category, but they are not entirely distinct from it either. What they do is explore the *nature* of aphorism, which means in effect the nature of tradition, of language, and of the role of the individual in the process.

No. 59 in the first sequence makes this clear:

A stair that has not been deeply hollowed by footsteps is, from its own point of view, merely something that has been bleakly put together out of wood.

If the general sentiment reminds us of innumerable Romantic and post-Romantic writers, such as Hölderlin, Rilke and Heidegger, only Kafka would have had the wit and imaginative empathy to see things from the point of view of the poor modern staircase, 'bleakly put together out of wood'.

This finds an echo in the entry for 13 January in the second sequence:

Everything he does seems to him extraordinarily new, but at the same time, because of this unbelievable spate of novelty it seems extraordinarily amateurish, scarcely even tolerable, incapable of finding its place in history, breaking the chain of the generations, cutting off at its most profound source the music of the world for the first time, which before then could at least be divined. Sometimes in his arrogance he has more anxiety for the world than for himself.

'In his arrogance' is typical of the way these little pieces keep throwing up counter-thoughts, counter-pressures, which unsettle and disturb. But if we leave that aside for the moment, the thought expressed by the passage, that everything 'he' does, far from helping him and us understand our condition, only helps break the chain of tradition and render inaudible the music of the world, helps to explain the harshness of 52:

> In the struggle between yourself and the world, second the world.

That is why he insists: 'Never again psychology!' (93), for that would merely lead us further into the swamps of guilt and self-justification; and that is why here, more than anywhere else in his writings, he ponders the implications of the stories and teachings of the great religions: the Hebrew stories of the Garden of Eden, the Christian teachings on renunciation, the Eastern teachings on the Way.

But even as he does so he keeps coming back to the central problem, that, whatever he does,

> He has the feeling that merely by being alive he is blocking his own way. (13 January)

Every attempt even to formulate the problem is dogged by human impatience, which leads to 'an apparent fencing-in of what is apparently at issue' (2). At moments he dreams of a view of life which would grasp it simultaneously in 'its natural, full-bodied rise and fall' and 'as a dream, as a hovering' (15 February). But he knows that such dreams are beyond him, that

> The bone of his own forehead blocks his way (he batters himself bloody against his own brow). (17 January)

Besides:

> Truth is indivisible, hence it cannot recognise itself; whoever wants to recognise it must be a lie. (80)

Yet this does not result in a plea for quietude – and how could it, since that too would suggest that 'he' had the answer.

Instead, these little pieces are vibrant with the sense of quest, with delighted and horrified surprise at where the act of thinking and writing is leading him. Were this simply a book of aphorisms we could learn them by heart and then throw the book away. But these meditations constantly evade our mental grasp even as they persuade us instantly of their absolute authenticity. That is why this book is one we will want to carry with us and take out whenever we feel the need to draw closer to ourselves, knowing as we do that introspection will never be the answer, that what we need is another voice, is, in fact, *this* voice.

12. Listening to the Voice in *Four Quartets*
in memory of Chickie

I

T.S. Eliot's *Four Quartets* must be read not as a philosophical examination of the problem of time but as the narrative of a person talking to himself at four o'clock in the morning. Listen:

> Time present and time past
> Are both perhaps present in time future,
> And time future contained in time past.
> If all time is eternally present
> All time is unredeemable,
> What might have been is an abstraction
> Remaining a perpetual possibility
> Only in a world of speculation.
> What might have been and what has been
> Point to one end which is always present.

The words are chosen with the exaggerated care of one who does not know what is going to come next, and the syntax reflects this, with its simple parataxis ('time present and time past... And time future contained in time past... What might have been and what has been...') and its pervasive conditionals ('perhaps ... if... what might have been...'). When the word 'present' returns for the fourth time in ten lines it carries with it the finality not so much of a problem solved as of a painful effort at clarity come to nothing. We may not be at the mad extreme of Lucky's feverish monologue in *Waiting for Godot*, but we are certainly nearer to that than we are to the meditations on time of St Augustine or Bergson.

The first effort at understanding having apparently got nowhere, the voice changes direction completely:

> Footfalls echo in the memory
> Down the passage which we did not take
> Towards the door we never opened
> Into the rose-garden. My words echo
> Thus, in your mind.
> But to what purpose
> Disturbing the dust on a bowl of rose-leaves
> I do not know.

A body has entered the scene previously occupied by abstractions. With 'footfalls' comes a 'we', a 'me', a 'you'. And with this peopling of the scene comes memory. But a very peculiar kind of memory, one which seems to consist only of negatives – the passage which we did not take, the door we never opened. And yet, as Freud noted, the unconscious does not know the word 'not', and neither does the imagination. The words are no sooner read than we have taken the passage, opened the door, entered the rose garden.

Eliot, who is as great a master of enjambment as Wordsworth, uses all his skills to make us advance, hesitate, enter, hesitate again: 'Towards the door we never opened/Into the rose-garden.' And then, when the voice changes direction once again, syntax, punctuation and enjambment all contribute to the effect: 'My words echo/Thus, in your mind.'

The voice stops again. But this time the organisation of the words on the page makes the break both more and less than that of a return to the beginning of the line, something akin to a dash or bracket yet different from both, something we take in at once as we look at the page but which the speaking voice can never quite convey – for if what we first encounter is a voice it is also, and primarily, words aligned on a page in a certain order. Indeed, this is what the words are now saying: they emerge, they are aligned:

> But to what purpose
> Disturbing the dust on a bowl of rose-leaves
> I do not know.

It is as if the speaker can at last utter that first-person pronoun only because it is immediately followed by a confession of ignorance. The words which have emerged from the silence, from the blankness of the page, have disturbed long-settled dust, but why they should do so, or what meaning they have, appears to be secondary to that first, unexpected, unasked-for effect.

The shift from abstractions to memory has, however, given the voice a new lease of life. Instead of the premature closure of 'which is always present', which required a massive effort to restart, new links in the chain now come easily, lightly:

> Other echoes
> Inhabit the garden. Shall we follow?
> Quick, said the bird, find them, find them,
> Round the corner. Through the first gate,
> Into our first world, shall we follow
> The deception of the thrush? Into our first world.
> There they were, dignified, invisible...

The bird's urgent imperative is also a statement. We have moved from the half-life of the opening, so reminiscent of the world of Eliot's early poetry ('You tossed a blanket from the bed,/You lay upon your back and waited;/You dozed, and watched the night revealing/The thousand sordid images/Of which your soul was constituted') to life, to the quick as opposed to the dead. So powerfully is Eliot able to convey this by his sudden quickening of the rhythm that we hardly notice the word 'deception' at the end. But once it has appeared, poly-syllabic and Latinate in a context mainly monosyllabic and Anglo-Saxon ('quick' 'find', 'first', 'gate', 'world', 'thrush'), it puts a drag on the rhythm and returns us to the slow and ponderous movement of the opening. There is a difference though. As always in this poem the way back is the way forward, and the calling up of an earlier experience only helps to move us into new territory. Now the slowing down of the rhythm prepares us for a ritual procession which will lead to a kind of epiphany:

> There they were, dignified, invisible,
> Moving without pressure, over the dead leaves,
> In the autumn heat, through the vibrant air,
> And the bird called, in response to
> The unheard music hidden in the shrubbery,
> And the unseen eyebeam crossed, for the roses
> Had the look of flowers that are looked at.
> There they were as our guests, accepted and accepting,
> So we moved, and they, in a formal pattern,
> Along the empty alley, into the box circle.

We are not told who 'they' were, and we do not need to be told; it is enough that 'there they were as our guests, accepted and accepting', and the new life which seems to imbue this relation of host and guest turns the occasion into more than a visit, it turns it into the ultimate expression of reciprocity, a dance.

Until now movement in this poem has been abrupt, the voice constantly shifting gear in an effort not to grind to a halt. Now host and guest, accepted and accepting, move in a reciprocal motion; the stark opposition of stasis and movement, silence and speech, has been overcome by the meaningful exchange of the dance:

> So we moved, and they, in a formal pattern,
> Along the empty alley, into the box circle,

> To look down into the drained pool.
> Dry the pool, dry concrete, brown edged,
> And the pool was filled with water out of sunlight,
> And the lotos rose, quietly, quietly,
> The surface glittered out of heart of light,
> And they were behind us, reflected in the pool.

Joining the dance, we become witnesses to a transformation: the dry pool is suddenly filled with water and in its midst rises the lotus which, like Stevens' jar in Tennessee, draws the surrounding elements into a meaningful pattern. 'The surface glittered out of heart of light.' We didn't recall this and we didn't imagine it: the experience occurs as the lines are spoken, it is inseparable from the words, which are impossible to paraphrase and yet immediately comprehensible.

But nothing in this poem ever stays still for long. No sooner has the lotus emerged 'out of heart of light' than

> a cloud passed, and the pool was empty.
> Go, said the bird, for the leaves were full of children,
> Hidden excitedly, containing laughter.
> Go, go, go, said the bird: human kind
> Cannot bear very much reality.
> Time past and time future
> What might have been and what has been
> Point to one end, which is always present.

The bird's 'go', like his 'quick', is a sign of life, an index of sheer being. The cloud has passed, the pool is revealed once more as empty, but there is the sense of life in the leaves. At the same time the bird is urging us away. It is unclear if it is the bird or the speaker who says that 'human kind' 'cannot bear very much reality'. But it does not matter, for the abstraction of the phrase is itself a proof of the truth it states. At the same time to take it by itself, as a philosophical statement, is to misread the way this poem works. Here, following on from the sense of laughter in the leaves and the voice of the bird, it has something comforting about it, seems to be not so much an indictment of mankind as a necessary part of the dance of life.

Nevertheless, the words seem to call back the language of the opening. It emerges now, though, with a new authority, quietly assertive rather than tentatively groping. It sends us back to the beginning with a new understanding: we are beings who exist in time, beings with memories and imaginations; nothing we have done and thought simply disappears or solidifies into a lump we are forced to carry forever on our backs. Time and meaning constantly escape us as we move through our lives, but this is a reason for hope as much as for despair. As Beckett so memorably said of Proust: 'Only he who forgets remembers.' The way Eliot puts it is: 'If all time is eternally present/All time is unredeemable', with the corollary that since all time is not eternally present, time is indeed redeemable. Since we live in time we also live in memory and hope. We use both wrongly when we use them as a means of escaping the present through nostalgia or apocalyptic yearnings; the right use is to be alive to the present, to see it always as what Walter Benjamin called 'the time of Now'. When we do that we realise that neither past nor future is locked into the iron tracks of necessity, that the past can always be transformed and the future holds a wealth of possibilities. 'Time past and time future/What might have been and what has been/Point to one end, which is always present.'

The word 'present', which threatened to bring the voice to a stop after a mere ten lines, triumphantly closes the first movement of *Burnt Norton*. The voice can now advance with a new confidence, and it immediately does so by celebrating the dance of the entire universe in a lyric outburst which easily accommodates both the patterning of the cosmos and the multiple horrors of our world:

> We move above the moving tree
> In light upon the figured leaf
> And hear upon the sodden floor
> Below, the boarhound and the boar
> Pursue their pattern as before
> But reconciled among the stars.

Now the meditative voice can re-enter, exploring the implications of such patterns:

> At the still point of the turning world. Neither flesh nor
>   fleshless;
> Neither from nor towards; at the still point, there the
>   dance is,
> But neither arrest nor movement. And do not call it fixity,
> Where past and future are gathered. Neither movement
>   from nor towards,
> Neither ascent nor decline. Except for the point, the still
>   point,
> There would be no dance, and there is only the dance.
> I can only say, *there* we have been: but I cannot say where.
> And I cannot say, how long, for that is to place it in time.

The experience cannot be put into words, but it is no simple rapture but rather 'both a new world / And the old made explicit, understood...' What we experience now, if rightly understood, will affect the past as well as the future.

Many years earlier the radical young Eliot had written in his 1919 essay, 'Tradition and the Individual Talent': '[T]he difference between the present and the past is that the conscious present is an awareness of the past in a way and to an extent which the past's awareness of itself cannot show.' And again: '[H]e is not likely to know what is to be done unless he lives in what is not merely the present, but the present moment of the past, unless he is conscious not of what is dead, but of what is already living.' There is nothing surprising in this conjunction of ideas across a span of sixteen crucial years, for, as the poem is to say later, 'what there is to conquer/...has already been discovered', and 'There is only the fight to recover what has been lost/And found and lost again and again.' But it does remind us that the division of Eliot's career into an early secular and a later religious phase is quite beside the mark. As Yeats said, we most of us discover what we have to say by the time we are twenty and spend the rest of our lives finding different and better ways of saying it.

The paradoxes with which this portion of the poem is concerned have already been touched on in the first section. This is a poem that grows by coils, not by marching forward in a straight line. As we have seen, the experience of pattern in the universe, of dance as its central principle, is not one that can last: the water in the pool and the lotus vanish as abruptly as they had come. This is natural, for such experiences seem to be outside time, and 'the enchainment of past and future' is '[w]oven in the weakness of the changing body'. And yet that is a mixed curse, for such weakness '[p]rotects mankind from heaven and damnation'. Even that, however, is to put it negatively. Putting it positively we can say that it is only because we are creatures of time that we can glimpse that which is outside time:

> But only in time can the moment in the rose-garden,
> The moment in the arbour where the rain beat,
> The moment in the draughty church at smokefall
> Be remembered; involved with past and future.
> Only through time time is conquered.

Having arrived at this, the central paradox of the entire sequence, the voice changes direction again; for there will be time to explore its ramifications, there is no rush. What follows in section III is an examination of the world of Eliot's early poetry, a world whose inhabitants are neutrals, neither hot nor cold, spewed out by both Heaven and Hell, who pass their lives 'distracted from distraction by distraction/Filled with fancies and emptied of meaning/Tumid apathy with no concentration/Men and bits of paper, whirled by the cold wind...'

Instead of the ordered movement of the dance there is only the meaningless whirling of men and bits of paper, picked up by the wind and tossed aside again. And yet here too it is only the possibility of such a state of 'tumid apathy' which guarantees quite other possibilities: 'In order to possess what you do not possess/You must go by the way of dispossession.' The exploration of this state is therefore followed by a brief and powerful lyric, its total opposite both in its confident rhythm and in its content:

> Time and the bell have buried the day,
> The black cloud carries the sun away.

Instead of apathy there is the clear recognition that after day night must come, after life death. And the acknowledgement of this brings relief and release:

> After the kingfisher's wing
> Has answered light to light, and is silent, the light is still
> At the still point of the turning world.

Now, the lyric being over, we return to the longer meditative line as the voice, having faced both ecstasy and apathy, prepares for one final assault on meaning. This time it will question its own performance as well as the other issues which have been touched on and then left in the air in the course of the poem:

> Words move, music moves
> Only in time; but that which is only living
> Can only die. Words after speech, reach
> Into the silence. Only by the form, the pattern,

> Can words or music reach
> The stillness, as a Chinese jar still
> Moves perpetually in its stillness.
> Not the stillness of the violin, while the note lasts,
> Not that only, but the co-existence,
> Or say that the end precedes the beginning,
> And the end and the beginning were always there
> Before the beginning and after the end,
> And all is always now.

This is the Symbolist aesthetic, made manifest by the poem ('Words, after speech, reach/Into the silence...') as well as elegantly summarised. The last three lines deftly relate it to the earlier thoughts on time, so that we are not far here from Yeats's meditation on the 'great-rooted blossomer' and from his rhetorical question: 'How can we know the dancer from the dance?'

But, as we know, the way human beings are constituted makes this only an ideal, never a liveable reality. For, in reality

> Words strain,
> Crack and sometimes break, under the burden,
> Under the tension, slip, slide, perish,
> Decay with imprecision, will not stay in place,
> Will not stay still. Shrieking voices
> Scolding, mocking, or merely chattering,
> Always assail them.

I find these lines among the most moving and *encouraging* in the entire poem. By admitting what he does, the speaker reaches across to me in a way he has not quite done so far. For this is something we all know, how our need to speak, to articulate our fears and desires, is always frustrated by the fact that words seem to have a life of their own, how they refuse to perform as we want them to, how they slip and slide away from us and how other voices, voices we did not know existed and didn't want to hear, voices which shriek or merely chatter, constantly interrupt, disrupt and mockingly destroy even our most heart-felt efforts.

Already in *The Waste Land* Eliot had been able to articulate in memorable poetry the failure of poetry and of memory:

> On Margate Sands
> I can connect
> Nothing with nothing.
> The broken fingernails of dirty hands.

We have all felt this but literature has, by and large, colluded in a conspiracy of silence on this point, as though there were something shameful about it — except for a few maverick works like *Tristram Shandy*. Proust, Eliot, Kafka and Beckett, though, affect us as they do precisely because they break the silence on this point. They assert that this inability to connect anything with anything, this failure of the will to organise language so that it can express what we feel and want to say, is perfectly natural, is in fact *the* natural condition of man. Here, they say, is where we must start from, not the ideal of the finished, the well-made work. And by so saying they release us from our sense of personal failure and give us back hope.

This, it seems to me, is the true heart of Modernism. We find it in Yeats' 'Circus Animals' Desertion', where the poet, seeking a theme in vain 'for six weeks or so', finally realises that he must start 'where all the ladders start,/In the foul rag-and-bone shop of the heart'. We find it in the later philosophy of Wittgenstein, where the philosopher, instead of attempting to produce the impossible, perfect match of word and world, accepts that thought will most often come up against a dead end, and accepts that *this is in itself an interesting phenomenon*, worthy of comment. For the mind is not a sealed chamber and words are not mine to do what I want with. Indeed, it is precisely at the moment when the mind, in solitude, tries to bring ultimate clarity and precision to bear on a recalcitrant world, that it is most vulnerable. As Eliot puts it:

> The Word in the desert
> Is most attacked by voices of temptation,
> The crying shadow in the funeral dance,
> The loud lament of the disconsolate chimera.

The Romantic myth of the single pure voice, of the poet as filled by the divine afflatus and speaking forth in inspiration, is here deftly countered by what Eliot sees as a myth which is truer to our creaturely possibilities. By capitalising the word 'word', he effortlessly brings to bear on the question of language and will the implications of Christianity: Christ came to save mankind in human form and lived out a life that, by the criteria of the world, could only be seen as a failure; but that failure, that criminal's death, is both illustration and guarantor of the place where our human potential lies: in the acceptance of our weak and vulnerable human bodies, our weak and vulnerable spirits, our weak and vulnerable minds. Anything else, being a denial of the human, is a false lure, 'the loud lament of the disconsolate chimera'.

There is, after this, nothing more to say. All that is required is to celebrate this hard-won insight. In the final lines of *Burnt Norton* the lyric and meditative strands come together for the first and only time:

> The detail of the pattern is movement,
> As in the figure of the ten stairs.
> Desire itself is movement
> Not in itself desirable;
> Love is itself unmoving,
> Only the cause and end of movement,
> Timeless and undesiring
> Except in the aspect of time
> Caught in the form of limitation
> Between un-being and being.
> Sudden in a shaft of sunlight

Even while the dust moves
There rises the hidden laughter
Of children in the foliage
Quick now, here, now, always —
Ridiculous the waste sad time
Stretching before and after.

II

Eliot published *Burnt Norton* in 1935. It thus grew from the same
soil as *Ash Wednesday* and *Murder in the Cathedral*. But the voices he
had released in the writing, it turned out, still had much to say
before they would finally be still. At some point, it seems, Eliot
must have conceived the project of writing four poems which
would be linked both thematically and structurally: each would
have five movements, of which the first would establish the
place referred to in the title and its particular aura, the second
would start with a lyric, the third would deal with the negative
aspect of the quest, the fourth would be purely lyrical and the
fifth would bring art itself and the writing of the poem into the
focus of the meditation. To talk of the quartets of Beethoven
or Bartok here, is to risk overlooking the deep continuities in
Eliot's life as a poet. *The Waste Land* too, after all, had eventually
fallen into five parts, and there as here there is no sense of the
poet imposing the structure on his material but rather discovering it in the process of composition. But even to speak of five
parts gives slightly the wrong impression, for already in the first
sections of *The Waste Land* and *Burnt Norton* there are many voices,
many starts and stops. But where *The Waste Land* gives the impression of 'fragments shored against my ruin', the disparate pieces
lying side by side, often in fierce juxtapositions, *Burnt Norton*,
following on from *Ash Wednesday*, is both more tentative and
more capable of growth. Growth, change, is only a distant possi-

bility in *The Waste Land*, heralded by the rain which arrives as
the poem ends, but *Burnt Norton* is from the start poetry of
exploration, of coils rather than straight lines, of paths which
seem about to peter out but which open suddenly on to larger
vistas. The voice accepts that there is no final resting place, no
perfect way to say things, just as there is no perfect existence.
It launches itself into a meditation on time, or into a story, but
then it can stop and question the validity not only of what it
has said but of the way it has said it:

> That was a way of putting it – not very satisfactory:
> A periphrastic study in a worn-out poetical fashion,
> Leaving one still with the intolerable wrestle
> With words and meanings.

But even this is only another way of putting it, not the final
truth. What it does for the poet is to put the voice 'on hold'
until a new foray can be initiated.

But the confidence that came with the completion of *Burnt
Norton* gave the quartets that follow a new authority:

> The poetry does not matter.
> It was not (to start again) what one had expected.

Time does not bring wisdom, merely a different perspective;
there is

> At best, only a limited value
> In the knowledge derived from experience.
> The knowledge imposes a pattern, and falsifies,
> For the pattern is new in every moment
> And every moment is a new and shocking
> Valuation of all we have been.

Twenty years earlier, in 'Tradition and the Individual Talent',
he had written:

> [W]hat happens when a new work of art is created is some-
> thing that happens simultaneously to all the works of art

which preceded it. The existing monuments form an ideal order among themselves, which is modified by the introduction of the new (the really new) work of art among them. The existing order is complete before the new work arrives; for order to persist after the supervention of novelty, the whole existing order must be, if ever so slightly, altered; and so the relations, proportions, values of each work of art towards the whole are readjusted; and this is conformity between the old and the new.

The focus now, however, is not on the entire history of culture but on the history of a single human being; the laws adumbrated in the essay, though, remain valid.

In the fifth section of the second Quartet, *East Coker*, Eliot, true to his new formal and thematic constraints, picks up the themes of the second section and applies them to his own life in art:

> So here I am, in the middle way, having had twenty years —
> Twenty years largely wasted, the years of *l'entre deux guerres* —
> Trying to learn to use words, and every attempt
> Is a wholly new start, and a different kind of failure
> Because one has only learnt to get the better of words
> For the thing one no longer has to say, or the way in which
> One is no longer disposed to say it. And so each venture
> Is a new beginning, a raid on the inarticulate
> With shabby equipment always deteriorating
> In the general mess of imprecision of feeling,
> Undisciplined squads of emotion.

The poet is a person who tries to speak truthfully and accurately in order to make sense of things to himself; he is not the unacknowledged legislator of the world. Like Proust and Kafka and Wittgenstein, Eliot insists that his is a personal quest — and then immediately insists that this personal quest is one all human beings undertake:

> And what there is to conquer
> By strength and submission, has already been discovered
> Once or twice, or several times, by men whom one
> cannot hope
> To emulate – but there is no competition –
> There is only the fight to recover what has been lost
> And found and lost again and again...

Terms like 'gain' and 'loss', 'success' and 'failure' belong to the world of material transactions; they do not apply here: 'For us there is only the trying. The rest is not our business.'

The trouble is that as soon as something is formulated it is in danger of becoming an idol. We start to worship its exterior form and lose any sense of its urgency. Kafka and Wittgenstein sensed this and the feeling made it extremely hard for them ever to complete anything. *The Castle* and *The Philosophical Investigations* remain unfinished because no arrangement of the material could satisfy their exacting authors. Proust and Eliot felt this too, but they accepted it and built their unease into their works. That is why, in these Quartets, it is of both aesthetic and ethical importance that the voice keep moving, that it never rest content with any one formulation, even so apparently innocent a one as 'for us there is only the trying'. So the next poem in the sequence, *The Dry Salvages*, returns to the theme and comes up with an even starker formulation:

> this thing is sure,
> That time is no healer: the patient is no longer there.

This third poem, dealing as it does with the power of the sea to destroy, as *East Coker* had dealt with the power of the land to regenerate, is fully aware of the fragility of life:

> Here between the hither and the farther shore
> While time is withdrawn, consider the future
> And the past with an equal mind.

> At the moment which is not of action or inaction
> You can receive this: 'on whatever sphere of being
> The mind of a man may be intent
> At the time of death' — that is the one action
> (And the time of death is every moment)
> Which shall fructify in the lives of others:
> And do not think of the fruit of action.
> Fare forward.

What had earlier been a groping for meaning through the support of rhythm has now become a confident assertion of the limits of human comprehension:

> right action is freedom
> From the past and future also.
> For most of us, this is the aim
> Never here to be realised;
> Who are only undefeated
> Because we have gone on trying.

III

The fruit of this new-found confidence — found through and by means of the *Quartets* themselves — was *Little Gidding*. The other three titles had referred to places which had personal associations for Eliot, places he had known or lived in or which his family had links with. Little Gidding, on the other hand, is the Huntingdonshire village where in the early seventeenth century Nicholas Ferrar, a close friend of George Herbert's, retired with his family to live a life of ordered devotion. It is significant only because of the actuality of the lives that were once lived there. And the poem invites us to visit it not as a shrine but rather as a place which forces us to question the whole nature of shrines and holy places:

And what you thought you came for
Is only a shell, a husk of meaning
From which the purpose breaks only when it is fulfilled
If at all. Either you had no purpose
Or the purpose is beyond the end you figured
And is altered in fulfilment.

We have to understand that anywhere can be a place of significant encounter – 'at the sea jaws,/Or over a dark lake, in a
desert or a city' –

But this is the nearest, in place and time
Now and in England.

The voice has ceased once and for all to be one which gropes
for meaning in the early hours of the morning. It is now quite
clear about what it wants to do and say:

You are not here to verify,
Instruct yourself, or inform curiosity
Or carry report. You are here to kneel
Where prayer has been valid.

But what is prayer? (What is poetry? What is speech?)

prayer is more
Than an order of words, the conscious occupation
Of the praying mind, or the sound of the voice praying.
And what the dead had no speech for, when living,
They can tell you, being dead: the communication
Of the dead is tongued with fire beyond the language of
the living.
Here, the intersection of the timeless moment
Is England and nowhere. Never and always.

There is a short story by Henry James called 'The Middle
Years'. It tells of a middle-aged writer whose latest book has
just been published and who meets a young doctor at a seaside
resort who is a great admirer of his work. At the climax of the

story the writer, dying, laments the fact that he has barely begun to achieve what he felt he had been put on earth to do. I'm only in the middle, he groans, I had hardly begun to say what I wanted to say. The doctor disagrees passionately: No, he says, you've given the world so much, you've given *me* so much, you mustn't talk like that. The beauty of the story lies in the fact that both are probably right. Were the writer to believe he had said what he needed to say he would come across as insufferably smug; he is right to feel that he has only just begun. On the other hand the doctor also speaks the truth when he tells him his work does form a meaningful whole, that he has given to others far more than he gives himself credit for. Mallarmé put it another way when he said of Poe that death had changed him into himself – 'Tel qu'en lui-même l'éternité le change.' That, I think, is what Eliot means here when he says that 'what the dead had no speech for, when living,/They can tell you, being dead'. Their speech is no longer made of words or phrases but of their whole lives. That is why critics' talk of the works of artists being in some cases successes and in others failures is nothing but chatter. To anyone who has responded to Cézanne or Picasso, Dostoevsky or Kafka, Schoenberg or Stravinsky, the awarding of points for different works seems like an irrelevance. We respond to the whole enterprise, and success and failures together make it up. Our lives normally make little sense to us as we live them, but they speak to others even when we are long gone: '[T]he communication/Of the dead is tongued with fire beyond the language of the living.' Nothing is wasted, not the years of 'l'entre deux guerres', not the unhappy years of Eliot's disastrous first marriage, not Proust's forays into the world of high society or Wittgenstein's into that of Austrian village schools. Nothing you have done. Nothing I have done. To us it may seem like that, but not to those we have come in contact with, or to God (if there is a God), who can see the whole trajectory of our lives.

That having been said, the poet can now formally pay homage to those who helped him find his voice: Yeats, Donne, above all Dante. The second part of section two of *Little Gidding*, Eliot was to say later, cost him more hard work than any other poem of his. Written in a loose form of Dante's *terza rima* (a form far easier to work with in Italian than in English), it brings the present of London during the blitz into conjunction with the eternity of Dante's great poem. The 'familiar compound ghost' he meets in the bombed-out city does not come to offer superficial balm but the deep comfort of truth. First he repeats, in Dantean language, the lesson already learned, that we cannot rest on our laurels:

> Last year's fruit is eaten
> And the fullfed beast shall kick the empty pail.
>> For last year's words belong to last year's language
>> And next year's words await another voice.

Then he reveals to him 'the gifts reserved for age':

> First, the cold friction of expiring sense
> Without enchantment, offering no promise
>> But bitter tastelessness of shadow fruit
>> As body and soul begin to fall asunder.
> Second, the conscious impotence of rage
>> At human folly, and the laceration
>> Of laughter at what ceases to amuse.
> And last, the rending pain of re-enactment
>> Of all that you have done, and been; the shame
>> Of motives late revealed, and the awareness
> Of things ill done and done to others' harm
>> Which once you took for exercise of virtue.
>> Then fools' approval stings, and honour stains.
> From wrong to wrong the exasperated spirit
>> Proceeds, unless restored by that refining fire
>> Where you must move in measure, like a dancer.

By now, though, such lashings are purgatorial, not infernal, a positive spur to the spirit rather than a reason for despair. The speaker has accepted himself as a being living in time, responsible for past actions as well as future ones, and memory, so ambiguous earlier, has now become one of the chief weapons at his disposal:

> This is the use of memory:
> For liberation – not less of love but expanding
> Of love beyond desire, and so liberation
> From the future as well as the past.

The mood is no longer hesitant but firm and clear-sighted: 'History may be servitude,/History may be freedom.' And so the voice moves into the mode of prayer and celebration, which is the mode of those who recognise the openness of both past and future and are themselves open to both:

> And all shall be well and
> All manner of thing shall be well
> By the purification of the motive
> In the ground of our beseeching.

The lyric which has to follow encapsulates for one last time the paradox of love:

> Love is the unfamiliar Name
> Behind the hands that wove
> The intolerable shirt of flame
> Which human power cannot remove.
>   We only live, only suspire
>   Consumed by either fire or fire.

But there is one more theme to take up before the voice can at last be still. The 'familiar compound ghost' in the ruins of London had quoted Mallarmé at him:

> Since our concern was speech, and speech impelled us
> To purify the dialect of the tribe...

But this familiar phrase is capable of two distinct interpretations. For Mallarmé it tended to mean the creation of a language free of the crudities of daily speech; for the speaker here, who has, from the first, been concerned with the acceptance of the human condition in all its weakness and disarray, and who, in the Incarnation, has seen the vindication of that very weakness, the implication is very different, and he now, in the last section of the last poem of the sequence, makes that clear. He begins by recalling the opening words of the first poem in the sequence, acknowledging, across the mighty arch that now lies between them, that other, hesitant voice which was nevertheless his own:

> What we call the beginning is often the end
> And to make an end is to make a beginning.
> The end is where we start from.

We can start from the end because it is not so much a point along a line as a new form of understanding, which brings with it a new relationship to language:

> And every phrase
> And sentence that is right (where every word is at home,
> Taking its place to support the others,
> The word neither diffident nor ostentatious,
> An easy commerce of the old and the new,
> The common word exact without vulgarity,
> The formal word precise but not pedantic,
> The complete consort dancing together)
> Every phrase and every sentence is an end and a beginning,
> Every poem an epitaph.

We are weak creatures, who cannot bear very much reality; who cannot articulate what we feel and desire without the words slipping and sliding away from us; who have flashes of understanding, but only when what has been understood is no longer relevant; who are always in the middle years, though we long for the fulfilment of a true end, a true beginning — and yet, by virtue of our humanity, of our acknowledgement of these weaknesses, we form part of a larger community, and so we are neither lost nor alone:

> We die with the dying:
> See, they depart, and we go with them.
> We are born with the dead:
> See, they return, and bring us with them.
> The moment of the rose and the moment of the yew-tree
> Are of equal duration. A people without history
> Is not redeemed from time, for history is a pattern
> Of timeless moments. So, while the light fails,
> On a winter's afternoon, in a secluded chapel,
> History is now and England.

Eliot, the scion of a New England family growing up in the mid-West, the adolescent with his memories of St Louis and the Mississippi, undergoing his education at Harvard, the American in London, the Anglo-Catholic in a secular world — Eliot, no less than Kafka, speaks for all those who, in the twentieth century, have found themselves in a country not their own, speaking a language which resonates differently for them than it does for the natives. Wherever chance has happened to bring them — London or Prague — is more cherished by such people than it is by the natives, who take what surrounds them for granted. To the religious mind, of course, none of us is a native, we are all merely sojourners, pilgrims in this world, having been lent our lives for a short time to make of them what we will. That is why the marginality of both Eliot and Kafka has turned out to have a universal appeal: it is they, in the end, who speak for us all.

In his beautiful essay on reading, Proust makes the point that the works of art which mean most to us are those which are spurs to our own imaginations and endeavours, those which lead us to the threshold and then invite us to enter the house ourselves. That, of course, is what his novel does, and it is what *Four Quartets*, which is in so many ways parallel to *A la recherche*, also does:

> What we call the beginning is often the end
> And to make an end is to make a beginning.
> The end is where we start from.

As *Little Gidding* and the entire sequence draws to its end we have the sense not so much of a path having been traversed as of a field having been gone over until every patch of ground has been touched. Then it is time to stop. But now stopping will not be a sign of failure but of triumph, the voice will cease not because it cannot find a way forward but because nothing more needs to be said. Speaker and reader have been carried to the threshold, and it is time for us, all of us, to make a start:

> We shall not cease from exploration
> And the end of all our exploring
> Will be to arrive where we started
> And know the place for the first time.
> Through the unknown, remembered gate
> When the last of earth left to discover
> Is that which was the beginning;
> At the source of the longest river
> The voice of the hidden waterfall
> And the children in the apple-tree
> Not known, because not looked for
> But heard, half-heard, in the stillness
> Between two waves of the sea.
> Quick now, here, now, always —
> A condition of complete simplicity
> (Costing not less than everything)

And all shall be well and
All manner of thing shall be well
When the tongues of flame are in-folded
Into the crowned knot of fire
And the fire and the rose are one.

13. Borges and the Plain Sense of Things

THE NAME OF BORGES, among readers of modern literature, has always been synonymous with labyrinths, Babelic libraries, gardens of forking paths, parallel universes, refutations of time and all sorts of cunning intellectual paradoxes. I want to argue, however, that these are merely the means whereby this profoundly modern writer seeks to make manifest the importance of the ordinary and the contingent in our lives and to remind us that this is the only life we have, that death will bring it to an end, and that every moment of it is infinitely precious. In this he is at one with Proust and Wallace Stevens, Beckett and Nabokov.

In saying this I am not saying anything particularly revolutionary. It is, after all, the message of one of Borges' greatest stories, the one he chose to place at the head of his finest collection, *Ficciones* (*Fictions*), the story called 'Tlön, Uqbar, Orbis Tertius'.

Let me remind you, briefly, how that story goes. With all the circumstantial detail that is the hallmark of his work, he describes, in the first person, how an alternative universe gradually encroached upon our own. It first enters his consciousness when his friend Bioy Casares refers in passing to the opinion of one of the heresiarchs of Uqbar, 'that mirrors and copulation are abominable, because they increase the number of men'. Asked by the narrator for the source of this, Bioy Casares mentions an encyclopaedia entry on Uqbar, but when the two men look up the relevant volume they find no such entry. However, the next day a triumphant Bioy Casares calls him to say that he has found it, at the end of Volume XLVI of the encyclopaedia he has at home, though the spine of that volume asserts that the contents run only from *Tor* to *Ups* and the four pages on that country are found to figure in no other copy. Nor is there any reference to it in any of the atlases and travellers' accounts in the National Library. A short while later, however, Tlön and Uqbar manifest themselves to the narrator again, this time in the form of an entire volume found in a packet left in a bar, on his death, by a mysterious Englishman. This allows the narrator to put together rather more fully the history and intellectual ambience of that strange country.

Its culture is strictly idealist, and thus neither causality nor language as we know it exist: 'The world for them is not a concourse of objects in space; it is a heterogeneous series of independent acts. It is successive and temporal, not spatial. There are no nouns in Tlön's conjectural *Ursprache*... The perception of a cloud of smoke on the horizon and then of the burning field and then of the half-extinguished cigarette that produced the blaze is considered an example of association of ideas.'

'Centuries... of idealism have not failed to influence reality', the narrator goes on, in a nice double negative. 'In the most ancient regions of Tlön, the duplication of lost objects is not infrequent.' Two persons look for a pencil; the first finds it and says nothing; the second finds a second pencil, 'no less real, but closer to his expectations'. These secondary objects are called *hrönir*, and these *hrönir* have little by little been ousting the real, banal objects, so that the world of Tlön is approximating more and more to the expectations of its inhabitants.

The rest of the story tells how this fantastic world has slowly invaded our own, helped on by a secret society dedicated to Tlön and its propagation. This society, we are told, is 'benevolent', and included George Berkeley among its founder members. At first there were only isolated examples of infiltration, but these gradually turned into a trickle. By 1944 the trickle has become an avalanche:

> Manuals, anthologies, summaries, literal versions, authorised re-editions and pirated editions of the Greatest Work of Man flooded and still flood the earth. Almost immediately, reality yielded on more than one account. The truth is that it longed to yield. Ten yeas ago any symmetry with a semblance of order – dialectical materialism, anti-Semitism, Nazism – was sufficient to entrance the minds of men. How could one do other than submit to Tlön, to the minute and vast evidence of an orderly planet?

Our world, it seems, will soon be indistinguishable from Tlön:

> Already the schools have been invaded by the (conjectural) 'primitive language' of Tlön; already the teaching of its harmonious history (filled with moving episodes) has wiped out the one which governed my childhood; already a fictitious past occupies in our memories the place of another, a past of which we know nothing with certainty – not even that it is false... If our forecasts are not in error, a hundred years from now... English and French and mere Spanish will disappear from the globe. The world will be Tlön.

At this point the narrator, who has not been much more than a literary device, suddenly takes centre stage: 'I pay no attention to all this', he writes, 'and go on revising, in the still days at the Adrogué hotel, an uncertain Quevedian translation (which I do not intend to publish) of Browne's *Urn Burial*'.

It is easy enough to see the 'point' of the story: it is an anguished cry in the face of the persuasive ideologies which swept the world in the 1930s, and a kind of stoic refusal to submit to them. There is a puzzle about the dates: the story came out first in the collection *El jardín de senderos que se bifurcan* (*The Garden of Forking Paths*) in 1941, and was reprinted in the larger volume of 1944, *Ficciones*. Yet the latter part of the story is relegated to a postscript dated 1947. I presume this is a projection forward in time by the author, writing in 1940 or 41. He imagines then a world overtaken by Nazi ideology and dramatises what he would like his reaction to be: not so much passive resistance as a kind of quiet active resistance, the activity consisting of a completely selfless (he has no intention of publishing) translation into Spanish of a minor seventeenth-century prose work in English. The voluntary submission to a selfless task, to the carrying over into his native language of an author and a language far removed from him in space and intellectual interests, is the only way this quiet intellectual feels he can avoid being sucked into the idealist world of Tlön, that he can assert what he feels to be fundamental human values in a world rapidly turning into a mirror of our desires and imaginings.

It might be felt that the lumping together of dialectical materialism, anti-Semitism and Nazism makes for a rather limp critique of the times, and that to see them all as one thing, and that thing as an example of the idealist world of Tlön suggests a lack of political and historical acumen. Yet other stories – notably 'Deutsches Requiem' – as well as remarks he made in interviews, makes it clear that the anglophile and democratic Borges was far from the uninvolved creator of private labyrinths he is often taken to be. On the other hand there is no doubt that the references to current events do seem rather perfunctory and that those stories, such as 'Deutsches Requiem', which deal with contemporary matters are not among his most successful. Indeed, one might say they feel slightly false precisely because he assimilates political issues a little too easily to his own concerns with the dangers of the imagination, It may be that

Borges' mode of writing is not such as to engage fully with politics and history, like that of Sartre and Malraux; yet I would suggest that despite this his central contrast of the melancholy and resigned translator and the idealist world of Tlön is more deeply political than Sartre and Malraux could ever be, and that it helps to bring out something that is often overlooked in studies of literary Modernism: that to write about politics without recognising the complicity of forms of writing with the formation of political consciousness is to betray the cause one thinks one is serving, and that writers like Eliot, Stevens, Beckett and Borges may in the end be better guides to the times than Malraux, Sartre, Camus, Silone and the rest.

What are the implications of the contrast between the narrator and the world of Tlön? And why, if Borges sees Tlön as a dangerous temptation and a fallacy, does he spend so much of his time and ingenuity in the construction of idealist universes? To answer this question it is necessary to understand the critique of traditional fiction that drives Borges' literary innovation.

Let us go back to the burning cigarette: 'The perception of a cloud of smoke on the horizon and then of the burning field and then of the half-extinguished cigarette that produced the blaze is considered an example of association of ideas.' Not in the real world, we retort. But what of the world of fiction? After all, in that world there is no causality, only the semblance of causality, for the smoke is not real smoke, the field not a real field, and the cigarette not a real cigarette. The writer has put these three elements together on paper, but we read it as a story of how a fire was started. We only do that, however, because we know about the real world. The men of Tlön do not read it as a story but as an example of association of ideas, because '[t]he world for them is not a concourse of objects in space; it is a heterogeneous series of independent acts.' In other words, the world of Tlön is the world of literature shorn of its realist illusion.

We can now see why Borges is so fond of detective stories and why detective stories should have emerged out of the crisis of Romanticism with the work of Poe. For detective stories go to the heart of the nature of literature and raise questions about the difference between causality in real life and causality in the imagination: 'The Murders in the Rue Morgue' is the flip side of 'The Raven'. Were we to find those three elements, the smoke on the horizon, the burning field, the half-extinguished cigarette, in a detective story the deduction that the cigarette caused the smoke on the horizon would figure as the first, obvious, banal explanation, later to be shown up by the detective to be false. It would have to be false because as it stands it is too obvious. Too boring. No reader would bother with a writer of detective fiction who presented us with such a story and left it at that. Thus in Borges' story, 'Death and the Compass', the dull police inspector Treviranus, faced with a number of facts – a dead body in a hotel room, precious stones in the next room – comes up with the obvious explanation: 'No need to look for a three-legged cat here. We all know that the Tetrarch of Galilee owns the finest sapphires in the world. Someone, intending to steal them, must have broken in here by mistake. Yarmolinsky got up; the robber had to kill him. How does it sound to you?' 'Possible, but not interesting', replies the detective hero, Lönnrot. 'You'll reply that reality hasn't the least obligation to be interesting. And I'll answer you that reality may avoid that obligation but that hypotheses may not. In the hypothesis that you propose, chance intervenes copiously. Here we have a dead rabbi; I would prefer a purely rabbinical explanation, not the imaginary mischances of an imaginary robber.'

Lönnrot is of course right. But his intuition leads to his own death, for the murderer is, in this story, one step ahead of the detective, has in fact produced an 'interesting' series of crimes precisely because he knows that Lönnrot has a weakness for the interesting. The ultimate victor, though, is the story: Borges has produced a classical detective tale with not one element of chance in it and not one but two twists in the plot, and only the most ingenious reader could have guessed the second one.

Borges' fondness for detective stories stems from his dislike for the classical novel. For the detective story, unlike the novel, accepts from the start that the logic of fiction is not the logic of life and that as a fictional construct its prime duty is to be interesting, not realistic. The novel, on the other hand, is a curious hybrid: it wants to assert at one and the same time that it is dealing with life in all its boring contingency, while at the same time telling a story which implies that life has a meaning, is always more than mere contingency. This is the secret of its hold over us, as Sartre, for one, understood so well. We open a novel, Sartre says in *La Nausée*, and read about a man walking down a road. The man seems free, the future open before him. At once we identify with him, for that is how our own existence seems to be to us. We too are walking down the road of life, not knowing what is to come. But the pleasure of reading a novel stems from the fact that we know that this man is in fact the subject of an adventure that is about to befall him. How do we know this? Because he is there at the start of the novel and he would not be there if nothing were going to happen to him. Thus, Sartre concludes, 'the end is there, which transforms everything. For us the guy is already the hero of the story.' The extraordinary power of the novel lies in this, that it makes us feel that our lives are both free *and* meaningful. It does not say this, for it neither needs to nor is it fully aware of it, but nonetheless that is its essence, the secret of its power.

Borges, like Beckett, dislikes the novel for two reasons, one having to do with literature and the other with life. He dislikes it because he finds it tedious and uninteresting to imitate reality, and he dislikes it because he feels that it propagates a false view of life which stops us seeing what life is really like.

It is easy enough to understand the first reason: since literature is not tied to causality, why not let the imagination free to discover its own rules and laws? But the way this first reason is tied to the second is, despite the clarity of Sartre's analysis, rather more difficult to grasp. Let me turn briefly to another writer who may help us do so, Søren Kierkegaard.

Kierkegaard's great decade of writing took place exactly a century before Borges', in the years 1840–50. Nevertheless, the problems he explored were almost identical to those of the Argentinian writer. Kierkegaard is concerned with what he calls 'actuality', with the stuff of life as it is lived, and with the way narratives about living, whether they be those of novelists or of a philosopher like Hegel, covertly falsify actuality. '"Actuality" cannot be conceived,' he writes in his notebook for the year 1850:

> To conceive something is to dissolve actuality into *possibility* – but then it is impossible to conceive it, because conceiving something is transforming it into possibility and so not holding on to it as actuality... But there's this deplorable confusion in that modern times have incorporated 'actuality' into logic and then, in distraction, forgotten that 'actuality' in logic is still only a 'thought actuality', i.e. it is possibility.[1]

Everything would be fine if works of fiction and works like Hegel's *Phenomenology* presented themselves as hypotheses, but they do not, they present themselves as actuality. And it is the same with history:

> But isn't history actual? Certainly. But what history? No doubt the six thousand years of the world's history are actuality, but one that is put behind us; it is and can exist for me only as thought actuality, i.e. as possibility. Whether or not the dead have actually realised existen-

1 Søren Kierkegaard, *Papers and Journals: A Selection*, tr. Alastair Hannay, London, 1996, p.470.

tially the tasks which were put before them in actuality has now been decided, has been concluded; there is no more existential actuality for them except in what has been put behind them, which again, for me, exists only as ideal actuality, as thought actuality, as possibility.[2]

I can think of history as actuality, but the very thinking robs it of its actuality. If I am to grasp the actual I have somehow to think against thinking, to imagine against imagination. Already in 1837 – before, that is, he had published any of his books – Kierkegaard had struggled to make sense of this conundrum. He had done so by drawing a contrast between the indicative, the mode of actuality, and the subjunctive, the mode of possibility: 'The indicative thinks something as actual (the identity of thinking and the actual). The subjunctive thinks something as thinkable.'[3] The writer sensitive to the gulf between thinking and living will reflect this distinction by choosing the subjunctive, not the indicative, as his mode: 'One should be able to write a whole novel in which the present tense subjunctive was the invisible soul, as light is for painting.'

This helps explain why so many modern writers have been at pains to stress that their fictions are only fictions, not reality. This is not in order to play games with the reader or to deny the world, but on the contrary, out of a deep sense of the wondrous nature of the world and a determination not to confuse the world as it is with the world as we imagine it to be, not to confuse actuality with possibility. Borges is quite clear about this in both the parable and the poem he has devoted to the tiger: 'Never can my dreams engender the wild beast I long for' he writes in the parable. 'The tiger indeed appears, but stuffed or flimsy, or with impure variations of shape, or of an

2 Ibid.
3 Ibid., p.91.

implausible size, or all too fleeting, or with a touch of the dog or the bird.'[4] And the poem ends by directing us away from poetry to the living beast: 'I go on/Seeking through the afternoon time/The other tiger, that which is not in verse.'[5] In his stories he invents plots that help bring out the contrast between the indicative and the subjunctive: the man who waits for his killers to come, imagining again and again the moment of their arrival, until he can no longer distinguish reality from his nightmares; the creature lost in the labyrinth of his melancholy life, welcoming with relief the coming of Theseus, who will put an end to his solitude; the Symbolist writer who refuses the pleasures of mere imagination and sets out to write that which is quite other than any of our imaginings. As with Beckett and Stevens, Borges' imagination keeps trying to imagine the death of imagination, but it is only when the imagination has been given its head that it can be effectively exorcised and so allow actuality to shine through.

For imagination to be exorcised it must be released from the constraints of causality that operates in the real world; by so doing it will make clear what realistic fiction obscures, drive a wedge between imagination and reality. But that is only the first step. The second is to try, by means of the imagination, to reveal the nature of reality. 'In spite of having been a child in a symmetrical garden of Hai Feng, was I – now – going to die?' asks the Chinese agent in 'The Garden of Forking Paths', and the story is designed to bring him – and us – to an understanding of what that 'now' means, of what, in effect, death means – not in imagination, but in reality.

First of all we must be weaned from our lack of curiosity about 'nowness', from our taking it for granted. To do so we

4 *Dreamtigers*, tr. Mildren Boyer and Harold Morland, London, 1973, p.24.
5 *Ibid.*, p.71.

must be made to realise how very strange it is that everything that happens to us happens, precisely now. And this can be done by making us grasp *that things could have been otherwise but were not*. 'In all fictional works,' Stephen Albert, the sinologist, explains to the Chinese agent,

> each time a man is confronted with several alternatives, he chooses one and eliminates the others; in the fictional world of Ts'ui Pên he chooses – simultaneously – all of them. He *creates*, in this way, diverse futures, diverse times which themselves also proliferate and fork. Here, then, is the explanation of the novel's contradictions. Fang, let us say, has a secret; a stranger calls at his door; Fang resolves to kill him. Naturally, there are several possible outcomes: the intruder can kill Fang, they both can escape, they both can die, and so forth. In the work of Ts'ui Pên, all possible outcomes occur; each one is the point of departure for other forkings. Sometimes the paths of this labyrinth converge: for example, you arrive at this house, but in one of the possible pasts you are my enemy, in another, my friend...

The traditional novel, by refusing to countenance the fact that things could have been otherwise, stops us also from understanding the strangeness of the fact that they are *not* otherwise, but thus. 'Thus "now" can never be written, for that would turn [it] from actuality again into possibility.' 'Now' can only be pointed to, not uttered: 'In a riddle whose answer is chess,' Stephen Albert asks the Chinese agent, 'what is the only prohibited word?' 'I thought a moment and replied: "The word *chess*."'

The classic novel, unaware of its complicity with the forces of falsehood, imagining that it deals with actuality when it deals only with possibility, blithely includes such words in its discourse. The more fastidious writer, aware of what he is doing, knows that his only way of conveying the sense of the word is to construct a riddle or labyrinth whose answer is the missing word. He cannot speak the word, for that will immediately turn it from actual to possible. He must find a way of making that word emerge through the construction of a fiction. That is what the Chinese agent has done, though because he is acting in the real world and not creating fiction, the consequence, for himself and others, is dire. Realising that his human voice is 'weak' and cannot rise above 'the uproar of war', he has worked out that the only way to send his message to Germany is to murder a man. 'I have won out abominably,' he concludes:

> I have communicated to Berlin the secret name of the city they must attack. They bombed it yesterday… The Chief has deciphered this mystery. He knew my problem was to indicate (through the uproar of the war) the city called Albert, and that I had found no other means to do so than to kill a man of that name. He does not know (no one can know) my innumerable contrition and weariness.

What is the missing word of 'Tlön, Uqbar, Orbis Tertius'? The answer is 'the actual', what Wallace Stevens called 'the plain sense of things'. A conventional narrative would, like mirrors and copulation, merely double our confusions; Borges' narrative, recognising that 'the absence of the imagination/Had itself to be imagined', manages to convey the 'nowness', the 'thusness' of actuality, to which the narrator commits himself at the end. There is no better gloss on it, and on all Borges' work, than the poem Stevens called 'The Plain Sense of Things':

> After the leaves have fallen, we return
> To a plain sense of things. It is as if
> We had come to an end of the imagination,
> Inanimate in an inert savoir.
>
> It is difficult even to choose the adjective
> For this blank cold, this sadness without cause.

The great structure has become a minor house.
No turban walks across the lessened floors...

Yet the absence of the imagination had
Itself to be imagined. The great pond,
The plain sense of it, without reflections, leaves,
Mud, water like dirty glass, expressing silence

Of a sort, silence of a rat come out to see
The great pond and its waste of the lilies, all this
Had to be imagined as an inevitable knowledge,
Required, as a necessity requires.

14. Aharon Appelfeld: Three Novels and a Tribute

1. The Retreat

ONE OF THE PLEASANTER RESULTS of the confusion of tongues consequent upon the fall of the Tower of Babel is that we can discover, late in the day, a major writer who has been quietly establishing himself in his native country and who, at the height of his creative powers, suddenly appears to us when his works start to be translated. Such is the case of Aharon Appelfeld, who now, at fifty-two, and with over fifteen books in Hebrew and the distinguished Jerusalem Prize behind him, is at last beginning to appear in English.

Appelfeld was born in 1932 in Czernovitz, Bukovina, in what was once the Austro-Hungarian Empire and is now Ukraine, but was then Romania. Twelve years earlier Paul Celan had been born in the same town, which meant that Celan was nineteen when the war broke out and fate had already determined that he would become a German writer. Appelfeld was eight when the Nazis rolled in, shot his mother and sent him and his father to a camp. He promptly escaped and spent the next three years hiding in the Ukrainian forests before joining the Russian army and eventually, in 1946, making his way via Italy to Palestine. Today he lives in Jerusalem, teaches at the University of Beersheba, and writes in Hebrew. Naturally, though, his novels are closer in feeling to the work of other Israeli writers born in Europe, such as the poets Yehuda Amichai and Dan Pagis, than to that of a native Israeli like Amos Oz. In Appelfeld's work, as in that of Celan, one hears the distinctive voice of Jewish

221

European culture, the strains of Hölderlin and Kleist and Kafka, as well as the Bible and Talmud.

The novels of Appelfeld's that have so far been translated into English all deal with a single subject: the plight of the Jews in Europe, their impossible desire for assimilation and the fools' paradise in which so many of them chose to live, and their subsequent fate. *Badenheim 1939* focuses on a group of Jews in an Austrian holiday resort in that fateful year; *The Age of Wonders* deals with one family, and in particular with the child of that family, in the years 1932–9, and then with the return of the child to the town he grew up in many years after the end of the war; *Tzili* also concentrates on a child, this time a girl, who wanders in the forests out of reach of the Germans during the war years; and *The Retreat* takes up the theme of Badenheim once more, though this time the place in which the Jews gather as the decade draws to its close is not a spa but a big house high up in the Austrian Alps, where the owner, Balaban, seeks to eradicate the Jewishness of the residents with a strong dose of physical exercise and mental bullying.

But to describe the theme of a novel by Appelfeld is to say hardly anything about it. Like Kafka's, his stories are both precise and unrealistic; like Kafka's, they cannot be allegorised. But they are not, like Kafka's, irreducibly enigmatic. They are in fact extremely simple. Their uniqueness derives from their combination of such simplicity with extreme density and richness. In *The Retreat*, as in *Badenheim*, there is a sense in which nothing at all happens, but another sense in which more happens in each paragraph than most novelists manage to convey in an entire book. Here, for example, is a brief, dry summary of why Lotte Schloss finds herself, at the start of the book, on her way to the mountain-top retreat with her daughter:

> In the winter of 1937 the mother had still played a few small parts in the theatre. And that was the end. No one

had given a farewell party for her, and it soon transpired that her pension too was in question. For a few months she ran from place to place, called on old friends, knocked on doors. In the end, penniless and at the end of her tether, she arrived on her daughter's doorstep. Her daughter did her best but her husband, George, did not make her welcome. He did not think much of actors.

And here, in the same laconic, almost hurried style, is the description of the life of the non-Jewish janitor, Robert:

In his youth he had worked in a Jewish department store, then he had run away and tried country life again. But not long afterwards he had returned to the city. He was strong and handsome, many women fell into his net. He had always worked, with occasional interruptions, for Jews. In their shops and their gardens. He did not like them, but he had grown used to their ways. They were easier to satisfy than the farmers and estate owners, it was easier to talk to them. They had good-looking women, and the women were generous with their favours. What more could a man ask for? A man should be content with his lot. There was truth in his quiet voice. As if he wasn't talking about his own fate, but about a law of nature. Now he was sixty-five years old, an age when a person should rest and not trouble his mind with strange ideas. If there was anything he missed, it was the mountains of his native village. But the village was far away and it was better not to think of it.

'And you have no complaints.'

'No.' As he said this he seemed to recover his peasant's face, and to Lotte he looked strong and ageless.

The peculiar quality of the writing stems, I think, from the fact that what at first looks like purely neutral description turns out to be description which is, in fact, straining to remain neutral. We hear a voice telling a story; it is not the voice of an impersonal narrator, but neither is it the voice of Lotte or Robert. Rather, it is one possible voice, with which they recount their story to themselves as much as to others, a voice which both accepts and refuses to accept what life has done to its owner, and which discovers what it wants to say only as it starts to speak.

Nor can this voice always be located in a character: 'For two months the quarrel between them had raged. Now all that was left was an echo, not lacking in sharpness, however. The storm refused to subside.' The voice here is that of both Lotte and her daughter and of the charged and complex feelings that flow between them. Appelfeld can say so much so briefly and simply because he recognises that life does not stand still, waiting to be described. We have to catch it as it flies past. Contrast this kind of description with one of the innumerable descriptions that litter the novels of a writer like Graham Greene:

> The place reminded her of a seedy hotel, yellowing mirrors in the bathrooms, broken toilet bowls and dripping taps, where the chambermaids spoke in impertinent voices and the doormen reached out to them with their big, strong hands.

A novelist like Greene is always out to make an effect; his eye is on the reader. Appelfeld, by contrast, is trying to catch the truth: his eye is on the object. Summing up the world in a gesture which is neither quite internal not quite external, he reminds one of Eliot ('Hakagawa bowing among the Titians'). In both we recognise that the miracle of literary art is that by a fusion of the imaginative and the verbal the entire complex tangle of reality which would otherwise remain forever closed to us is caught and conveyed.

Balaban's dream is to eradicate the defects of the Jews. Nearly everyone in the retreat is conscious of the urgent need for this. On her first day in the house Lotte hears from the violinist Engel about his dogged attempts to improve:

> 'My dear lady, I have made great efforts over the years. The will exists, but that one little defect makes any real progress impossible.'
>
> 'What defect are you speaking of?'
>
> 'Internal, in the main. The great Sebastian, with whom I studied, even succeeded in locating it exactly. It's the shoulder, the right shoulder upsets the balance, and with it the sound and all that implies.'
>
> ' Strange,' said Lotte. She was still thirsty.
>
> 'The defect is essentially hereditary, that's why I was so glad when I was invited to come here and eradicate it once and for all. The rest of the time I spend in exercise.'
>
> 'A kind of refresher course, in other words.'
>
> 'You might say so. The truth of the matter is that I was dismissed from my job. I don't blame them. When all is said and done you can't hide a defect for ever.'

This is funny, but it is also dreadful. The idea that a defect of this sort can be precisely located – in the right shoulder; that it is hereditary; and that Engel can so calmly and rationally agree with those who dismissed him – what a confusion of self-doubt, brutality, resignation and irony is mixed up in this brief exchange.

Appelfeld is not interested in repeating once again the story of German atrocities. 'What happened to the Jews in the Second World War is beyond tragedy,' he has said in an interview. 'It is impossible to understand it. We are not able to think about the death of a single individual, a close person, a single one. How can we think about hundreds and thousands of people?' With this one clear-headed remark he implicitly condemns the thousands of more or less artistic, more or less sensitive fictionalisations of the Holocaust. For him, to use art to describe those events is an insult to those who suffered, for it suggests that we can understand; our sympathy is a worse betrayal than indifference.

Instead, he concentrates on those things that *can* be imagined, on the temptations of the imagination. His theme is the folly of wilful blindness and the inability of the imagination to face reality. In the spa of Badenheim the Jews imagine that they can relax and enjoy themselves, that time and history will simply go away if they do not think about them. Gradually we realise how mistaken they are. At the end they are herded into the waiting trains, many of them still trying to believe that all is for the best and that soon they will awake from the nightmare. In Balaban's mountain retreat too there is a gradual encroachment by the outside world and a gradual disintegration of the imaginary world the inhabitants have erected in its place. Suicides occur. The people give up their exercises, turn back from goyish billiards to Jewish poker. Balaban himself falls ill and in one go forgets all his German and reverts to the hated Yiddish. Finally he dies. But for the survivors life goes on:

> And the summer grew broad and hot. Herbert now returned from the village beaten and wounded. Ruffians fell on him and beat him up. His appearance towards evening was excruciating in its silence. Betty tended his wounds with wet compresses.

We are in the summer of 1938, but these people seem unaware of the significance of that date, and, more disturbingly, so does the narrator:

> The world seemed to be narrowing down to its simplest dimensions: breakfast, supper. And if anyone said, I would like – all he had in mind was a cup of coffee… And when all the coats had been sold, the jewels and the suits,

Herbert went into Balaban's room, sorted out his clothes and tied them up in a sheet. Tomorrow he would sell them to the farmers.

The book is coming to an end, but the tone does not change. We want to shake the inhabitants of this retreat, to shake the narrator, to hear them react appropriately, but no, they are forever shut off from us, enclosed in the cocoon of their desires, their fears, their thoughts, their language.

Appelfeld's books are far more disturbing than any account of Nazi atrocities and Jewish suffering just because they are so quiet. They will not let you go. For the imagination he sets in play in the reader is one with the imagination used so desperately by the inhabitants of the retreat. And this suggests that though his subject matter is relentlessly singular and Jewish, it is also universal. The dream that drives Balaban and most of those in the retreat is not an exclusively Jewish dream. It has its roots in Romanticism and the French Revolution, and what it ultimately desires is so to transform man as to eradicate all trace of hesitation, fear and remorse that he will become as simple, as much at one with himself, as an animal:

> 'One sin leads to another, as I've always said,' pronounced [Balaban] in a bucolic voice. 'Today Swiss chocolate and tomorrow tidbits of cheese and the body which I have worked so hard to cure will be beyond redemption again, as hopelessly Jewish as it was in the beginning.'

But is such redemption possible? Can man really be so transformed? Eating healthy food and undertaking physical exercise is no doubt good for one, but it is a dangerous illusion to imagine it can stop us having bad dreams. Like Malamud's *Dubin's Lives,* with which it shows surprising, but perhaps not totally unexpected affinities, *The Retreat* calls out to the post-Romantic West: no matter how healthy a diet you adopt, how much exercise you take, there is one thing you cannot eliminate, and that is death. And if we are all to die, we all have only a single life – so what should we do with it?

These Romantic dreams take many forms: there is the Nazi dream of a thousand-year Reich; the American dream of eternal youth; the Israeli dream of a soldier citizenry which will put paid once and for all to the idea that Jews can only be victims. Appelfeld does not doubt the potency of these dreams; Lotte has often fallen victim to her version of them:

> There were times, not so long ago, when she still believed that her tired body would find a resting place by the side of some simple man in a remote cottage where the bread was fresh and warm, vegetables grew outside the windows, horses grazed in the meadow and the fences were covered with creepers. From her youth she had been drawn, probably because of the literature she had read, to these wild outposts of nature, and sometimes when the company toured the mountain regions she would say to herself: I'll stay here. The man loves me. What do I care about the theatre?
>
> But the simple men were not so simple.

It was perhaps the dubious privilege of the Jews to have forced upon them by history the madness of such dreams. What the pressure of reality reveals to the Jews in the retreat is, ultimately, their common humanity in the face of the one fate we all have to share. And so the book ends not with despair and destruction but with a quiet dignity which is all the more unnerving for what it leaves unsaid about the way that dignity will be tested in the years that lie ahead:

> Herbert went into Balaban's room, sorted out his clothes and tied them up in a sheet. Tomorrow he would sell them to the farmers. At night, of course, people were afraid. But they helped one another. If a man fell or was beaten he was not abandoned.

Appelfeld's uncanny power stems from the fact that he knows the limitations of the imagination, and hence of art. Novels are not the world, they are spas, retreats. By demonstrating that retreats can never be more than temporary refuges Appelfeld creates novels which point beyond themselves to what no novel can ever say. And so, though there is no peace at the heart of the retreat, there is the peace of great art, of an art which is fully aware of its own condition and of the condition of man, at the heart of this gentle and terrifying book.

2. The Age of Wonders

This is a marvellous and disturbing book. From the opening sentence – 'Many years ago Mother and I took the night train home from the quiet, little known retreat where we had spent the summer' – *The Age of Wonders* works at a level which is so close to one that it is difficult to take one's bearings in relation to it. Yet, unlike Kafka's work, of which this could also be said, it is, on the surface, perfectly straightforward and easily summarised. The book is divided into two parts: the first deals with the family of a Jewish-Austrian writer on the eve of the Second World War, seen from the point of view of the writer's twelve-year-old son; in the second part the son returns, thirty years later, to the town where he grew up, and notes what has changed and what has remained the same.

Having said that, though, one has hardly said anything at all. One has, of course, said nothing about the peculiar tone of the book; but one has even passed over some of the obvious questions that cannot help but trouble the reader. Why, for example, is the first part in the first person and the second in the third? And can we be sure that the protagonist of Part II is in fact the child of Part I? Could Bruno not be imagining a past for himself, or meditating on the past of someone else? Or could it be that it is Part II which consists only of thoughts and imaginings, perhaps Bruno's, as he moves about his adopted home, Jerusalem, wondering what return to his native town would be like?

These are not idle questions, for this book, as the opening sentence suggests, is just as much about our relation to ourselves – our past, future and present selves – as is *A la recherche du temps perdu*. And just as the opening sentence of Proust's novel miraculously incorporates all its major themes, so here, in those few simple words, we already have the book in embryo: the boy's closeness to his mother; the train journeys which are to grow more and more useless and frenetic until, as the last sentence of Part I has it, 'By the next day we were on the cattle train hurtling south'; and finally, the question, never resolved, of where precisely this memory is coming from in space and time. As with Proust, the status of the person remembering is impossible to determine, because, like Proust's, this is a book about continuity in discontinuity: the continuity of memory in the body; of the body in time; and of humanity through the generations – for as we are reminded in the second part, when the fathers have eaten sour grapes it is the teeth of the sons that are set on edge.

Part I is in a sense a rewriting, in a more personal vein, of Appelfeld's best-known book, *Badenheim 1939*. Like that novel this deals with Austria, and specifically with the Jews in Austria, on the eve of the Second World War. Appelfeld has no illusions about the way people behave under stress. The most terrible scenes here are not those depicting Austrian anti-Semitism, but those which show the Jews turning on each other, the intellectuals blaming the *Ostjuden* for simply being present, the *petits bourgeois* blaming the intellectuals for their 'decadence', until, in the climactic scene of Part I, as the Jews wait in the temple for the trucks to come, they turn on the rabbi and first insult then assault and torture him. But Appelfeld is no cynic. Rather, we get from this book the same sense of wisdom as we get from Kafka's conversations with Janouch or from Rosenzweig's letters from the Eastern Front in the First World War. The wisdom consists of the recognition of the weakness of men in the face of terror and suffering, but a recognition too that men are capable of unexpectedly noble responses, which must be celebrated and which implicitly indict the failures of the weak. Yet it is not moral judgements that are being made. In the end, we feel, people are not merely better but happier for having had the strength to make certain decisions, not merely less good but unhappier for having made others.

And *The Age of Wonders* is a book about decisions, responsibilities. As that opening sentence hints, it is in the first place about the child's emergence from the paradisal world of irresponsibility into the baffling world of adolescence, where adults are suddenly seen as weak, frightened and uncertain, and where the adolescent is forced to recognise that he has only himself to depend on. Here, again as in Proust, the transition involves the child's sudden awareness of his parents' mortality, combined with a growing awareness of sex, of bodily desires which as yet seem to have no focus. But of course it differs radically from Proust in that we are not in the France of the end of the nineteenth century but in the Austria of the 1930s, a time and a place where it is becoming more and more difficult to evade choice and responsibility.

A large number of servants, friends and relatives pass through the book, bent on self-protection, escape, even self-sacrifice, hounding the weak and turning a blind eye to what is really going on. But it is on the narrator's immediate family that the book focuses. The mother is mainly a silent, increasingly unhappy presence, though Appelfeld wonderfully conveys the bond between her and her child. Her death, which, like nearly all the deaths in this book, happens in the space between the two parts, is mentioned only in passing: 'From then on until the day she died I did not see a soft line on her face.' In contrast to her silence and submissiveness is the father's frenetic activity. Friend of Brod and Zweig, admirer of the still barely known Kafka, a complex tormented man whose talent is sadly not equal to his ambitions, he starts out as a universally respected Austrian writer and ends ostracised by the establishment, his works banned and rejected, his spirit broken. We last see him deserting his wife and escaping to Vienna to mingle with an aristocratic salon in the hope of getting a liberal intellectual journal started, though everyone can see that the time for such ventures is long past.

How much self-deception is involved here? Though he is right to go on protesting, to refuse to see himself in racial terms (isn't anxiety, after all, a human trait, he asks an anti-Semite who claims he can always tell a Jew by the anxiety written on his face), right to go on insisting that he is a man and a writer first and a Jew second, his responses come to seem more and more inadequate to the events which overtake him. Perhaps for all of us there is a time when it becomes a matter of either accepting history or trying to escape it. In this instance, for him as for so many others, to accept one's Jewishness meant accepting one's humanity, one's existence in this precise time and place, and the denial of that meant a denial of life. Escape, in any case, may never be possible, as Jonah discovered. In Part II we are briefly told that the father probably died, mad, in Theresienstadt.

In this second part Bruno, himself escaping from a childless and unhappy marriage ('her parents,' he says of his wife, 'had bequeathed to her too much suffering. They had met in Auschwitz. The year after the liberation, Mina was born.'), seizes the excuse of renewed interest in his father's work in Austria to revisit the town of his birth. Through him we experience the strangeness of seeing the very houses that had witnessed the events of 1939–45 still standing as though nothing had happened. For those with a memory, however, the only way of describing the present is with the words which form the title of Part II: 'Many years later when everything was over.' 'Everything' is the horror, of course, but it is also life itself. The Jews Bruno comes across, who converted, married their house-keepers or in some other way kept alive, seem to be ghosts who have gone on breathing, but who, with the denial of their roots, have given up any real reason for living. And even among those who died there are gradations. Bruno, we sense, has less respect for the vet and his wife who hanged themselves rather than be deported than he has for the four brothers who, though converts, took their place at the crucial moment in the temple with the other Jews.

What then of Bruno himself? In a sense he too is a ghost. It is true that he was born just late enough to have been spared the need for choices. Yet the book is clearly about his own attempts to bring together the scattered and repressed parts of himself. Does he succeed? In the town he finds nothing of importance relating either to himself or to his father. He talks to a few people, pursues a few others, ends, uncharacteristically, by beating up an old renegade Jew on a park bench when the latter insults him and tells him to go away and not rake up old embers. But the book offers no answers. The trip has not been a success, but it has not been a failure either. It may even not have taken place at all. At the end of Part II, as at the start, Bruno finds himself speaking words that do not seem to be his, as he stands waiting for the inevitable train, 'empty of thought or feeling'.

Yet of course something has happened. What Bruno had tried to destroy in himself was the memory of his father, out of shame at his treachery, but part of the reason for this repres-sion, we are made to feel, is that Bruno has not sorted out whether the treachery was to his mother (and so to himself) or to humanity. And for him even to think of returning implies a change in his attitude: 'He gave his father no credit at all. But in recent years, perhaps because he himself was already approaching his father's age, he felt the old wretched shame swelling inside him in a different way, no longer hatred but a kind of distance and even wonder.'

That distance must be seen in two ways. It is negative, a distance from himself, an inability to link the 'I' of his child-hood with the 'he' of the present, and so to make sense of either. But it is also positive, for with the recognition of this distance, which is both the first experience the book records and its secret cause, comes the possibility of renewal, of mending the broken halves.

And this is the measure of the book's greatness. The gap between the first and second parts and the disorientating switch from first to third person is not a clever formal device. It is what makes the book possible: for it is only by recognising that there is a gap, an unspeakable, unimaginable time 'between' that the healing process can start.

Implicitly, the way this book is written is a condemnation of those authors, Jewish and Gentile, who, in the past few years, have made use of the events of 1940–45 for their own private purposes. Appelfeld's silence admonishes them – and us. Each of us, of course, must sort it out with his own conscience; Appelfeld at least is clear that the real difficulty, human and artistic, is how both not to distort and not to pass over in silence. For to write a story about these events, however admirable one's motives, debases them: to use those events for mythological purposes, as so many novelists seem to do, is to go on playing the Nazi game. Appelfeld's is an exercise in demythologising, a making clear of the roots of responsibility before the terrible choices history imposes on us – not as groups or nations, but as individuals.

All art after Kafka is a lie, says the father; yet he, we are made to understand, goes on writing his Werfel-like books. Appelfeld, though, has taken his point. Not that Kafka was simply 'prophetic', or that the Nazis made language 'unusable', but that the events of those years forced on the consciousness of people everywhere, but on Jews in particular, an understanding of what Kafka, like Kierkegaard before him, had put at the heart of his work: that we are never at one with ourselves; that we can never speak the truth, only show it; that we can only grow into what we are; that we refuse our destiny at the cost of our humanity. And the writer too is implicated. Appelfeld shows how people use words and their imaginations to deny reality and themselves; the truth, when it comes, is silent.

With this book, indeed, post-war writing has come of age, for it has grasped and made palpable for us the relation of the great Modernist tradition of Kierkegaard, Nietzsche, Proust and Kafka to the crucial events of modern times, and it has done so not by being clever but by being wise, not by numbing us with images and ideas but by looking quietly and steadily at what is central to our lives. It is absurd to ask which part of the book is real, which imagined. Both are real because the juxtaposition of the two makes us capable of imagining both. And so, at the end, we go back and start the book again, aware that it will give us neither a story nor an answer, but instead something far more precious: a stirring of what was dead in us back to some kind of life, an experience both painful and joyous:

> The Fürsts were honest people. A strange honesty. A sick honesty. And in the evil days they stood up to be counted and joined the queue with all the other deportees. The way they stood by themselves in the locked temple stirred the hearts of the beaten people with wonder for the last time. There were four of them and all the way to Minsk they did not remove their caps. Not all the Fürsts possessed the same strength, however. August stayed in his shop. And he was still sitting in it. And all night long Bruno continued to see the converts standing at attention in the temple like reprimanded soldiers. And afterward too, in the cold and close to death, they did not utter a sound.

3. For Every Sin

The war is over. The camps have been liberated and the survivors set free. A young man, Theo Braun, makes his way on foot across Europe to his home town somewhere near Vienna. He walks over hills and through valleys, avoiding the other released prisoners when he can, finding shelter and food in the huts and stores abandoned by the retreating Germans.

The first sentence puts it clearly: 'When the war ended Theo resolved that he would make his way back home alone, in a straight line, without twists or turns.' But, clear as this is, this first sentence is also deeply puzzling. What does it mean, 'in a straight line without twists or turns'? That is not how one ordinarily speaks of a long journey. So is this perhaps an allegory? Is it a spiritual journey we are dealing with, and is this desire of Theo's to go in a perfectly straight line and to separate himself from the other ex-inmates of the camps a description of an inner urge rather than of a practical plan? As with Kafka – and this is the most Kafkaesque of Appelfeld's novels – there is no answer forthcoming. What takes place is described precisely and without comment or elaboration, yet this very factuality seems to call out for explanation in other terms. On the other hand, as with Kafka, as soon as we leave the factual detail and try to understand matters in moral and spiritual terms those terms seem crude and inadequate. As with Kafka, we come to realise that this very paradox is in a sense what the book is about, what troubles Theo without his even being aware of it, and what troubles and intrigues us.

Theo has a desperate need to be alone. He cannot stand the togetherness that the prisoners and now the ex-prisoners seem to prize so highly. 'For many years we were together,' he tells a refugee on the road. 'Now the time has come for everyone to be by himself. That togetherness brought many calamities down upon us. Now it is every man for himself. Let no one mix into anyone else's business.' That's why he wants to hurry forward, go in a straight line, keep to the hills and not go down into the valleys where the wretched hordes of refugees are winding their way or sleeping wearily in makeshift encampments. 'Any delay was sinful. From now on, only his route. Without any deviations or compromises.'

At the same time he cannot quite rid himself of vestiges of guilt at the attitude he has adopted. 'It's easier for you. You're walking by yourself. You have no supplies,' a refugee says to him early on. 'You could also do the same thing,' Theo replies. 'True,' says the man, 'but we've sworn to each other that we'll never separate again.' 'So why are you complaining?' 'I'm not complaining,' says the man. 'True, I also feel like getting up and going sometimes.' 'The men around him', the narrator goes on, 'didn't react to that statement, as though they realised it was only a vain wish. But that very statement aroused a kind of hidden guilt in Theo. He had abandoned his companions in suffering.'

Later, in an incident that affects him more profoundly than he realises, Theo gets into an argument with another refugee. The man grabs his coat and Theo pushes him away. But his action must have been more violent than he realised because the man stumbles, falls, and lies still. Terrified, Theo drops to his knees beside him. A trickle of blood is running down the man's forehead. 'What's the matter with you? What's the matter with you?' Theo shouts angrily at him. As with Kafka, it's impossible to tell when people are play-acting or over-dramatising and when they are being natural. People gather round them. 'He's breathing,' a woman says. But other than that the man shows no sign of life. A doctor is called. Everyone crowds round as he examines the man, who seems to be known to the others. Then the doctor is called away to what he says is a more urgent case and everyone waits about, looking at the fallen man. The woman who had first knelt by him goes up to Theo: 'Get out of here. I don't want to see you again.' 'I'm prepared to stand trial,' Theo says. 'If I deserve punishment, I'll bear it.' 'What kind of trial are you talking about?' she says. 'You killed him.' 'I?' 'You.' But even as the woman speaks the man opens his eyes 'Since no one had expected to see his eyes again, it seemed like a strange sign from heaven. The people knelt down in their places, not believing what they saw.'

The reason for the altercation with the man lay in Theo's sudden remark that he was going to convert. The man is puzzled: 'What brought you to that difficult decision?' 'Faith', Theo answers. The man can't get over what he has just heard: 'What harm did the Jews ever do you?' 'It's hard for me to bear that togetherness,' Theo answers, and when the man remains puzzled, saying that *he* wouldn't convert under any circumstances, that he fears and despises graven images, Theo tries to explain: 'I'm used to it. My mother took me to churches to hear the music.' And then, as the man remains angry and suspicious: 'Music preserved my sanity in the darkest of times.' But surely, the man says, you can listen to Bach without converting? How can a Jew come to have faith in Jesus? 'It's beyond my understanding. I raise my hands in surrender.' 'How can words explain to you?' Theo answers, and then: 'But if you insist on asking, sir, I shall explain: Bach's cantatas saved me from death. That was my nourishment for two and a half years... I'm going back to the church because Bach dwells there.' But this seems to rouse the man even more: 'The thought that someone who was in a camp until just a month ago should set out for his native city in order to convert to Christianity drives me mad. That's all. I have nothing to add.'

As Theo's journey unfolds his memories of his childhood and youth start to flood through him. Memories of his father, a quiet, thoughtful librarian; but especially of his mother. It is she, as he says, who introduced him to Bach and Mozart, she who took him to churches to hear their music. Beautiful and wilful, she seems to feel trapped in the stuffy bourgeois life she is expected to lead. She takes to going on sudden trips to beautiful places and usually insists on taking the boy with her. He remembers her in trains, in station waiting-rooms, asking for coffee, talking to strangers. He remembers his father remonstrating with her: You can't let the boy miss school like that. He'll fail his exams. But she won't listen: 'If not now, when?' 'He loved the trips with his mother', says the narrator, 'mad trips that would last all day. Museums, theatres, churches and chapels, views of the snow and views of the sunset. More than once he had opened his eyes and found himself in a remote country inn, far from any road, drowsing in his mother's arms.'

At first she seems merely high-willed and eccentric. She has become, or perhaps always was, an ardent believer in the afterlife: 'Don't worry, dear. This dreary day is only an illusion. We're slowly sailing on to another world. Believe me.' The boy is puzzled: 'Where is it?' he asks. 'Beyond the mountains,' she replies. 'A distance of thirty miles, no more.' And one day, after a Bach concert: 'We just spent a full hour in the world to come. Marvellous. Too bad we were driven away from there. But I'm not worried, my dear. For we're sailing there.' Her need to be always on the move grows more and more pronounced. The father is in despair. You're ruining us, he says. What is money? she replies grandly, there are more important things than money. Even the boy now realises that there is something wrong with her. Several times she is taken away to a sanatorium but each time she returns unchanged. 'We must get to Salzburg,' she tells Theo. 'There pure streams of music flow. Only someone who has been to Salzburg and drunk in those pure tones knows what music is. Only there can one be purified.' 'Mama,' he says, 'we haven't got any money.' 'You're talking like Papa,' she snaps back at him. 'You mustn't talk to me like Papa.'

In the sanatoria she charms the doctors and nurses and seems oblivious to her surroundings. And even when the end comes she does not seem to be aware of what is happening. 'She went to the train dressed carefully, as she used to go to the railroad stations in the past. She refused to take a knapsack. As she left the house she looked very lovely. Her illness wasn't visible in her. Expressions of pride and softness were mingled in her face.'

This is the burden Theo carries with him as he slowly makes his way back to his home town. Memories of her beauty. Of her exhilarating words. Of her last gestures. But memories too of his father as he stands in despair in the middle of the room trying to reason with her, or as he and the neighbours are rounded up and taken in turn to the station. A policeman orders them to pray. 'We aren't religious,' says his father. 'We don't know how to pray.' 'So, you're heretics.' 'We're not religious.'

As Theo advances it becomes obvious to him that things are not working out as he had planned. It all seemed so simple at the start: he would go in a straight line, he would not be deflected, he would return to his native town and there convert. But against his will he has kept getting involved with the other refugees, with the confusion in his own memory, and too often he has found himself circling back on his tracks or descending from the high ridges to the overcrowded valleys. Suddenly he realises 'that he would never return to his home town. From now on he would advance with the refugees. That language which his mother had inculcated in him with such love would be lost forever. If he spoke, he would speak only the language of the camps. That clear knowledge made him dreadfully sad.' Out of nowhere a man addresses him: 'Where did you intend to go?' 'To my home town, to Baden-bei-Wien.' 'There's no need to go there. Stay here. We have everything you need. The shed is full of supplies. There's no sense seeking something that can never be attained. We won't bring the dead back to life. You understand that. Here we're together, I won't conceal from you that it isn't always comfortable, but still, we're together.'

It is a kind of defeat. The book ends: 'Fatigue and helpless-
ness assailed him. He placed his head on a bundle, curled up as
if after a big quarrel, a desperate quarrel, closed his eyes, and
collapsed.'

Is Theo's misery due to the fact that he has succumbed after
all? That he has not been able to live up to the hopes of his
mother? Or on the contrary, that he has not been ready to recognise his solidarity with the other refugees, with other Jews?
'Hatred stirreth up strife; but love covereth all sins', says the
proverb (Proverbs, 10:12). The first part is easy to understand,
but the second? If love overcomes the transgressions (perhaps
a better translation of the Hebrew word pesha'im in Appelfeld's
title) of others, then is Theo lacking in love for his mother or
for his father? For himself or for his fellow-inmates?

The beauty of Appelfeld's works is that he refuses to
moralise, that his protagonists are as puzzled and confused as
we all are and that there is no book or person or set of laws to
which we can turn for clear guidance. Theo has lost his struggle
to enter a purer life, to escape the horror of the camps. That
happier life, cleansed of the compromises and disillusionment
of this life, of which the music of Bach and Mozart give us a
glimpse, will never be his. But then perhaps he is, now that the
lure of that purer life has been removed for ever, in a better position to make a new life for himself out of what he has. The
straight way home is a dream, a beautiful dream but a dream
nonetheless, as is the purity of the world to come. It is a dream
which we all dream, and which drives every artist. But Judaism
teaches that we live in this world and must make the best of
that. And the greatest art reveals to us, against our stubborn
wills, that though dreams are a part of what we are and cannot
be cynically dismissed, they have in the end to be accepted as
only dreams. We do not advance in a straight line, we are not
alone in the purified air. At the end of the road we can only lie
down exhausted, as after a terrible quarrel, our goal unattained.

But the miracle of art is that at the same time, having walked that road with Appelfeld and his protagonist, we also feel in our veins the same kind of renewal as is given us by the greatest music of Bach and Mozart.

A Tribute

I come before you today with two conflicting emotions. On the one hand pride and pleasure that I should have been asked to contribute to the celebration of the artistic and spiritual quality of the work of Aharon Appelfeld on the occasion of his retirement from the University of Beersheba; and on the other hand, intense embarrassment. Why embarrassment? Imagine a Japanese critic who does not speak or read English coming to Britain to speak about the work of Virginia Woolf or Muriel Spark. No matter how intelligent or sensitive he might be, no one would take him seriously. Why was he invited? people will ask. How can he presume to talk about these writers with any kind of authority when he cannot read them in the original? In my case the presumptuousness is even greater, for Appelfeld has often said in interviews that it was the Hebrew language that led him both to literature and to the Jewish people. To Philip Roth he even confessed that 'the Hebrew language taught me to think'. What is someone who has only learned biblical Hebrew late in life and who can only read with any confidence the narrative portions of the Hebrew Bible, who cannot therefore read modern Hebrew prose, to do in the face of such remarks, except keep quiet?

And yet, when I put those scruples to the organisers of this happy event they were brushed aside. It seemed that I was wanted, Hebrew or no Hebrew. Why? What, I wondered, might I, in my ignorance of the Hebrew language and my relative ignorance of Jewish traditions and of East European Jewry, all of which would seem to be central to Appelfeld's work, have to contribute? Though my own family name is Romanian, and my father's family came, apparently from Iasi, not a million miles from Czernowitz, where Appelfeld was born, there is no way in which I can think of myself as a Romanian Jew. My father's family had settled in Egypt in the nineteenth century and left their roots behind, and anyway I last saw my father when I was three and know very little about his side of the family. Though my mother's father came from Odessa, he died when she was five and I have no contacts with any members of his family either. Only my mother's maternal family are known to me, Jews partly Italian and partly Egyptian for many generations. Again, though I was touched by the war, as a child in France, my mother and I escaped incarceration and the horrors inflicted on others. Though I have in recent years become interested in the Jewish side of my being and very interested in the Hebrew Scriptures, in part due to my acquaintance with Aharon and his work, I have no real inwardness with these matters.

What then? Perhaps I have been invited as a fellow-writer? But though I share Appelfeld's passion for Kafka, I belong, by and large to a very different tradition of writing: Proust, Eliot, Wallace Stevens, Claude Simon and Marguerite Duras are some of the writers who helped me to discover who I was and what I wanted to do – the artists of European Modernism and its aftermath. What has such a writer to do with Appelfeld?

As it turns out, quite a lot. I discovered early on that I was not interested in the realist novel, either in its classic or its contemporary form: Balzac and George Eliot, even Tolstoy, felt very alien to me, as did writers like Anthony Powell and David Lodge in England, though I could admire and enjoy their books. They seemed to belong to a French or an English or a Russian society in a way that kept me outside, excluded me, and their mode of writing – perhaps for that reason – left me cold. Perhaps my sense of closeness to European Modernism stemmed from the fact that I myself felt displaced, writing in a language not my own, but without feeling – like Nabokov or Beckett – that there was a native language I had abandoned, willingly or unwillingly. Even more difficult was the sense that if I was not inward with the English language I was even less inward with English society, and never would be, not even with Anglo-Jewish society, which was and is largely East European in origin. Proust and Eliot and Kafka, on the other hand, gave me a sense of how one can start with an acknowledgement of failure, with a sense that one will never succeed in saying – or even knowing – what one wants, but of how one can *use* that as a way in to greater authenticity of speech. And, in the wake of these writers, others, like Simon and Duras, showed me how one could dispense with anecdotes, plotting and all the – to me – tedious machinations of the realist novel, and make works that would grow like plants or acquire the firmness of a piece of crystal. And in the wake of these writers I discovered a number of others, slightly older contemporaries, in every country in the world, who seemed to be working from the same premises and moved me for the same reasons, no matter how different the surface of their work: Perec in France; Bernhard in Austria, Shabtai in Israel. And Appelfeld. For on first reading him I felt at once that *here was something for me*.

That was in the early 1980s, and I have been reading him ever since. Some of his books I have liked more than others; but always I have felt this double sense of being at once completely at home and yet meeting something that was clearly Other; of hearing a voice that was utterly different from mine, yet could help me find my own. It matters, of course, that I cannot read him in the original, but even in translation I hear that voice, just as Keats heard the voice of Homer, loud and clear, when he first looked into Chapman's translation.

What I want to do today, then, in the short time at my disposal, is to try and understand, for myself and with you, why it is that Appelfeld's books speak in this immediate and powerful fashion to one who is in so many ways a foreigner.

There is a novel of Appelfeld's called *The Conversion*. It is set, as always with him, in an indeterminate time and place, though, like the bulk of his books, the time is the 30s of the last century and the place Eastern Central Europe. It deals with people who convert from Judaism to Christianity to further their careers and also to get rid of the burden of alienation; and it shows how, by so doing, they lose an essential part of themselves and condemn themselves to a kind of secret despair. This is a relatively straightforward scheme, and in that it is uncharacteristic. Usually Appelfeld's novels are more complex, dealing with the conflicting pressures on Jews at that time and place, but also with the variety of responses to those conflicts.

In one of the richest and subtlest of these, *The Healer*, a family travels from Vienna to the Carpathian Mountains in search of a wonder-working rabbi who might be able to cure the daughter of a mysterious disease afflicting her. For the mother this is a return to her roots; for the father it is a shameful and shaming pandering to superstition. For him the sight of his wife and daughter listening to the old rabbi and following his instructions, learning Hebrew and Hebrew prayers, is a source of irritation, even anger, in ways he can't quite explain to himself. He has the feeling that the two women are in the process of entering a convent – an interesting variant on the conversion motif, and one which in this book we are not allowed to view in a purely negative way. In fact we as readers are made to work to decide where *we* stand on this: is Felix simply a typical example of the assimilated urban Jew, whose only desire is to put his Jewishness behind him, and whose scepticism about the wonder-working rabbi is the result of his unwillingness to see the truth about himself and his Jewishness? Is the healer right when he implies that nothing he says will be of any help to the girl or her parents if it is met only by Felix's scepticism? Or is there perhaps something in Felix's sense that the kind of conversion experience the rabbi is offering and the mother and daughter are embarked on is something profoundly un-Jewish, something profoundly Christian? What does conversion mean now?

As Felix and his son return to Vienna on the train, leaving mother and daughter behind, he enters into conversation with a beautiful and distinguished-looking woman in the dining-car. For some reason which he cannot explain to himself he is drawn to this woman, even though she appears to want to be left alone. As in all the conversations in this novel – and in Appelfeld generally – it is less a dialogue than a case of each person speaking out their hidden thoughts and obsessions, using the other as a way of discovering themselves. 'One must return home in gladness,' Felix says to her, 'especially when home was Vienna.' 'If one loves a city,' he goes on, 'it becomes ones native city... Closeness is important, delicate contact with the trees.' 'Are you a religious man?' she asks, and he, though at first taken aback, responds that he is not religious, though he has a feeling for the arts and in his youth had wanted to study medicine. 'Too bad,' she says, and when he asks why, she responds: 'Because the Church gives life meaning.' Felix is stunned, takes a while to respond, but then comes back with: 'I am Jewish, madam, Jewish by birth.' At which she says: 'I too was a Jew.' 'You converted?' he asks. 'I did.' 'What brought you to such a decision?' ' What do you mean?' she asks. 'Faith. Without faith one doesn't take a step like that.' 'I have never been close to religious faith,' whispers Felix. 'Nor was I,' she responds, 'until I discovered the Church. The Jews have long since lost their faith. What remains to them is only a routine maintained by force of habit, but they have no living faith.' 'And the Church has it?' he asks. 'I, at any rate, found it,' she answers. ' Strange,' he says. 'It's hard for me to imagine myself kneeling.' 'That's precisely the beginning of faith,' she replies. 'You must learn self-abnegation.'

The lady, it turns out, is a doctor herself. When she hears of the reasons for Felix's having left Vienna she is full of sympathy: it's marvellous, she says, that his daughter has 'accepted the faith of her ancestors'. Every doctor knows, she says, that without faith there is no healing. And when Felix asks if she thinks his daughter has done the right thing, she comes out with: 'Bear one thing in mind: one must never give in to melancholy and despair. Despair, more than anything else, is man's enemy. Despair is heresy. A man must cling to the virtues of the Creator and he is forbidden to despair.' But she at once feels that she has gone too far. 'Pardon me. I didn't intend to give a sermon.'

Shortly after, the train is stopped and officials come on board to check their papers. When they pull Felix out with the remark: 'We've got ourselves a Jew,' the lady imperiously commands, from the other end of the carriage: 'Leave that man alone,' and they return the documents and leave the carriage. Felix goes to thank her and discovers that the book she is reading is, as he had suspected, St Augustine's *Confessions*.

I have quoted this little exchange at considerable length because it helps us to see the remarkable way in which Appelfeld complicates what had at first seemed like a simple enough equation: the urban assimilated Jew denies his roots, while his more open and flexible wife finds a way to return to them. Suddenly we begin to wonder if there may not perhaps be a grain of truth in Felix's assertion that his wife and daughter are in effect entering a convent. Conversion, even conversion to this simple pietistic form of Judaism, is suddenly seen to be a deeply Christian and un-Jewish act. Cultural historians have pointed out the parallels between Christian pietism and the Hasidic revival in Eastern Europe, but Appelfeld is not making a historical but a general point. Was Felix right all along then?

The scene we have been looking at is the penultimate one in the book. The train arrives in Vienna, Felix and his son get home, and he finds, to his horror, that their old maidservant, whom they had left in charge of the house, has rummaged in all the drawers, drunk all their liquor, slept in the marital bed, taken down the pictures in the living room and bedroom and replaced them with cheap examples of Christian iconography. The last paragraph goes like this:

> Two awkward pictures hung over the head of the bed. One was Jesus at his mother's bosom and the other the crucifixion. Drops of blood dripped from his arms. 'Take that out of here,' he wanted to shout. But he was exhausted. Weariness penetrated every limb of his body. Nevertheless, he gathered his strength and plucked the images from the wall. He opened the window and threw them out into the garden. That act, accomplished with his last strength, prostrated him on the pillows like a corpse, and he immediately sank into sleep.

Felix has acted at last, instead of merely reacting, as he has been doing all along. But that action has in it also a quality of despair, as the last sentence, so reminiscent of Kafka, makes clear. And we remember the lady doctor's words: 'Despair is heresy. A man must cling to the virtues of the Creator and he is forbidden to despair.' This is a Jewish as well as a Christian injunction. Typically, it has been theologised by Christianity, where despair is seen as a form of inverted pride, the first sin, an assertion that 'I alone cannot be saved by Jesus Christ', and so a repetition of Satan's original refusal to submit himself to the will of God. But though it is put differently in the Jewish tradition, it is the same imperative, and Appelfeld has often repeated it: keeping life going even in the darkest times, even where there appears to be no hope at all, is absolutely fundamental, for by one's very existence one testifies to one's belief in God, who made us. He talks, in one of his lectures, for instance, about what those who died in the Holocaust have left us: 'In their self-sacrifice on the brink of the abyss they were bequeathing us not only life but also the ultimate significance of their own existence.'

In the light of this, how are we to read the end of *The Healer*? (In novels like those of Virginia Woolf and Aharon Appelfeld, where there is no obvious closure at the level of plot, the ending of the book acquires enormous significance.) Does it not bring to the fore what has been latent throughout, that Felix is a being in despair, a being who refuses to recognise himself and therefore finds no reason for existing? The end merely shows us Felix giving way to that latent despair. Would not faith of the kind demonstrated by his wife and the lady doctor have saved him from this?

I'm not sure. Felix's action and collapse in that last paragraph can be read as despair, but they can also be read as a triumphant assertion: at the end of his tether, exhausted by the journey and all he has been through, he finally makes one vital and significant gesture, which shows him who and what he is. Both readings are simplifications. Both readings would fit a theological or even a psychological tract; the wonder of art, of fiction, of *this* fiction, is that it holds both readings in tension. As in life, there are no final answers, and the task of the artist, if he is to be true to life, is precisely not to give us answers but to *reveal an action*.

This is so important that we need to spend a little time exploring what it means. Why do I use the term *reveal* here? Why do I use the term *an action*?

Let us turn to another of Appelfeld's finest works, *The Age of Wonders*, to help us in our exploration.

That novel, as you all know, is divided into two parts. In the first a nameless boy is growing up in an intellectual and assimilated family somewhere in Bukovina, with a growing awareness that the clouds are darkening the sky, and that part ends, shockingly, with the Jews of the town being herded into cattle trucks en route to the camps. In the second part a man called Bruno, who might or might not be the same as the 'I' of the first part, returns from Jerusalem, where he now lives, to his home town in Bukovina and spends three weeks wandering around it, taking in the way it has changed and the way it has remained the same, and bumping into people he had known as a child and who have survived. Most of these have done so by conversion and by various acts of cowardice. For them Bruno is an evil spirit come to torment them, to remind them of what they would rather forget. One of these is the convert Fürst. Actually it is the grand-father who had 'managed to get himself baptised in the quiet and easy-going days of the Emperor Franz Josef'. Bruno enters the tobacconist's shop where he sees the old man sitting, smoking his pipe. Confronted with this ghost from the past the old man utters a series of confusing and disconnected phrases: 'My brother – my brother. I myself did not have the courage.' And, hitting himself fiercely on the forehead with his fist: 'This is the louse. His name is August. This is the louse. His name is August.' Bruno, in the paragraph which ends this chapter, quietly fills us in:

> The Fürsts were honest people. A strange honesty. A sick honesty. And in the evil days they stood up to be counted and joined the queue with all the other deportees. The way they stood by themselves in the locked temple stirred the hearts of the beaten people with wonder for the last time. There were four of them and all the way to Minsk they did not remove their caps. Not all the Fürsts possessed the same strength, however. August stayed in his shop. And he was still sitting in it. And all night long Bruno continued to see the converts standing at attention in the temple like reprimanded soldiers. And afterward too, in the cold and close to death, they did not utter a sound.

Appelfeld does not condemn or explain, he narrates. The preservation of life may be a Jewish imperative, but there is a greater one: truth to oneself. There are other kinds of heroism than that of the partisans and the ghetto fighters, Appelfeld reminds us in the introduction to his three lectures, *Beyond Despair*: 'For example, young people who might have been able to save themselves preferred to accompany their aged parents, staying with them until the last moment of their lives.' In *The Age of Wonders* one of the Fürst brothers stays behind and survives, to live out the rest of his life in guilt and despair; the other four take their place with the other deported Jews and die. They do so in silence. They do not explain, to others or to themselves, why they made that choice, and neither does the narrator. Perhaps they do not know why, yet they do it. Perhaps the narrator does not know why, yet he recounts it. And we cannot say they do it for unconscious reasons: one does not take so momentous a step as though one were a sleepwalker. No. What this shows is that our deepest decisions are taken at a level beyond speech and reason, not because they are unconscious but on the contrary because they are decisions of the whole self, body, mind and spirit.

Even the term 'decision' here is misleading, for it suggests one decisive moment, like St Paul's moment on the road to Damascus, whereas what we are talking about here is that interaction of chance, choice and mode of life which used to be called destiny and which, in the time of Homer and Greek tragedy, in the time of the Hebrew Scriptures, it was the purpose of narrative to bring into the light of day. That Achilles chooses to withdraw from the conflict on the plains of Troy; that Agamemnon chooses to kill his daughter so that the fleet may sail; that Abraham chooses to listen to God's command and leave his home and family — these are not choices in the sense in which we might use the word when we decide to have a pear instead of an orange for dessert. They are both shrouded in mystery and yet, having been made, seem inevitable, seem to be part of the character of Achilles, Agamemnon and Abraham.

And the writers who have given us these stories respect that mystery, carefully protect it, recognise it for what it is. Those later disciplines of philosophy, theology, psychology and sociology, on the other hand, cannot deal with it, for they deal only with the inner or the outer, only with the private or the public, whereas what is at issue when we talk of destiny is precisely the interaction of inner and outer, individual and society. And only narrative can reveal it to us.

If, as I suggested at the start, all of Appelfeld's books can be seen as stories of conversion, that only means that they are stories about the discovery by the protagonist of who and what he is. But if that is the case, do they not have much in common with the great German tradition of the *Bildungsroman*? Yet where Goethe and Mann were encyclopaedic and expansive, Appelfeld is compressed and elliptical. And this is not just a matter of personal preference or of the age in which he is writing; such compression and ellipsis is also a critique. For the *Bildungsroman* leads us to the self-awareness of the protagonist, to a new psychological state, and it is a self-awareness which the writer shares and imparts to the reader. In Appelfeld, as we have seen, such self-awareness cannot be called conscious and it manifests itself not by thought or inwardness, but by action, whether trivial in appearance, as with Felix at the end of *The Healer*, or momentous, as in the case of the Fürst brothers in *The Age of Wonders*. But this, as I have been suggesting, is not the result of a failure on Appelfeld's part, of an inability to 'understand' the 'inner workings' of the mind of his protagonist; rather it is what aligns him to what was once the main tradition of story-telling, a tradition which almost disappeared from the world under the impact first of Plato and then of Christianity, and later of the rise of the novel in the seventeenth and eighteenth centuries.

God says to Abraham, 'Go!' and he goes; we are not told why, nor does Abraham ask himself why; Jacob falls in love with Rachel and is tricked by her father into marrying Leah; we are not told what he feels ('and it came to pass that in the morning, behold, it was Leah' is all the Bible says). Not that he feels nothing, obviously, but that psychological explanations, in this as in all other biblical cases, would never be adequate explanations. The important thing is the narrative, the *mythos*, as Aristotle called it in his discussion of tragedy, the *shape* of the action, which we understand perfectly and yet can never fully express in conceptual or psychological language – which is why these stories remain as fresh today as they were when they were first told.

And it is the same with Appelfeld's work. Why does Felix act as he does? Why do the Fürst brothers act as they do? We feel that there is a deep rightness about it, that by so doing both act in accordance with their characters and that at the same time by this action they finally become themselves. What this calls forth in us is not understanding but awe and wonder.

And this leads me to my final point. In his lectures Appelfeld talks a great deal about the perfectly understandable but false ways of dealing with the Holocaust. He talks about the struggle to speak truthfully about his experiences and feelings. We are here at the point of intersection of an existential and a literary struggle, and see how each can help the other. Appelfeld's simple, direct style, which he has attributed to his reading of Kleist and Kafka and of biblical narratives, is more than a style. Why his books mean so much to any reader, Jew or non-Jew, born in 1920 or 1970, why I feel the same excitement and pleasure reading his work as I do reading very different authors with very different concerns, such as Proust or Bernhard or Muriel Spark, is because he has found a way of giving expression to that interplay of character, chance and choice which is destiny, and which we cannot grasp in our own lives except refracted through the narratives of another. It is the highest task of art and very few artists today even understand what it means. How fortunate we are to have Aharon Appelfeld among us.

15. Andrzej Jackowski: Reveries of Dispossession

1. Refuge/Refugee

A WOODEN HUT. Five broad horizontal planks of wood make up one wall, against which lean two narrower planks. The rough surface of the wood catches the light from the open door, through which one can glimpse a patch of blue sky and other buildings, one of which is topped by a narrow chimney or spire. The light clings to the edges of the boards and nestles in the roughness of the planks. On the right side of the room, which is otherwise empty, stands a mysterious construction, a sort of Noah's Ark on wheels, glowing in the semi-darkness.

There is nothing cold about this room. It is not something we look at so much as something we inhabit. We experience the light and the wooden boards as that which surrounds us, not something merely open to our gaze. Here is a place of refuge.

Because this place of refuge is made of wood it does not feel permanent; yet because it is made of wood it feels protective, human, natural. Each plank has been planed and cut and joined by human hands out of what had once been living trees. The mysterious contraption on wheels, on the other hand, is totally self-contained and faintly threatening, a hooded mover. It has come from another place and will perhaps soon be moving on. Yet the door is wide open, nothing is holding us in here, in this silent empty hut, whose only inhabitants, other than ourselves, seem to be the light and the shadows, the wheeled ark and the dust on the rough wooden surfaces. And though the silence and emptiness are slightly eerie, they also seem conducive to meditation and the work of memory. No blood will spatter these walls, no screams punctuate this silence. Here we can gather our memories, dream, and wait.

No doubt the hut will one day be dismantled, the whole wooden village too perhaps, and in its place there will, once again, be nothing but fields and trees and mud.

But if the hut is to be dismantled, if the inhabitants will inevitably move on, then this painting, made with as much care, and with its loving workmanship as fully exposed as the hut, will remain. It will encapsulate memory at the same time as it is witness to an activity. Without the memory there would be no activity, but without the activity memory itself would have disappeared.

This painting then, is no icon. It is not an object of religious or aesthetic contemplation. Rather, like Chardin's great images of silent concentration, it draws us into the process of living and making as something both wondrous and ordinary, into a space of both refuge and renewal, where we may acquire the strength and confidence to leave when the time comes, as it surely will.

2. The Tower of Copernicus

There is that mysterious wheeled ark in its corner on the right again, but here it only seems to be a big toy, for we half look down upon it. It is difficult to see how it got here, and how it will ever get out, for the last rungs of a ladder, appearing at the bottom of the picture, tell us we are on some sort of platform. Clouds whirl down into this space, which seems to be enclosed on all four sides yet open to the heavens above. Mysterious shadows play on the wooden walls, and, against the wall, next to a tree-stump of a stool, a small black cat sits staring unblinkingly past us.

Nothing is happening here. The objects appear to have been

left standing in this place for a long time. Perhaps once someone climbed the ladder and dumped the wheeled ark in a corner, sat perhaps for a while on the tree-stump and then climbed back down again. Only the cat sits, unmoving, staring into the darkness, and the sun and moon cast their shadows in turn upon the walls.

Copernicus perhaps once came here to study the stars and work out that the earth is not the centre of the universe but only a peripheral planet moving round the sun. But this deserted platform does not convey anything like Pascal's fear of infinite spaces. There is too much sense of the natural and the man-made for that, and the presence of the cat and the little wheeled ark are strangely reassuring. The earth may no longer be the centre of the universe and man no longer thought of as made in God's image, but for whoever comes here this is a kind of centre, a place to gather oneself together and come to some sort of accommodation with the indifferent elements. The whirl of cloud or the tumbling falls of snow of *Tower of Copernicus – Winter*, the beautifully shaped shadows nestling in the wooden beams of the construction, even the eerie light which catches the walls and floorboards in *Tower of Copernicus – Autumn* – these are not threatening but show rather the wondrous nature of the world in which we move and have our being. It is a beauty which does not ask to be admired, like the beauty of a sunset or a seascape, but which surrounds us and reveals itself to us as we go about our human work of making ladders, calculating the movement of the stars, or painting pictures. It is a beauty which is never still and will never be caught, but this is a part of what we are as we are part of the world of shadows and clouds and stars, of tumbling fluffy snow and whirling summery light, a beauty which is always textured, dense, yet evanescent, the beauty too of layered pigment and raw canvas, testifying to the work of the hand and the brush, themselves a part of our common world.

3. The Burying

A table is the sign and symbol of the human. Animals need no tables, and we need them for the two quintessential human activities of communal eating and solitary working. An altar too is a kind of table, on which that other quintessential human activity takes place: the sacrifice to the God, whether of the household or the universe. In Judaism and (in different fashion) in Christianity, sacrifice has been replaced by ritualised communal eating.

In Andrzej Jackowski's recent table paintings there appears at first to be no community. There is a solitary figure standing beside or in front of a table, or, in one instance, seeming to be part of the horizontal surface of the table itself. But these are not images of solitude. The walls here are painted with a vibrancy and warmth which, even when only a naked bulb hangs from the ceilings, endows the space with that nesting, comforting quality already evident in the hut of *Refuge/Refugee*. And on the table are boxes, sieves, cut flowers in vases, whole cities even, suggesting that the table is less a simple surface than a laboratory for human making and remaking.

The strangest of these paintings is *The Burying*, but it is also the key to them all. This is another human ritual: the burying of something precious. Surprisingly in this painter, who has brought back to painting the notion of the dappled, what the Greeks called *poikilos* and admired above all other effects, what Hopkins adored and saw as the sign of life itself, and which had been lost to the visual arts since the death of Bonnard, the background to this painting is bright and harsh, almost painful to look at. And then the river of light snaking across the bottom – is that where the burying is to take place? Or has it already taken place and has the object to be buried been safely sealed inside the box on the table? It is an elegant box, carefully constructed. Beside it is a circular white metal sieve or colander, the only round shape in the picture apart from the girl's head, echoing the wavy line of the river of light below. It is made to contain (like the box), but also to let out, to sift and allow to be dispersed, an emblem of the whole painting and the entire series. The girl, standing on the edge of the chair in her bare feet, has not climbed up out of fear or the desire to escape, but seems rather to be lifted up by the glowing presence of the colander. Yet she, like everything else in the picture, is not flying but is firmly rooted by the force of gravity.

The title tells us not about her or her feelings, but about an activity, perhaps a ritual. It takes no sides, refuses to tell us if this is a repression or an expiation. That gives it the authority of ancient story-telling, an authority which it carries effortlessly and which inheres in every part of the canvas, which is, like all these table paintings, completely open to our gaze and yet mysteriously withdrawn from it, returned to itself. It thus, like the Chardins again, makes no claim on the viewer but allows him to enter or leave at will, to wander over the surface or pause over a detail. Something is taking place and, if we wish, we too can be a part of it.

Patience and Anxiety

Temptation, of course, is always present in this work: the temptation of the uprooted to find refuge in myth, to plant the painted tree in painted earth and hope that in this way the foundations can be laid of a home to call ones own; the temptation to renounce the perpetual uncertainty of making, the perpetual reordering of elements which are without prior resonance or significance, in favour of the already made, the already known, of the dream image, complete, coherent, assertive.

'Because of impatience men were expelled from Paradise,' Kafka once wrote, 'because of impatience they do not return.'

The temptations of the artist are always the result of impatience: impatience with the world which will not see what he has made for it; impatience with oneself for failing to find the right objective correlative for the mingled sensations of exhilaration and anxiety which assail one; impatience at the thought that there is not, finally, any refuge from time.

But, set against impatience is trust. Not confidence, not arrogance, not faith, but trust, trust in the slow and silent work of the hand, in the possibilities of paint and canvas, trust, finally, in the world of light and shadow, sunshine and snow, of trees and sea and sky. For him who starts with nothing and expects nothing, who accepts weakness and vulnerability, who has learned to live with the fact that even trees do not last for ever – for such a person everything is always possible. As the uprooted tree testifies to the greater power of the storm, as the cut tree brings into the room at Christmas the smell and feel of the forest, so the uprooted exile brings with him far more powerful feelings of what it means to be rooted in our world than those who have always stayed at home can ever know.

Time and memory, anguish and desire, tug at us and it is necessary to keep diving back into the wreck, going on through the long night, making our temporary refuges and being prepared, when the time comes, to abandon them without regret. No final revelation is at hand but, with trust and patience, something can be made which will speak truthfully of the joys and sorrows of our condition. And that, surely, is enough.

16. The Singer on the Shore
in memory of Rachel Trickett

Dante and Casella

DANTE AND VIRGIL, on the shore at the foot of the mountain of Purgatory, 'alongside the ocean yet, like folk who ponder on their road, who go in heart and linger in body' (*che va col cuore e col corpo dimora*; *Purgatorio*, II.12), encounter a group of pilgrims newly arrived from earth. Among them is Dante's friend, the singer Casella. The poet tries to embrace him, but in vain, for though *he* has come to this place in his body, those he meets are only spirits. Nonetheless, Dante addresses him with a plea: 'If a new law does not take from you memory or practice of the songs of love which used to quiet me in my longings (*che mi solea quetar tutte mie voglie*), may it please you therewith to comfort my soul somewhat, which coming hither with its body is so wearied...' (106–11): Casella immediately responds by beginning to sing one of Dante's own early poems, and the effect is instantaneous:

> *Love that discourses in my mind*, he then began so sweetly that the sweetness still [i.e. now he is back in the world and writing his poem] within me sounds. My master and I and that folk who were with him appeared content as if naught else touched the mind of any. We were all rapt and attentive to his notes, when lo, the venerable old man [Cato, the guardian of that realm], crying, 'What is this, you laggard spirits? What negligence, what stay is this? Haste to the mountain to strip off the slough that lets not God be manifest to you.'

At once, like feeding doves frightened off by some noise, the group disperses and hastens towards the slope, 'like one who goes, but knows not where he may come forth'; nor, he adds, 'was our departure less quick'. (112–13).[1]

This episode of the *Commedia* raises questions about art, ethics and the nature of our deepest longings that still resound today. At its simplest, the lesson Dante seems to want us to draw from the episode is that art cannot really appease the unquiet heart, that in fact it is a distraction, a drug, which must be removed if we want to go on the pilgrimage that will lead us to true fulfilment and peace. It belongs to the body, which wishes to linger, not the heart, which is eager to go.

And yet from the start Dante clouds the issue. For one thing, Casella seems to belong more with those, like Virgil, who guide Dante on his way, than with those, like the sinners in Hell, who seek to detain him. For another, the phrase 'the songs of love which used to quiet me in my longings' suggests that such quiet-ings are beneficial, while the longings are only the thrashings of the unquiet spirit. And this still seems to be the role of art, since when Casella sings the effect is so powerful that Dante, to describe it, uses a phrase he will use again at the very end, when he has his final beatific vision: 'that the sweetness (*dolcezza*) still within me sounds…'. And, finally, we have to remember that the austere lesson to be learned from this episode, and the final vision itself, are both conveyed to us by means of poetry and fiction.

In other words, try as we may to draw distinctions between idolatry and true devotion, between worshipping the Golden Calf and the invisible Creator, we cannot do so with any confi-dence. The distinctions grow slippery even as we try to make them, and we, as readers, must live this poem, as Dante lived

---

1 I use Singleton's distinguished prose translation throughout: *The Divine Comedy*, translated with a commentary by Charles S. Singleton, Princeton, 1973.

his vision, and find ways to confront the contradictions: art must be transcended, yes; but only art can show us how.

Wordsworth and the Leech-Gatherer

The artists who followed Dante did not, by and large, feel the need to dwell on these paradoxes. Art, for the Renaissance, whether it was justified by Aristotelian or neo-Platonic doctrines, seemed an inalienable good, one which went hand in hand with ethics and metaphysics. Those who did dwell on them, like Rabelais, Cervantes, Herbert, Swift and Sterne, are very much in a minority. But by 1800 the issue had surfaced again, much more confusedly and confusingly – so much so that many of the greatest artists of the nineteenth century, who seem to us to be impaled on the horns of the Dantean dilemma, hardly seem to be aware of it themselves.

Take Wordsworth, and one of his greatest poems, 'Resolution and Independence', also known as 'The Leech-Gatherer'. 'There was a roaring in the wind all night', the poem begins, and we are immediately immersed in the natural world. But as so often with Wordsworth's best work, this is not the world of Dutch landscape painting but a fierce apocalyptic world, one where, after the storm, 'The sky rejoices in the morning's birth.' 'I was a Traveller then upon the moor', the poet tells us, 'I saw the hare that raced about with joy; /I heard the woods and distant waters roar.'

But just as the stormy weather suddenly and inexplicably turns fine, so the poet's joy turns suddenly to melancholy, a kind of 'dim sadness' which cannot be named or placed. Yet he does to try to explain it, and comes up with the thought that it was brought about by brooding on all the fine poets whose youth began in gladness but who in the end succumbed to 'despondency and madness'. In this dream-like state he

6   Andrzej Jackowski, *Refuge/Refugee*, 1982. Private collection © Andrzej Jackowski

7   Andrzej Jackowski, *The Tower of Copernicus*, 1980. Arts Council Collection, South Bank Centre © Andrzej Jackowski

8   Andrzej Jackowski, *The Burying*, 1994. The collection of the artist ©
Andrzej Jackowski

9   Andrzej Jackowski, *Beneath the Tree*, 1994. Private collection © Andrzej Jackowski

suddenly comes upon a strange sight: 'Beside a pool bare to the eye of heaven/I saw a Man before me unawares;/The oldest man he seemed that ever wore grey hairs.'

This figure seems to be both human and a part of the land-scape: 'As a huge stone.../Couched on the bald top of an eminence', or 'Like a sea-beast crawled forth', sunning itself on a shelf of rock. 'Such seemed this Man', says the poet, 'not all alive nor dead,/Nor all asleep – in his extreme old age.' As the poet draws near the old man remains 'motionless as a cloud', 'That heareth not the loud winds when they call;/And moveth all together, if it move at all.'

Coming up to this strange creature the poet engages him in conversation and at this point an odd and even ridiculous note enters the poem. 'This morning gives us promise of a glorious day,' he says, as though their meeting was of the most ordinary and everyday kind. He goes on to ask what the old man does and the other explains that he is a leech-gatherer. But even as he talks 'his voice to me was like a stream/Scarce heard; nor word from word could I divide,/And the whole body of the man did seem/Like one whom I had met with in a dream.' His former deadening thoughts return, but he struggles free of them to ask again, almost like a sleep-walker: 'How is it that you live, and what is it you do?' The old man repeats what he had just said and then proceeds to give a potted history of leech-gathering. But again the poet's mind wanders, and 'In my mind's eye I seemed to see him pace/About the weary moors contin-ually,/Wandering about alone and silently.' But, says the poet, the cheerfulness of the old man's speech and the warmth of his personality force him to see that despair, such as he had been in danger of succumbing to, cannot be the right response to life when it contains such splendid examples of fortitude and uprightness. And he ends:

I could have laughed myself to scorn to find
In that decrepit Man so firm a mind.

'God', said I, 'be my help and stay secure,
I'll think of the Leech-gatherer on the lonely moor!'

Lewis Carroll, seventy years later, homed in on what is wrong
with this poem with the unerring instinct of the born parodist:

> I saw an aged aged man
>   A-sitting on the gate.
> 'Who are you, aged man?' I said,
>   'And how is it you live?'
> And his answer trickled through my head
>   Like water through a sieve.
>
> He said, 'I look for butterflies
>   That sleep among the wheat;
> I make them into mutton-pies,
>   And sell them in the street.
> I sell them unto men,' he said,
>   'Who sail on stormy seas;
> And that's the way I get my bread —
>   A trifle, if you please.'
>
> But I was thinking of a plan
>   To dye one's whiskers green,
> And always use so large a fan
>   That they could not be seen.
> So, having no reply to give
>   To what the old man said,
> I cried, 'Come, tell me how you live!'
>   And thumped him on the head.

Wordsworth the poet wishes to write about a strange and
powerful experience: his encounter on the bare moors with a
figure who is both human and, somehow, a part of the landscape, like Lucy, 'rolled round in earth's diurnal course / With
rocks and stones and trees.' But Lucy is dead while the old man
lives and talks. This is a problem for Wordsworth. He wants,

rightly, to make it clear that this was no vision, that the old man both existed and seemed to be a sign or index of something else. The enterprise itself is not risible. Shakespeare rose to the challenge in *King Lear* as did Beckett in *Endgame*. For parts of the poem Wordsworth too succeeds in conveying the old man's elemental and frightening quality. But then it's as if he doesn't trust in his own vision, and feels the need to give the man an occupation and a form of speech that goes with it, as though only in this way would we be convinced by him. He seems to be caught between two modes *and to believe that they are one.* As so often in his poetry an optimistic Protestant morality tries to recuperate a much darker and more unsettling vision, but without success.

Wordsworth, we could say, has mistrusted himself; the enemy here is not the fetishisation of art, as it was in Dante, but the erosion of the poetic vision by morality.

Prejudice and Art: Wagner and Dostoevsky

What had been a clash between morality and art in Wordsworth becomes a clash between prejudice and art in a wide range of later nineteenth-century artists. Let me pause briefly with two of them, Wagner and Dostoevsky. This time the clash does not occur within the work but rather between the artist's pronouncements *in propria persona* and his work.

Wagner's anti-Semitic tracts are notorious. His views made him popular with the Nazis and led to his work being banned from performance in Israel. But while it cannot be said that there is *no* connection between his views on life and his views on music, there is clearly nothing in the music that could be called anti-Semitic. One can show – and people have shown – that the deep yearning in his music and librettos for redemption, for freedom from the petty troubles of this world, reveals them as coming from and contributing to the climate of German idealism which provided such fertile ground for Nazi propaganda. But that is all. The man was prejudiced; the music is not.

The same thing could be said of Dostoevsky, but, because he is a writer, it is easier to see what is at stake in the distinction. If one reads the newspaper articles that form what is misleadingly called *A Writer's Diary*, one finds a man who is seemingly nothing but a bundle of prejudices: virulently anti-Semitic and anti-Catholic; bent on promoting the idea of an Orthodox Greater Serbia with its capital in Constantinople; and with a visceral horror of Moslems and Turks – reading him today it is easy to understand what has been happening in the Balkans recently and why Russia played the role it did there. How, we feel, can a man with views like that be a great novelist?

The answer is, easily. All these views are present in the novels, but set in dialogue with others and so expressing not Truths but very human desires and attitudes. As Bakhtin saw, what Dostoevsky does in the great novels is to set prejudices against one another, to allow these voices of obsession and bigotry and madness to enter into dialogue with one another, so that the reader is left feeling, not, 'This is the Truth', but 'This is what the world, what human beings, are like.' As in Dante, we have to make up our own minds; but here there is no sense of direction in the work to guide us and the singer on the shore has become one of the many devils in Hell.

Romanticism and Protestantism

What distinguishes Dostoevsky's characters from those in so many nineteenth-century novels is that they themselves are split and fragmented, engaged in a frenzied and inconclusive dialogue with themselves. Dostoevsky's butts are the figures of certainty and rectitude who imagine that there is a single unified self and that they speak for it, just as there is a single set of truths in the world for which they speak: these are the Jesuits, the district Governors and all the idealistic believers in 'The Good and the Beautiful'.

That last phrase, which is to Dostoevsky the novelist as the proverbial red rag is to the bull, alerts us to the fact that there are two divergent aspects of Romanticism. The first, idealist, is summed up in this phrase of Schiller's, and is the Enlightenment legacy to Romanticism. It is what lies behind Wordsworth's admiration for the old leech-gatherer's fortitude and moral worth, and it is also what fires Robespierre and the worst excesses of the later years of the French Revolution. The second, which we might call realist, recognises the darkness and mystery at the heart of human motivation, recognises that for human beings there is no such thing as 'being natural', that 'speaking the truth' or 'saying what you mean' is not at all easy, since we are never clear what precisely 'the truth' is or even what we really mean. Dostoevsky's novels and the greatest moments of Wordsworth's poetry give us access to this second strand.

But of course when put like that it becomes clear that both aspects of Romanticism have their roots in Protestantism. If Socrates's 'Know Thyself' heralded a new attitude to the self in fifth-century Athens, then Luther's 'Here I stand; I can do no other' – *ich kann nicht anders* – did the same for sixteenth-century Europe: it both summed up what many people felt at the time but had not been able to express and it pushed their feelings in that direction. But, again, Luther's principled stand leads in two opposite directions – and Shakespeare has the appropriate formula for both. First:

> This above all, to thine own self be true
> And it must follow as the night the day
> Thou canst not then be false to any man.

That, however, is Polonius, not Shakespeare. And *Hamlet*, that extraordinary exploration of Romanticism *avant la lettre*, 'places' Polonius in a nexus of conflicting and contradictory voices, as Dostoevsky 'places' Kirilov and Alyosha Karamazov and all the others. What, the play asks, does it mean to be true to yourself? Is there a self to be true to? How comes it, Hamlet wonders, that the Player King can weep at purely imaginary woes while he, whose father has been murdered and whose mother has married the culprit, cannot shed a single tear?

Eliot and Cliché

'It is impossible to say just what I mean!' exclaims Prufrock. In the room, though, the women 'come and go,/Talking of Michelangelo', and the couplet suggests both their complete confidence in talking about Michelangelo and the absurdity and banality of such talk. For Prufrock, on the other hand, to speak is to say the wrong thing. The women, like Polonius, can, without a second thought, pin him wriggling to the wall, but he can only reiterate: 'And should I then presume?/And how should I begin?'

Of course this puts him at a terrible disadvantage, leaves him bewildered, helpless and ridiculous, but there is nothing to be done about that. If he is to be true to himself he will have to be true to the emptiness that is his self. He may dream of a more elemental life, like Wordsworth's Leech-Gatherer, reduced to a pair of ragged claws scuttling across the floors of silent seas – but in the world in which he finds himself, a world of cities and salons, of decisions about tie-pins and appropriate partners, he is at a loss as to how to conduct himself. Yet he will not succumb to the temptation to ape the women, but will remain true to his sense of how impossible it is to say just what he means – he clearly has too high a regard for the world and the truth to do otherwise.

And the same holds for his creator. Clichés of language and behaviour occur when we assume without question that there are words for every occasion and that they are immediately accessible; but the responsible poet can only wonder: 'And how should I begin?' He is not a prophet, like John the Baptist or Shelley, he has not, like Lazarus or Dante, come back from the dead, 'to tell you all'. All he can do is to bring out into the open the awful and destructive power of cliché, in life and art, and to pluck fragments out of the past to shore up against his ruin, hoping that, out of the collision of one cliché, one fragment, with another a kind of truth will emerge; that in the desert of the wasteland rain will, somewhere, start to fall.

These early poems of Eliot's show people locked into the prison of themselves because they are simply not conscious of other ways of being and talking – the women in the room, Hakagawa bowing among the Titians, Madame de Tornquist and Madame Sosostris with their absurd rituals, Pipit, Sweeney, Burbank with his Baedeker and Bleistein with his cigar, the Princess Volupine and Mr Eugenides the Smyrna merchant. These are both clichés in themselves, acting out the roles the world has provided them with, and clichés for the poet, nightmare figures who have to be exorcised if he is to find life-giving rain for his spirit and his poetry. It is no use trying to ignore them, going on writing like Swinburne or Masefield; only, like Dante, by descending into the depths and giving them bodies and words, can he ever hope to rise up to the point where he can see the stars again, feel the wind in his sails or ruffling his feathers.

Kierkegaard, in the nineteenth century, had tried to show that this negative way was the only way forward; and had demonstrated brilliantly how great is the temptation for the negative thinker to turn positive even in his negativity. The difficult thing, he said, was to keep 'the wound of the negative' open; for if it is prematurely closed the resulting infection will affect the entire body. We can see Eliot struggling with this in his later poetry and in his prose essays. The temptation is to suggest a way for mankind, and for the poet, to go. 'Ash Wednesday' and *Four Quartets* are aware of the temptation and enact a resistance to it; in the prose that is not always the case.

But for a number of writers who followed Eliot the temptation was too strong to resist and we see Prufrock turning into the women in the room before our eyes.

Waugh and the Temptations of Tradition

'I will show you fear in a handful of dust', says one of the voices in *The Waste Land*, and Evelyn Waugh seized on the phrase as a fragment to shore against *his* ruin, using it as the title of what many regard as his greatest novel. Yet if early Waugh is very close in spirit to early Eliot, what we find in his case is the curious phenomenon of the principled stand against cliché turning, in the life and the art, into a stance of cliché-like rigidity. Let me try to outline this painful trajectory.

In Waugh's early novels, as in early Eliot, the protagonists are the inarticulate victims of articulate predators. Paul Pennyfeather's first words in *Decline and Fall* do not occur till he has been debagged, dumped in the fountain, and then sent down for indecent behaviour:

> 'Just off?' said the Junior Dean brightly. 'Yes Sir', said Paul. And a little farther on he met the Chaplain. 'Oh, Pennyfeather, before you go, surely you have my copy of Dean Stanley's *Eastern Church*?' 'Yes, I left it on your table.' 'Thank you. Well, good'bye, my dear boy. I suppose that after that reprehensible affair last night you will have to think of some other profession. Well, you may congratulate yourself that you discovered your unfitness for the priesthood before it was too late.'

It is only as he is being driven to the station that Paul suddenly comes out with: 'God damn and blast them all to hell', though the narrator tells us he said it meekly to himself, and then felt rather ashamed of himself for swearing. Adam Fenwyck-Symes in *Vile Bodies*, watching as the book he has just written is seized by a Customs Officer, who pronounces that he will burn it, as he is by law entitled to do, can only come out with: 'But do you realize that my whole livelihood depends on this book?' 'And *my* livelihood depends on stopping works like this coming into the country,' replies the officer. 'Now 'ook it quick if you don't want a police-court case.' 'Adam, angel, don't fuss or we shall miss the train,' Angela Runcible adds as she leads him away and tells him about a party due to take place that evening. Arrived in London he phones his fiancée:

> 'How are you, Nina?' 'Well, I've got rather a pain just at present.' 'Poor Nina. Shall I come round and see you?' 'No, don't do that, darling, because I'm just going to have a bath. Why don't we dine together?' 'Well, I asked Angela Runcible to dinner.' 'Why?' 'She'd just had all her clothes taken off by some sailors.' 'Yes, I know, it's all in the evening paper to-night…' 'Oh, I say, Nina, there's one thing – I don't think I shall be able to marry you after all.' 'Oh, *Adam*, you are a bore. Why not?' 'They burnt my book.' 'Beasts. Who did?' 'I'll tell you about it tonight.' 'Yes, *do*. Good-bye, darling.' 'Good-bye, my sweet.'

Vile Bodies is, to my mind, Waugh's greatest novel, his *Waste Land*, though it's far more bitter than Eliot's poem, ending not with the thunder and *Shantih* but with an epilogue on 'the biggest battlefield in the history of the world', ironically entitled 'Happy Ending'. But only four years later, in 1934, with *A Handful of Dust*, a change is discernible. Tony Last is, like Paul and Adam, the inarticulate victim of shallow and brutal people. But now Waugh is starting to feel sorry for him, and starting to fill in his background in order to show us his qualities:

> *Between the villages of Hetton and Compton Last lies the extensive park*
> *of Hetton Abbey. This, formerly one of the notable houses of the county,*
> *was entirely rebuilt in 1864 in the Gothic style and is now devoid of*
> *interest...*

This passage from the county Guide Book did not cause Tony Last any serious annoyance. Unkinder things had been said... But there was not a glazed brick or encaustic tile that was not dear to Tony's heart. In some ways, he knew, it was not convenient to run; but what big house was? It was not altogether amenable to modern ideas of comfort; he had many small improvements in mind, which would be put into effect as soon as the death duties were paid off. But the general aspect and atmosphere of the place; the line of its battlements against the sky; the central clock tower where quarterly chimes disturbed all but the heaviest sleepers; the ecclesiastical gloom of the great hall, its ceiling groined and painted in diapers of red and gold, supported on shafts of polished granite with vine-wreathed capitals, half-lit by day through lancet windows of armorial stained glass, at night by a vast gasolier of brass and wrought iron, wired now and fitted with twenty electric bulbs...; all these things with which he had grown up were a source of constant delight and exultation to Tony; things of tender memory and proud possession.

Tony Last's inarticulate attachment to his house and the ways of the countryside is moving and well done. But we see Waugh here starting to champion those values against – what? Well, against the inroads of modernity, in the guise of the Beevers, mother and son, and of those who are attached only to themselves, like his wife. And once he does this it is not very long before he becomes, in both his writing and his life, locked into a posture of rigid conservatism. Prejudice has swung, as it were, from the thoughtless and selfish to the author himself. The wound of the negative has been prematurely closed.

Pretending to be me

To keep the wound open seems particularly difficult in an English context, perhaps because of the strong Protestant moralising background. We see its premature closure very clearly in the case of Amis and Larkin.

The early letters of Larkin and Amis show them, like the early Eliot and Waugh, turning inarticulateness into both a weapon and a source of humour. We might at times think we were reading Gertrude Stein as we read the letters Amis fired off to Larkin in the late 1940s and early 1950s, as typewriter errors are compounded in a wild excess of high spirits, and language thoughtlessly used by the famous and the established to pontificate about life and art mercilessly parodied.

Larkin said that Amis was the funniest man he had come across, and he describes his amazing gift for mimicry of both people and sounds. What both Larkin and Amis couldn't stomach was pretentiousness in any form. They recognised that the pretentious are so ridiculous because they are a walking bundle of clichés, and both Professor Welch and Margaret, in Lucky Jim, are just such bundles, Welch in a comic, Margaret in a tragic mode: 'She said this in a tone that combined the vibrant with the flat, like a great actress demonstrating the economical conveyance of strong emotion. This was her habit when making her avowals.' Jim, by contrast, is a living example of what Freud said distinguished the baby from the adult: polymorphous perversity. He has a different face for every occasion, and a child's love of practical jokes. What endears him to us is his awareness that he is confused and full of contradictory impulses.

'I don't want to go around pretending to be me', said Larkin in an interview, and by that he meant earning his living by being a 'poet' — reading his poems in public, talking about how he wrote and what his life was like. Perfectly understandable, and a welcome contrast to most writers. But, as both Larkin and Amis aged, they both of them, like Waugh before them, settled more and more into 'pretending to be me'. Their hatred of the English pretending to like and understand 'foreignness' turned into a hatred of foreignness; their hatred of intellectuals like themselves pretending to like modern art turned into a hatred of modern art. As with Waugh, the anarchic inarticulacy of the honest and self-aware, the visceral hatred of cliché in any form, gave way to a stance of bulldog Englishness, to apoplectic rage against all that was alien and thus threatening. For both of them Mrs Thatcher was a godsend. How sad.

17. Memory: Too Little/Too Much

'WE MUST NOT FORGET!' How often have we heard this cry, and each time we have heard it we have no doubt silently repeated it in our hearts. In the face of the growing tide of anti-Semitism once again sweeping Europe, both drawing strength from and giving encouragement to the kind of revisionism which, only a few years ago, seemed absurdly cranky and marginal, and in the face of the historical ignorance of those born long after the war, it has seemed blatantly obvious that every effort must be made to ensure that the atrocities perpetrated by the Nazis should not disappear from sight.

Moreover, it is not only today, fifty years after the liberation of the camps, that the injunction not to forget appears particularly forceful. It was there in the hearts and on the lips of all those who suffered precisely because one of the imperatives of the Nazis was to eradicate all memory of what they had done. They failed. But their failure only makes us conscious of the fact that they *might* have succeeded, that the eradication of memory was their aim, and not just in self-protection but as part and parcel of their determination to eradicate a whole people whose survival has, in the past, always depended on memory. The Nazi crime was a crime against countless individuals, but it was also a crime against a people who had, at the centre of their affective being, the injunction *zakhor*, remember – remember what God did to Israel. The question of memory, then, when dealing with this episode in European history, is not peripheral but absolutely central.

And yet, as soon as we pause to ask ourselves exactly what the injunction not to forget actually means, problems overwhelm us. How many of us have personal memories of those events? In fifty years' time the question will not even make sense any more. But how can we ask people not to forget what they have never experienced? Is not the word *forget* perhaps the wrong one? As I hope to show, this is not a mere semantic quibble.

We can deal with the revisionist challenge relatively easily. 'These things never happened,' says the revisionist, or 'They may have happened, but it was not nearly as bad as Jewish apologists try to make out.' Such views are not just uttered by obvious thugs or dimwits. They are put forward in books which look no different from the books which say that such things did indeed happen and that they were in fact far worse than any of us can ever imagine. How are we to distinguish between the two sets of books? Will our choice not depend simply on our upbringing and prior convictions?

I don't think we should worry about such problems in the abstract. Wittgenstein's answer to the sceptic who calls into doubt the fact that this mountain existed a hundred years ago and who greets all attempts to answer him with a smile and the question, 'Yes, but how can you be *sure*?' – Wittgenstein's response seems to me to be perfectly adequate to our needs. His point is that factual information does not come to us in discrete fragments but that we learn how to live in the world by learning various practices and by coming to understand how they interrelate. I would have to throw away too much in order to accommodate the sceptic, too many of the things I know to be the case and that allow me to function in my daily life. I can never refute him outright, but everything I know about the world persuades me that it was not created yesterday. Of course, each of those items of knowledge is also subject to the sceptical argument, but that does not make that argument more persuasive. I may have to revise my views about how mountains came into being, or I may have to live with the awareness that scientists cannot agree about just *how* they came into being, just as I may have to revise my views of what went on in the camps in the light of new evidence or by talking to someone who seems to have more knowledge of them than I do. But that is what human knowledge is like, and to strive for certainty, or to have such faith in certainty that whatever is uncertain is deemed not to exist at all, is a pathological condition, like having to check all the time to make sure I have exactly five fingers on each hand. Unfortunately it is a condition to which theorists are often driven when they lose their foothold in reality, in the actual ways we learn about, and act in, the world.

Nevertheless, even when we have put aside the pseudo-problem raised by the revisionist, there remain deep and troubling problems connected with the injunction not to forget. In the first place it puts us in company we would probably prefer not to keep, the company of Milosevic and Karadzic, of Paisley and Adams. For it is striking how often, in the past few years, we have heard that cry from the lips of those we regard as dangerous demagogues, people who seem to be locked into a world of fantasy and delusion. Coming from Serb and Irish leaders the phrase seems to be a way of denying others even the right to argue with them, a fanning of the flames of self-pity, bigotry and factionalism. 'Remember Kosovo!' 'Remember Bloody Sunday!' – what is the difference between these calls to memory and our cry: 'Remember the camps!'?

One immediate difference would seem to be that the one is a call to action and the other is not. But that is not quite right either. Anyone with an interest in the Middle East and the fate of Israel amongst its Arab neighbours will recall the way Begin and the Israeli right have used the injunction not to forget the Holocaust as a way of justifying aggression and warding off the moral indignation of the world at their treatment of Palestinians. There is no difference there between the injunction to remember Kosovo and the injunction to remember the camps. In both cases the implicit 'Never again!' is used to reinforce what Jewish historians have called a lachrymose version of national history ('Look how *we* suffered at *their* hands!'), and to justify actions which are morally and legally reprehensible.

But, it will be argued, Begin and the Likud have simply hijacked for their own ends perfectly respectable, indeed, highly desirable attitudes. Surely what they have done with the injunction not to forget has nothing to do with what millions of Jews and non-Jews have felt since the full extent of the Nazi atrocities came to light: that these things were so appalling that we need to keep them constantly before us if we are to make sure they are never repeated. This is perfectly true and indeed, as I suggested at the outset, it is a view which no right-thinking person could fail to share. Yet I don't think we can separate it quite so neatly from the views of the Serbian and Irish leaders and of Begin and the Likud.

Sincerity clearly cannot be a criterion of worthiness. There is no reason to suppose that the IRA and the Bosnian Serbs are not sincere, or that Begin was not sincere. Indeed, a pure conscience can be the most dangerous thing of all. What I think we need to do is to think not in terms of sincerity and hypocrisy but of openness and closedness, of memory as the mastering of reality and memory as the compulsive repetition of gestures and clichés, memory as the coming to terms with that which is painful and memory as the masochistic turning of the screw of pain. Then we need to understand that we are not speaking here of personal but of public memory, and we need to ask ourselves what it is that constituted public or communal memory in traditional societies and whether such a memory is still possible today.

I would like to suggest that communal memory in traditional societies can be thought of first of all as *dialogue*. Maurice Halbwachs, the distinguished Jewish sociologist who was murdered by the Nazis in the last year of the war, divides the latter part of his book, *Les Cadres sociaux de la mémoire*, into chapters on the family, religion and the realm of work.[1] In each case, as he shows, what is important is the continual dialogue which is involved: between parent and child, priest and parishioners, master and apprentice. Traditions are handed down by word of mouth, but not at all as one hands over a baton in a relay race, for what is passed on is inseparable from argument, discussion, meditation and practice. The child grows up hearing his parents and grandparents, his uncles and aunts, talking about earlier generations or distant members of the family of whom he has no personal knowledge; but he comes to know these people by means of the anecdotes he hears about them, the arguments his seniors get into concerning them, and the answers given to the questions he himself asks. And when the time comes he in turn passes these on to his own children, joined now to anecdotes and arguments about the parents, grandparents, uncles and aunts he has himself known.

And what do we find in the Hebrew Bible? Precisely such anecdotes and arguments, such multiple views of the ancestors, allied to injunctions not to forget. In the rituals of Judaism, particularly the Passover seder, we have a living example of this tradition at work. The guests, including the very youngest children, are encouraged to identify with their ancestors who escaped from Egypt and, through God's help, crossed over into safety. But they are also actively invited to discuss the details of the biblical story, to debate what seems problematic about such details, and to apply them to their own lives. The meal thus becomes at once a pleasant social occasion, a commemoration, a celebration, and a framework within which the year to come will be lived.

1   Maurice Halbwachs, *Les Cadres sociaux de la mémoire*, Paris, 1952.

The profound interconnection between family history and national history and between both and religion is probably unique to Judaism, but in the medieval Christian church the words of the priest celebrating mass entered into dialogue with the pictures on the walls and the stained glass windows of the church, with stories about local saints and with each person's sense of his or her own life as made meaningful by the central Christian story. In the Corpus Christi plays not only did the whole town mill about the streets watching the Christian story unfold from Creation to Last Judgement, but of course many of the citizens actually took part in the plays.

In the workplace the master passed on the skills he had himself learned from *his* master, explaining and teaching by example, as in the fields the father taught his children and in the house the mother taught hers what they had themselves learned from their fathers and mothers. But it is not just different living voices that carry the story forward, allow life to be lived and things to be made and mended. Where the family is concerned the story inheres in the very objects with which the child grows up. 'Les choses sont l'âme de la famille' (things, material objects, are the soul of the family), as Halbwachs says.[2] Today this may still be true for some peasant and aristocratic families, but the rest of us have to make do with a very few family heirlooms which, wrenched from their context in specific rooms and houses, have lost much of their significance or perhaps signify nothing so much as transition and loss. Once, they were triggers of memory, objects which had been known to have passed through many hands and which had many stories adhering to them, as swords do in Homer and in medieval epics. Now they seem to serve no purpose except as mute reminders of incoherence, and within a few generations it will be difficult

2 *Ibid.*, p.159.

to remember why they were ever preserved in the first place.

In our modern world, then, where families are fragmented, religion has lost its hold and the workplace is an impersonal factory or office, such memory grows scarcer by the day. The 'modern world', though, goes back a long way, and it would be foolish to grow too nostalgic about the world of our grand-parents. If the Roman peasant and the Roman patrician thought of history in terms of family land, family memories and family pieties, the city of Rome itself had, by the time of the first emperors, become a seething cauldron of the uprooted and the dispossessed: penniless war veterans, escaped slaves, immigrants from the regions come to seek their fortune, the destitute victims of personal and family feuds and public pogroms. This Rome was the first great city in our modern sense of the term, and it is no coincidence that it was also the arena where the first large-scale attempts were made to direct the memories of the masses. The combination of demographic explosion with a tradition of urban democracy led to struggles taking place, more or less consciously, for the minds and, in effect, the memories of the people. That is why Shakespeare's Roman plays strike us as so modern in their exploration of political realities and why they are so different in feel from his history plays, which explore the dynastic squabbles of feudal lords. For Shakespeare, reading Plutarch, sensed that the Roman mob was not a thing of the past but, sadly, of the future.

Julius Caesar was probably the first great manipulator of public memory. Single-handed, he created the notion that he was *Divus Iulius*, the divine Julius, and that his claim to the impe-rial throne was backed by the evidence of history. His successor Augustus even employed a court poet, Virgil, to write the history of the Roman people in such a way as to legitimate his personal claim to the throne and the Roman claim to the terri-tories he ruled over. But in the truly modern world it was with the French Revolution that this other form of memory, what I would call monologic or mythic memory, emerged and was developed in ways with which we have become all too familiar in the twentieth century. That is why the first volume of Pierre Nora's extraordinary series of books, *Les Lieux de la mémoire*, is devoted to the Republic, for the French Republic forged itself out of the transformation of the dialogic into mythic memory.[3] The result was, of course, that in the ensuing century different mythic memories struggled for dominance, struggled to impose themselves as the only true ones. That is why France, in the nineteenth century, remains the *locus classicus* for the study of such struggles.

Avner Ben-Amos, for example, in his essay on the funeral of Victor Hugo in Nora's first volume,[4] quotes Henri Rochefort in *L'Intransigànt* remarking that, had Hugo been laid to rest in the cathedral of Notre Dame, this would have been a triumph for the clergy akin to what the retaking of the Bastille would have been for Louis XVI. As it happened, Republicanism and secularism triumphed in this instance, and Hugo was buried in the Panthéon. Nevertheless, on the day of Hugo's burial, as Ben-Amos points out, it was not the poet but the crowd following his cortège that was the real hero. For it was a crowd such as had never been seen before, and it struck all who were present on that day as a truly wondrous phenomenon. Maurice Barrès, in his novel *Les Déracinés* (1897), describes it as the coming together in oneness of the real France, thus transforming a Republican occasion into a nationalist blood-and-soil myth. Without dialogic memory to guide them Frenchmen, in the years to come, would be free to choose between these and other competing myths, influenced only by demagogues and the media.

3 Pierre Nora (ed.), *Les Lieux de la mémoire*, Vols. I and II, Paris, 1984 & 1986.
4 *Ibid.*, Vol. I, pp.473–522.

The twentieth century, of course, was to see many such myths flourish and die, most notably of course the myth of the *Volk* under threat, so assiduously nourished by the Nazi propaganda machine. The urban proletariat, having no dialogic memory to fall back on but only a burning desire to be released from their poverty and the emptiness of their lives, were, as we know, easy prey to such propaganda. All that is needed is the powerful projection of a simplified version of history which stresses the wrong done to the community by others and the need to fight for one's rights in the face of an uncomprehending world. What is particularly frightening in all such cases is that nothing seems capable of making a dent in such myths since, as with paranoia, each new set of facts will immediately be reinterpreted so as to fit in with the myth.

I have been arguing that when communal memory, dialogic memory, breaks down or disappears, myth rushes in to fill the gap. And I have wanted to suggest that for many people the slogan 'We must not forget!', whether it is applied to the outrages committed by the cruel Turks on the defenceless Serbs, by the cruel British on the innocent Irish, by the cruel Germans on the helpless Jews, is just such a trigger to mythic thinking, or rather, mythic emotion. But, I hear you expostulate, how can you compare the two things? The point about 'We must never forget!' when applied to the Holocaust is precisely that we must move beyond myth, that we must steep ourselves in historical detail, that we must insist on study centres being set up, films being shown, trips to the sites of atrocity being organised. The whole point is precisely that education and history should replace myth.

My answer – and this is my penultimate point – is that this is an admirable goal, and that it is indeed the task of the historian and educator to dispel myth, but that it underestimates the potential of such an enterprise to be re-absorbed into myth, the way in which the obsession with history, particularly the history of catastrophe, can itself become a way of denying reality, can itself become pathological. Let me explain.

We are beginning to understand — thanks largely to the labours of historians — that there is nothing *natural* about historiography, that it is as much a cultural phenomenon as perspectival drawing. History, we are beginning to grasp, only emerges as a discipline as communal memory starts to decline. We can see this process at work in fifth century Athens, in Renaissance Europe, and, as Josef Haim Yerushalmi has shown, among the Jews of the Enlightenment.[5] Nietzsche was perhaps the first to understand this when, in one of his earliest works, 'The Use and Abuse of History', he raised the simple but devastating question: What is the *use* of history? The growing nineteenth-century passion for history and belief in the primacy of historical explanation, it seemed to him, needed itself to be explained. 'Consider the cattle', he begins,

> grazing as they pass you by: they do not know what is meant by yesterday or today, they leap about, eat, rest, digest, leap about again, and so from morn till night and from day to day, fettered to the moment and its pleasure or displeasure, and thus neither melancholy nor bored. This is a hard sight for man to see; for, though he thinks himself better than the animals because he is human, he cannot help envying them their happiness... But he also wonders at himself, that he cannot learn to forget but clings relentlessly to the past: however far and fast he may run, this chain runs with him.[6]

5 Josef Haim Yerushalmi, *Zakhor: Jewish History and Jewish Memory*, Washington, 1982.

6 'The Use and Abuse of History', the second essay, written in 1874, of *Untimely Meditations* (1876). The title is translated as 'On the Uses and Disadvantages of History for Life', which is closer to the German, in R.J. Hollingdale's translation (Cambridge, 1983), which I use here.

And the pressure of the past, Nietzsche goes on, 'pushes [man] down or bends him sideways, it encumbers his steps as a dark, invisible burden which he would like to disown'.

There is, Nietzsche argues, something profoundly pathological about our obsession with the past. It is akin to sleeplessness. Human beings need sleep, they need to forget, at least for a while, or they cannot function properly. The nineteenth-century public which feeds so avidly on history, he is suggesting, is in danger of simply breaking down through lack of sleep.

Nietzsche begins his essay by quoting Goethe: 'I hate everything that merely instructs me without augmenting or directly invigorating my activity.' And he returns to Goethe at the climax of one of his last books, *The Twilight of the Idols*.[7] What he admires in Goethe, he says there, is his 'limited perspectives', his ability to set himself a host of strictly limited and practical goals. Goethe is an ideal for Nietzsche not because he is one vague large thing, 'a genius', but because he is a man who did many things supremely well: he wrote poetry and plays, advised rulers, ran a theatre, gardened, studied the ways plants grow and how we perceive colour.

Perhaps Nietzsche's Goethe has a role to play for us today. And there are signs that his advice is being acted upon. For if Yugoslavia and Ireland and even Israel have, in recent years, been object lessons in the power and destructive potential of mythic memory, there have also been other, more heartening examples of how communities try to grapple with their past. We have had President Mitterrand's decree that the remains of the village of Oradour, so long presented as a monument to the Resistance and a memorial of Nazi war crimes, should be allowed finally to disappear. We have the Oslo agreements,

---

7 *The Twilight of the Idols*, tr. R.J. Hollingdale, Harmondsworth, 1968, pp.102–4.

suggesting that the only way forward in the Middle East is for Israelis and Palestinians, for Israel and her Arab neighbours, to accept that the past has somehow to be put aside. Above all, there is Nelson Mandela's remarkable attempt to heal South Africa's wounds by guiding its memory. The slogan here is not, 'We must never forget!' but, on the contrary, 'Let us leave the past behind us and look to the future!' For the sake of all, Mandela keeps insisting, we must make an effort of the will and of the imagination, not to forget the past – for how can we do that? – but to stop dwelling on it in such a way that it poisons the present. And as I write this it seems as though a similar effort is under way in Ireland. Of course in none of these places is it going to be easy, and in some it may well prove impossible for a long time to come. But if we think of communities as individuals, as Nietzsche urges us to, then we can see the wisdom of the attempt, its psychological necessity even. To recognise that there is a pathology of memory, that to cling to the past is a form of sickness, is to begin to return to health.

In his remarkable book, *Awakenings*,[8] Oliver Sacks examines a group of people who survived the great flu epidemic that coincided with the end of the First World War, but were severely damaged by it, many of them condemned to a twilight life, without affect; others developing acute forms of Parkinsonism, which meant that they felt impelled either to rush forward or to stand stock still, to gabble incoherently or to go dumb. When Sacks administered to them the newly-available drug L-DOPA he found that their memories came crowding back upon them, often so violently and causing them such anguish that many of them preferred to return to their previous vegetable state. With the most intelligent or those who, for one reason or another, were best able to cope, it became a question of balance: how to

8 Oliver Sacks, *Awakenings*, Duckworth, 1973.

administer just enough of the drug to allow them to 'wake up', but not so much that, having awakened, they would be overwhelmed by the weight of their memories and the sense of their wasted and empty lives. Similarly, it became a question of getting them to adjust their movements and their speech so that they could carry out at least a modified version of the activities of walking and talking which we all take so much for granted.

Sacks helps us to understand the complex series of adjustments we all have to make all the time in order to walk and talk in the 'normal' way we do. I would suggest – and this is my last point – that we have to think of memory in the same way. Too much and too little, the compulsive return to personal and communal traumas on the one hand, total amnesia on the other, are both examples of malfunctioning. And even proper functioning, we have to recognise, is not qualitatively different from the other two, only a way of managing our illness, which is being human.

The tragic suicide of Primo Levi makes it clear that for those who endured the camps such managing will probably often remain impossible. But for the rest of us it is not simply a question of trying. It is an imperative, something we owe the victims. For if we ask ourselves what it is that so horrifies and bewilders us about the events of those years, we see that it is the notion of so many innocent lives not given the chance to flower, destroyed in the name of an idea. The worst way we can pay homage to these victims is to stunt our own lives by letting ourselves be sucked into *the idea of horror*. We need to recognise our own weakness, our propensity to use the idea of the Holocaust as a form of masochism, to read books about it, to visit its sites, to attend lectures on it, at least partly as a way of testing our ability to imagine horror or even experiencing it vicariously. This aspect of our response has begun to be explored in works like Saul Friedländer's essay on the Holocaust and kitsch.[9] I find it present even in works like

Claude Lanzmann's *Shoah*, which take as their implicit injunction that we must experience these things whether we like it or not, that there is some sort of virtue in such experience and that not to wish to do so is a kind of moral evasion. I find this deeply repugnant. I feel that it fails to see that there might be a difference between reticence and wilful blindness, between modesty and evasion. It also fails to see that *all* works about these terrible events are subject to the same laws; that is, whether the film is *The Night Porter* or *Shoah*, it is always going to be a film, and we are always going to be voyeurs, looking on, looking in, able to grant or withold our sympathy. Our relationship to these works is therefore always going to be problematic. Which is why the greatest works that deal with these events, Primo Levi's first books, Aharon Appelfeld's novels, some of Paul Celan's and Geoffrey Hill's poems, deal with their subject tangentially, include within themselves the recognition that such events beggar understanding even as they cry out to be understood. After all, as Appelfeld once said, we cannot ever really come to terms with the death of a single beloved person, so how can we expect to come to terms with the death of millions?

Kitsch occurs when this is forgotten, when we are asked to respond in ways which it is beyond us to respond, and where there is a gap between these two kinds of response, generating guilt, and that guilt is then made into an aspect of the work. We must accept that we cannot respond as we ideally should, and that sometimes we cannot respond at all. We should ask ourselves how often our involvement with the details of the Holocaust has more to do with our own pathology, with our suppressed guilt and our suppressed masochism. We need to ask ourselves what we want of ourselves and how we can truly pay homage to the dead. For we are, if not free, at least immea-

9 *Reflections on Nazism: An Essay on Kitsch and Death*, New York, 1984.

surably freer than they were; our lives are, compared to theirs, our own; we are at least in a position to realise something of our potential. By doing so, in whatever field we happen to be working, we can pay our dues to the victims of the Nazis. Of course in order to do that we will need to master our own memories and myths, neither to blot out what happened nor to return to it compulsively. That won't be easy, and it won't ever be fully achieved. But it is the least we can do for those who died, and for those whose lives were ruined by the appalling deaths of those they loved.

18. This Is Not Your Rest

I HAVE OFTEN ASKED MYSELF what it is that makes me a Jew. Since I have not celebrated my bar mitzvah, do not attend synagogue or take part in any of the feasts or fasts (unless it is as the guest of friends who do), the answer ought to be simple: nothing. Yet all my ancestors were Jews, and, as I grow older, I feel more and more affinity with Jews and with their (our) past. I may not be much of a Jew, but I suppose I am more of a Jew than anything else.

What then is a Jew? As soon as I try to answer that question I feel my mind clouding over and panic rising in my chest. Exactly the same thing happens when I ask myself: What is a man? Perhaps that is why I am a writer and not a philosopher. As a writer I feel the panic subside and the clouds lift as soon as I move away from such large general questions and start to tell a story. Nor does this mean that I feel I am shelving important questions for the sake of trivia. The narrative writers I love – Homer and Dante and Proust and Kafka and Muriel Spark – do not seem to me to be doing something more trivial than the philosophers. On the contrary, when I start to read them I feel myself to be much more closely in touch with things that are central to life than when I start to read Plato or Descartes. It is as though the food they provide were more nourishing to me than that of the philosophers. And in my own writing of fiction, when things are going well, I also get the feeling that this is what is important and truly nourishing for me, and that the doubts that often arise about the value of what I am doing must be seen as temptations to which I must not succumb.

When things are going well. That is the operative phrase. And when do things go well with my writing? 'The idea you and George Balanchine have of doing a "ballet to end all ballet"', Stravinsky wrote to Lincoln Kirstein when they were discussing what was later to become *Agon* – 'well, limits are precisely what I need and am looking for above all in everything I compose. The limits generate the form.'[1] Every modern artist knows just what he means. Other people may talk in grandiose terms of a ballet to end all ballet, but what Stravinsky wants is a set of precise limits: so many minutes, so many musicians, so many dancers. Every modern artist also knows, however, that three-quarters of the problem lies in finding those limits. It may be easier for the composer, who does, after all, get precise commissions (unless he is as famous as Stravinsky!), and thus knows in advance what is required of him, at least in terms of length and size of orchestra. Even then, for the modern composer, who does not have just one patron, the problem will be what commissions to accept and what to reject. For writers it is even worse, and one could say that what every serious writer has had to do is establish for him or herself the parameters within which to work for each separate project. One can see Proust groping for ten years for the right parameters for a long novel, which he starts in the third person and then abandons, starts again as a critical onslaught on the method of Sainte-Beuve and then abandons, and only then finally sees what it is he is really after. Even then the search continues, and the new Pléiade edition of *A la recherche du temps perdu* gives us nine separate versions of the opening page in its section on variants. Virginia Woolf's *A Writer's Diary* gives a marvellous account of the agony and excite-

---

1   Igor Stravinsky, *Selected Correspondence*, Vol. 1, ed. Robert Craft, London, 1982, p.287.

ment of the process by which *The Waves* came into being. More recent writers, like Robert Pinget, have talked about the terrible period between novels, when one gropes in the dark for a voice, never knowing if one will find it. What Pinget means by 'voice' is in effect a mode of telling: *this* way, not *that*.

In my own work I have found that what I always need is for two kinds of pressure to come together. These could be described as an existential and a formal pressure, or as the need to explore and understand something about the world and its inhabitants (myself included), and the desire to solve a particular formal problem through the making of something out of words. I have found over the years that when one of these pressures exists without the other, no matter how powerful that single pressure, I can never bring the work to a satisfactory conclusion. The desire to speak about something without the corresponding desire to make something, or the desire to make without the desire to speak about – this can keep me going for several weeks or even months, but sooner or later I discover that nothing genuine is emerging and I lose interest.

On the other hand, when the two do come together I find that the work races ahead and there are just not enough hours in the day. This happened to me with my first novel, where it was the title, *The Inventory*, that generated both the plot and the form. I had been wanting for a long time to write about people and their possessions, about the fact that we humans are the only creatures who hoard and yet what good does that do us when we die, as die we must? And when a person dies the possessions he leaves behind both mock those who loved him and act as triggers for their memory. I was drawn to the idea of objects holding the traces of their previous owners. When the title came to me I felt my heart suddenly beating faster, and when I asked myself why, I realised it was because the word seemed to go in two directions at once, to hold within itself the traces of the word *invent*, with its strong subjective connotation, and yet refer to that most objective of things, an inventory. It came to me that the book would deal with the relatives of a man who has just died gathering at his house to make an inventory of his belongings, and that in the course of doing this we would find them trying to make sense of their relations to the deceased, their memory or invention (but which was it?) triggered off by the objects in the house. At the same time I realised that my book would do without a single narrative voice but would move forward by means only of dialogue and inventory lists. As soon as I had made these decisions the writing of the book became a challenge rather than an imposition. As I worked I found that the challenge of the form helped me to find the meaning, and by the time I had finished I had said more than I knew and made something that pleased me.

Three novels later it was again a title that showed me the way. In *Migrations* I wanted to explore what it means to belong nowhere, to be constantly on the move, with nowhere to settle and nowhere to return to. Before writing the book I read quite a lot about nomads and about modern migrant workers. At the same time I wanted to explore the way in which, in the telling of any story, the elements that make up that story have difficulty staying in place, want to migrate from one area to another, and are usually only held in place by the writer's firm commitment to some form of realism. This may be difficult to understand for someone who has not tried writing stories, so an example from the visual arts may help. It was Ernst Gombrich, I think, who pointed out that doodling is a much more primitive form of art than realistic representation. It takes a great deal of study to be able to draw a realistic representation. But it also takes a great deal of repression: the desire of the hand and spirit have to be subdued in the interests of realism. One way of looking at Modernism would be to say that the repression was removed – but then of course the problems of the limits of freedom arose with a new intensity.

In my own writing I found myself struggling with the over-whelming desire to let go, and with the need to keep some sort of order. What I wanted was a subject that would allow me to let go, to make letting go be a part of what the novel was about. In *Migrations* this became possible. The sense of having nowhere to settle and nowhere to go, but of having to be always on the move, became a condition both of the hero *and* of the narrative.

As I worked an image emerged and became central: that of Lazarus rising from the grave, wrapped in his grave-clothes, as I had seen him in Epstein's great sculpture in New College Chapel in Oxford. But for me Lazarus did not have the conno-tations he had for St John and the Christian tradition. I imagined a Lazarus who rises from the dead and starts to unwind the grave-clothes from his body; he unwinds and unwinds, more and more cloth falls to the ground around him, but when all has been unwound there is no glorious resurrected body but only a little heap of dust beside the folds of cloth.

This image did not seem to me depressing, and I did not use it ironically or satirically. Rather, it represented for me a triumphant insight, what all the slow unwinding of the narra-tive had been driving towards from the start. For the first time since I had begun to work on the book I grasped clearly what it was I was trying to say: Our lives and our art exist between the fully hidden and the fully revealed: there is nothing hidden which needs to be revealed; revelation means only the gradual unwinding of narrative till the end is reached.

I had been reading the minor prophets and came upon a phrase of Micah's that seemed so close to my sense of what I was trying to say that I immediately appropriated it as an epigraph: 'Arise and go now,' the prophet tells the Israelites, 'for this is not your rest' (2:10). This word *rest, menuchah*, is, I discov-ered, one that occurs frequently in the Hebrew Bible: the dove sent from the ark finds no rest for her feet, for example, and in the Book of Ruth Naomi tells her daughters-in-law: 'Go, return each to her mother's house... The Lord grant you that ye may find rest, each of you in the house of her husband' (1:9). The word *go*, *lekhu*, is also a key one in scripture. It is, after all, the primal injunction to Abraham: 'Get thee out of thy country,' God tells him, 'and from thy kindred and from thy father's house, unto a land that I will show thee' (Gen.12:1). *Lekh lekha*, God says to him, get up and go. And Abraham obeys, thus starting the long march of the Hebrew people, which is still going on and of which, willy-nilly, I am a part.

So, is the emphasis in the Bible on going or resting? Jon Levenson, in a fascinating book entitled *Sinai and Zion*, argued that the two mountains form two alternative centres to the Hebrew Scriptures, each exerting its pull over the surrounding material.[2] The first, the Mountain of the Law, is associated with Wandering, the Wilderness, Moses and the covenant; the second, the Mountain at the Centre, is associated with sacral kingship, David and the Messiah.

Both, it seems still exert their pull, on Christians as well as Jews. Some will see themselves and their history in terms of desert and wandering, or its Christian analogue of pilgrimage – 'we are pilgrims even as you are,' Virgil tells the souls he and Dante meet at the foot of Mount Purgatory; and Kafka, in a late diary entry, writes: 'Moses fails to enter Canaan not because his life is too short but because it is a human life'(19 October 1921).[3] But others will stress the goal, either the Heavenly Jerusalem or the actual city of Jerusalem as the capital of a Greater Israel, Judaea and Samaria. Naturally, my own sympathies are with Sinai rather than Zion, for I can see the fanaticism and hatred engendered by the latter, but I have to ask myself whether my total lack of feeling for any kind of Zion or the

2   *Sinai and Zion: An Entry into the Jewish Bible*, Minneapolis, 1985.
3   Dante, *Purgatorio* 11.63; Kafka, *Diaries*, ed. Max Brod, Harmondsworth, 1964, p.394.

advent of any Messiah is only the sign of my unredeemable secularity.

Be that as it may, I felt, when I came across that sentence of Micah's in the midst of my work on *Migrations*, that here, if anywhere, was the heart of a kind of Jewishness I myself could understand and imaginatively identify with. Micah does not say where rest is, only that *this* is not it, and *this*, I wanted to say in my novel, is never going to be your rest; while the belief that somewhere, sometime, there will be such a place of rest is misguided and misleading, only brought into being by a nostalgia similar to that for the fleshpots of Egypt which Moses, to his sorrow, found so prevalent among the generation he had led out from the bondage to Pharaoh.

Not only could I understand Micah's remark, or God's command to Abraham, but I found comfort and strength in the thought that something that was so central to my own experience and so alien to those amongst whom I found myself should also be so central to the Bible. It brought that book alive for me across the centuries and made me feel that if Judaism was somehow related to this then it was less foreign to me than I had hitherto imagined.

Central not only to my experience but also to everything I had been told about my family; for as far back as it can be traced my family has been doing what Jews everywhere have always done: leaving one place to go to another. My father's grandfather left the Romanian town of Iasi to seek his fortune, first in Constantinople, where he married, then in Egypt. My mother's great-grandfather must have left his native Ferrara as a young doctor a little earlier in the nineteenth century and, with the help of a whip-round organised by the local rabbi, sailed across the sea, also to Egypt. My mother's father, after studying medicine in Berlin, and having been wounded in the Russo-Japanese war, left his native Odessa and settled in Egypt, where he set up his practice. My parents in their turn left the Egypt in which they were born to study in France, where I was born on the last day on which my parents could have escaped from war-torn Europe. It was to Egypt that my mother returned with me after surviving the war in France, and from Egypt that we both came to England in the summer of 1956, so that I could in my turn pursue my studies.

I do not feel myself an exile, for an exile has a country to which he longs to return (but then neither did Abraham consider himself an exile). My home is not France, where I was born, nor Egypt, where I spent my childhood, nor England, where I have lived for three-quarters of my life. The feeling of a Stravinsky or a Nabokov for the Russia of their youth is quite alien to me. There is no land or language of which I feel I have been deprived by historical circumstances, nowhere to which I dream of one day returning.

If that leaves me without the bitterness of exile, it also leaves me without his sense of a lost paradise or of a native language. This is not a comfortable state to be in. What made it worse was my discovery that what I wanted above all was to write, for a painter or composer can more or less choose his 'language' today, but that privilege is not given to the writer. I write in English because that is the language I am most accustomed to by now, but of course I have none of that inwardness with English and its various registers that a native speaker would have, nor any of that inwardness with English culture (in the anthropological sense) that a native Englishman would have.

When one is young one is easily discouraged. 'How can I ever write as I had hoped to do when the cards are so stacked against me?' I thought. What saved me from despair was the discovery that my case was not unique, that other people had had to face similar difficulties. Thus I read with a quickening pulse Kafka's diary entry for 24 October 1911, in which he examines why the German language, which is the only one he really knows, is incapable of expressing in the word *Mutter* his own

(Jewish) sense of his mother; or Proust's description of Marcel's despair at not being able to express his sense of joy at the way the sunlight strikes the river, which leads to him banging his umbrella on the ground and crying 'Zut zut zut!' in frustration.

It was Stravinsky once again who most perfectly summed up the paradox. He remarks somewhere that had Beethoven had Mozart's lyric gift he would never have developed his own remarkable rhythmic talents. In other words, what is required is that we make the most of what we have and do not mourn the absence of what we do not have. Because circumstances have caused certain roads to be blocked to you, you are forced to discover others, which might never have been found had it not been for you and your circumstances. For what do Kafka's and Proust's remarkable fictions, Eliot's remarkable poems, emerge from, if not the profound sense that all the known ways were blocked to them?

I had to accept that I was not and never would be an English writer. Nor was I a French or an Egyptian writer who happened to write in English, as Julian Green was an American writer who happened to write in French and Wagih Ghali an Egyptian who happened to write in English. But what was I then? A Jewish writer? The answer, it seems to me, is a little complicated. Balzac is a French writer and Dostoevsky a Russian writer, but is Kafka a German writer? The word clearly covers two quite different meanings. Balzac writes in French and he is French; Dostoevsky writes in Russian and he is Russian. Kafka writes in German but he is not German. Nor is he, like Rilke, simply a native of the old Austro-Hungarian Empire who, coming from an educated family would, until 1918, have naturally had German as his first language. But if Kafka is not German he is not Czech either. Is he then a Jewish writer?

There are, I think, two categories to which the term can be applied. There are Jews who write about Jews and Jewish culture as they haved grown up with it, as Balzac and Dostoevsky wrote about French and Russian culture. The most distinguished representatives of this category in our century are I.B. Singer and S.Y. Agnon, who wrote in Yiddish and Hebrew respectivedly about a world and a tradition that were as familiar to them as nineteenth-century France and Russia were to Balzac and Dostoevsky. To me all these writers, though they may move and interest me, seem equally alien. For I am as unfamiliar with the worlds Singer and Agnon write about as I am with the worlds of Balzac and Dostoevsky.

But Kafka seems to be different. When he writes: 'What have I in common with Jews? I have hardly anything in common with myself', and talks about 'the impossibility of not writing, the impossibility of writing German, the impossibility of writing differently. One might also add a fourth impossibility, the impossibility of writing',[4] I feel I know exactly what he is talking about. And the same is true of Paul Celan when he says: 'Perhaps poetry, like art, moves with the oblivious self into the uncanny and strange to free itself. Though where? in which place? how? as what? This would mean art is the distance poetry must cover, no less and no more.' His translator, Rosmarie Waldrop, elaborates: 'He always finds himself face to face with the incomprehensible, inaccessible, the "language of the stone". And his only recourse is talking. This cannot be "literature". Literature belongs to whose who are at home in the world.'[5]

By this token Singer and Agnon write 'literature', Kafka and Celan do not. Singer and Agnon are at home in their world, at least as much at home in it as Balzac and Dostoevsky in theirs — and that world includes assumptions about what constitutes art, novels, and so on. Kafka and Celan are in flight from all

4 *Letters to Friends, Family and Editors*, Franz Kafka, tr. Richard and Clara Winston, London, 1978, p.289.
5 Paul Celan, *Collected Prose*, tr. Rosmarie Waldrop, Manchester, 1986, pp.44–5; vii–viii.

such assumptions. But the paradoxes multiply, for their remarks could be paralleled by those of many modern writers from Mallarmé to Beckett. Does this suggest that we should abandon my division of Jewish writers into two categories? That we should think of Singer and Agnon as Jewish writers and Kafka and Celan as international Modernists?

It may be that in a strange way the condition of Modernism meshes with the condition of Jewishness, just as the condition of English Romanticism meshed with the condition of being a rooted denizen of the English Lakes. This I think is what the painter R.B. Kitaj was getting at in the fascinating series of jottings he has called his *First Diasporic Manifesto*. Kitaj feels able to talk about Jews and Modernists in the same breath because he finds in both the marks of displacement. He sets Modernism against Romanticism as the art of rootlessness against the art of rootedness: 'To my mind,' he writes, 'the very deeply rooted Provençal Cézanne... had baked Impressionism into the final synthesis of his great southern baking machines, to which Picasso replied as a young relocated Spaniard in the *Demoiselles d'Avignon*.'[6]

I am sure there is something in this, but I can also see how such formulations can lead to misunderstanding, for it might look as though the terms 'rooted' and 'rootless' were purely descriptive and thus miss the tension (desperation might be a better word in some cases) in Modernism and in such Jewish writers as Kafka, Walter Benjamin and Paul Celan. It would be an understatement to assert that Kafka was not happy with the thought that he had 'nothing in common' either with himself or with Jews. If he was profoundly critical of his father's Judaism, which he saw as a religion of mere external conformity, he was also profoundly aware of the fact that his father just

6   R.B. Kitaj, *First Diasporic Manifesto*, London, 1989, p.87.

might be right and that his own inability to accept the externals of Judaism cut him off not only from others but from Judaism itself. Similarly his longing to settle in Palestine was perfectly genuine, and if he could not finally bring himself to do so it was himself he blamed and not Palestine. In a moving letter to Else Bergmann, who, as late as 1923, was trying to arrange his passage there, he confessed:

> I know that now I shall certainly not sail... Even assuming that I could carry out anything of the sort, it would not have turned out to be a real voyage to Palestine at this time, not at all... but in the spiritual sense something like a voyage to America by a cashier who has embezzled a large sum of money... No, I could not go that way, even if I had been able... That is how it is, and what a pity, but in the final analysis nevertheless quite right.[7]

We could say that what we find in Kafka is a continuing and powerful desire for rest, whether it be rest in marriage, in the religion of his fathers, or in the land of Palestine, along with an equally powerful sense that such rest was simply not an option *for him*. 'Nothing is given me,' he writes to Milena (admitting, in his usual way, that he may be exaggerating), 'I have to acquire everything, not only the present and the future, but even the past, that which is given to all men as of right, that too I have to acquire. It is perhaps the hardest task.'[8]

Each destiny is unique and it would be foolish to pretend that one can generalise from Kafka's life and his anguished twistings and turnings. Nevertheless it is striking that we find many of the same ambivalences in the lives of Walter Benjamin and Paul Celan. Both flirted with the idea of settling in

---

7 *Letters to Friends, Family and Editors*, pp.373–4.
8 *Letters to Milena*, ed. Willy Haas, tr. Tania and James Stern, London, n.d., p.118.

Palestine/Israel and neither could, in the end, bring himself to do so. Yet their tragic ends suggest that staying in Europe was no solution either.

I sense that Kafka, Benjamin and Celan all recognised that the idea that the true role of the Jew was to be a wanderer could itself be seen as a sort of nostalgia, a clinging to what one knows and a refusal to take the decisive step that would lead one out of the wilderness and into true community. Not for them Richard Shusterman's blithe remark that we can live as we choose, that 'we can just as well choose not to make anything of our Jewish identity without being guilty of trying to escape or deny it.'[9] The idea that we can make ourselves in any way we want, which Shusterman ascribes to Nietzsche and labels 'Postmodern', would have made no sense at all to them. Each of them had a longing for rest, for an end to wandering, which was as much a part of themselves as their impulse to refuse this rest or that. Shusterman would say that this was because they were still clinging to 'Modernist' notions of unity and the real-isation of the self. I wonder.

At the same time there are many voices, especially in Israel, claiming that Kafka, far from being representative of Jewry, was representative only of the kind of impotent Jewish self-hatred bred out of centuries of ghetto life and now finally put behind them by those Jews who have had the courage to return to the Promised Land. After all, God's injunction to Abraham does not stop with his telling him to get up and go. Go, says God, 'unto a land that I will show thee, And I will make thee a great nation, and I will bless thee and make thy name great' (Gen. 12:1–2). Is it not irresponsible to take the first part of the injunc-

---

9 'Next Year in Jerusalem? Postmodern Jewish Identity and the Myth of Return', in *Jewish Identity*, ed. David Theo Goldberg and Michael Krausz, Philadelphia, 1993, pp.291–308, 306.

tion to heart and not the second? Is not the condition of exile bound up with the notion of homecoming?[10]

That Kafka would have agreed with this criticism is no proof that it is right. I am aware of the element of masochism in Kafka, but I am aware too that to try to 'place' him by the use of terms like 'masochist' or 'neurotic' simply will not do. There is something too profound, too generous, too pure in his life and writings. It judges us, and it is a failure of our own imagination to think we can judge him by the use of terms drawn from any narrow discipline, psychoanalysis or theology or philosophy.

What both the Postmodernist and the Zionist position fail to register is the strength and richness of the tension we find in both Kafka and in Modernism. What both the Postmodernist and the Zionist imply is that the feeling of 'having nothing in common with myself' can be easily cured. But can it? Should it? Is that not itself a Romantic myth?

In an early letter Kafka recounts something that has recently happened to him:

> When I opened my eyes after a short afternoon nap, still not quite certain that I was alive, I heard my mother calling down from the balcony in a natural tone: 'What are you up to?' A woman answered from the garden, 'I'm having tea in the garden.' I was amazed at the ease with which some people live their lives.[11]

Kafka was so affected by this scene that he included it in one of his early, unfinished stories, 'Description of a Struggle'. It begins, as 'Metamorphosis' and *The Trial* begin, with the narrator waking up from sleep, unsure of who or what he is. It goes on,

10 For a forceful assertion of this view see Jonathan Sacks, 'A Challenge to Jewish Secularism', *Jewish Quarterly*, 36, no. 2 (Summer 1989), pp.30–7.
11 *Letters to Friends, Family and Editors*, p.17. I have modified the Winstons' translation, which is clumsy here.

like those other stories, to show us the narrator as outsider, listening and watching but forever debarred from 'the natural' in which others seem to live their lives. We have all undergone similar experiences. At the same time we can be certain that if others seem at times rooted and natural to us, it is doubtful if they feel that way to themselves. Most novels, though, in the very way they are told, even if they are in the first person, present life as if it was natural. But Kafka's tormented narratives – including the narrative of his own life as it emerges in his letters and diary entries – feel liberating rather than constricting precisely because they speak of what we normally have no words for: the sense of disorientation that results from the sudden feeling that nothing is given one, that it is only others who seem to lead their lives 'naturally'. At the same time it makes him – and his reader – recognise the wonder of life itself: even having tea in the garden is a kind of miracle.

Kafka's sense of his life as a state of 'in-betweenness' – between tradition and secularity, between East and West, between childhood and adulthood – gives him his sense of his own unnaturalness, but also of the wonder of the natural. And though of course it springs from his own unique temperament and circumstances, it is also perhaps closer to the mainstream of Jewish tradition than the unitary views of his critics. For if, in the Bible, certain absolutes are presented to us, such as strict adherence to the law on the one hand, and whoring after strange gods on the other, the Israelites are shown wavering uneasily between the one and the other, as the Jews of the Diaspora will later waver between an impossible adherence to the letter of the law and the ever-tempting embrace of assimilation. And if the prophets are the mouthpieces of the one view and certain kings emblematic of the other, those to whom the Bible gives most space – Jacob and David, for example – also hover between the two.

'In-betweenness' also seems characteristic of the lessons that the feasts of the Jewish calendar seek to inculcate. On Passover night Jews are enjoined to eat unleavened bread to remind them of their former captivity: 'This is the bread of affliction which our fathers ate in Egypt.' It is as if the celebration of true freedom must start with a remembering of bondage, not a denial of it. At the same time the Passover service is designed to elicit the question from the child: 'Why is this night different from all other nights?' It is meant to make the child understand that what he had simply taken for granted, his own existence, is the product of a miracle: had that not happened then, you would not be here now.

Again, on Sukkot, Jews are enjoined to build booths to remind them of their wanderings, but also of the fact that life itself is fragile, that we cannot ever build walls that will protect us completely.[12] And the Sabbath is seen as a day of rest not simply because on that day all labour stops, but because on that day will be celebrated God's own rest from his self-imposed labours. The institution of that day suggests the difference between God's making of the world and the ceaseless toil of the Israelites in Egypt. The daily prayer too, by insisting that this day is given by God and that it is a celebration of that 'perfect rest wherein thou delightest', transforms the notion of rest from being merely the cessation of work to being a day of active renewal in communal recognition and praise.

What all these feasts suggest is that we can understand some-thing only by understanding what it is not. In Aharon Appelfeld's wonderful novel, *The Age of Wonders*, the hero, whose childhood in an assimilated Jewish home in the 1930s we have followed in the first part, returns after the war to his native town somewhere in central Europe. He wanders in a sort of ghostly underworld not because so little of the town has survived but,

---

12 See the comments of Irving Greenberg, *The Jewish Way: Living the Holidays*, New York, 1988, *passim*.

on the contrary, because so much of it is still there, looking as though nothing had happened. And in the town he comes across the ghosts of men, too, for the Jews who have survived have done so through another sort of death, by converting, denying their Jewishness. They are, in one sense, alive, but in one sense only. They are no better than Achilles would have been had he escaped his destiny at Troy and fled back to Greece. That, of course, is not a choice Achilles would even contemplate, for how we are asked to view a man's life in Homer's epics does not depend on the length of his years but rather on the *kleos andron*, the fame of men, how he will be spoken of in times to come. Bruno's home town may seem far indeed from Homer's Troy, but that is perhaps an illusion. In contrast with the ghosts Bruno meets there is his memory of four brothers who, though converts already, chose to join the deportees when the moment came:

> The way they stood by themselves in the locked temple stirred the hearts of the beaten people with wonder for the last time. There were four of them and all the way to Minsk they did not remove their caps... All night long Bruno continued to see the converts standing at attention in the temple like reprimanded soldiers. And afterward too, in the cold and close to death, they did not utter a sound.[13]

The brothers had to choose. Not for them the delightful Postmodern freedom advocated by Shusterman. (One is tempted to say that in their choice they found themselves, as Achilles would find himself in his. But that is too positive, suggesting as it does the triumphant overcoming of suffering. None of us is permitted to say that of them and for them. All

13 *The Age of Wonders*, tr. Dalya Bilu, Boston, 1981, pp.246–7.

one can say is that in their choice they did not lose themselves forever, as the survivors that Bruno meets have clearly lost themselves.)

Most of us, fortunately, do not have to make such choices. But, as the example of Kafka shows, there is such a thing as coming closer to oneself or the contrary, falling away from oneself. Interestingly, though Kafka insists again and again on his inability to find true rest, there are places in his diary where something of the sense of Sabbath renewal comes through strongly. The first is when he reads aloud to a small gathering a speech he had written on the Yiddish language; the second is when, in one night, he writes the first story he truly acknowledges as his own, 'The Judgement': 'The fearful strain and joy, how the story developed before me', he writes, 'as if I were advancing over water... How everything can be said, how for everything, for the strangest fancies, there waits a great fire in which they perish and rise up again.'[14]

What I find, then, in Kafka, in Celan, in Appelfeld, in certain parts of the Bible and the liturgy, is the articulation of something that I myself have felt, but that I would not have been able to recognise and accept had I not seen it expressed in the words of another. Their words speak to me across the centuries and the miles, helping me to understand what I feel about not belonging, having no language, always being on the move; they make me realise that these are not things to be denied or overcome but are part and parcel of what I am, to be lived with and put into the service of that creativity which I recognise as a gift even if I cannot bring myself to believe in a Giver.

---

14 *The Diaries of Franz Kafka*, ed. Max Brod, Vol. 1 (1910–13), tr. Joseph Kresh, 25 February 1912; 23 September 1912. Peter Handke, in his beautiful poem, *Gedicht an die Dauer*, Frankfurt, 1986, brings out well the difference between the kind of rest given by a glorious holiday and that given by working regularly at what satisfies one in one's normal environment. He calls this 'true duration', but I think we are talking about the same thing.

19. Writing, Reading and the Study of Literature

SOME OF YOU MAY HAVE BEEN PRESENT on another such occasion, three years ago, when Jonathan Harvey delivered his inaugural lecture as Professor of Music at this university. If you were, you will recall that Jonathan began his lecture with a massive disclaimer: 'I am a composer first and foremost,' he said in effect, 'and so you will have to forgive me if I do not talk very well, for talking does not come naturally to one who works primarily with notes.' Actually, he began even more disarmingly, for before he said a word he switched on a tape recorder and played us the opening bars of his most recent composition. It was only *after* he had done this that he made the statement I have just quoted.

I listened to the lecture, as you must have done, with intense interest and admiration. It isn't often, after all, that we have the privilege of listening to a leading modern composer talking about his work. But I listened also, I must confess, with a certain amount of envy. For I thought: 'Yes, a composer can start a lecture in this way, but a writer can't.' And yet I, as a writer, feel myself to be in a position very similar to Jonathan's. I too feel that I am better, or, at any rate, more at ease, making artefacts than talking about them.

But surely, you will say, that is absurd. A composer, after all, works with notes, so that it is perfectly understandable for him to say that he is not very good at speaking. But what excuse does a writer have, since his medium is words?

I am not sure about excuses. But what I want to insist on is this: making an artefact with notes or paint or words is the same *kind* of activity, and it is quite a different kind of activity from *talking about* art or life or anything else.

In saying this I do not want to suggest that art is made out of some sort of 'pure' language that is unconnected with the rest of life. That is part of a Romantic dream, the same kind of dream which led to the assertion that all the arts aspire to the condition of music. That, it seems to me, does a disservice not only to the verbal arts, but to music as well, for composers too work with a language which has its own history, its own tendency to turn into cliché, its own syntax and grammar, which must be understood, respected and renewed. No, when I say that all the arts stand on one side of a line and discourse about art on the other it is not out of any wish to uphold fin-de-siècle notions of the intangibility of art and the ubiquitousness of some entity called 'genius'. In fact, what I hope to show in the course of this lecture, is that it is only by taking that divide seriously that we can actually understand the central place of art – of all the arts – in our lives and in the culture of the community.

However, I do not want to approach the subject through theory. Clearly the issue is a central one in aesthetics, but I am not a philosopher and I have no head for sustained rational argument. Moreover, I am not sure that the philosophical way is the best way to deal with this issue. It may be better – it certainly suits my temperament better – to deal with it on a more personal and exploratory basis. For what I have just said about the unity of the arts and their distinctness from any talk about art is to me both blatantly true and profoundly puzzling. What I want to do this evening is simply to try to share my puzzlement with you, to argue with myself, so to speak, in your presence. And if I cannot come up with any answers, I hope at least to persuade you that there are interesting questions to be asked.

I start then not with an idea but with a *need*. Not the idea of literature but the need to write. For me this need to write is an imperative which cannot and does not have to be explained. At times it feels almost as biological as the need for food, sleep and sex.

When I say 'the need to write', I do not mean primarily the physical urge to put words down on paper. It is more the need to *utter*, to talk, but to talk not *to* someone and not exactly to myself. Something is blocked up in my chest and I know that screaming won't help and keeping quiet won't help, only the transferring of this urge on to paper. At the same time, in my case, the recognition of this need to write goes hand in hand with the *impossibility* of satisfying that need. I would go further and say that the work of art only starts where that sense of impossibility makes itself strongly felt.

Why is there that sense of impossibility? Where does it come from?

At one level it is easy to understand. Every undergraduate meets it every week in the course of trying to get his essay written. He is bursting with ideas. He knows just what he wants to say. Yet as soon as he comes to write the first sentence down he is filled with a profound sense of dissatisfaction. He cannot seem to say what he wants. Suddenly every move he makes seems slow, clumsy, unbearably awkward. He finds himself using phrases and expressions that belong to other people, other places, other times. What has happened to all his exciting ideas?

Everyone who has had to write anything at all has met with this kind of frustration. With the writing of fiction the feeling is compounded. I am not sure if we are dealing with something of a different order or only with something more complex. Let me give some examples.

Here, to begin with, are five different versions of the same tiny fragment of dialogue, as one might encounter it in the pages of any novel. (Strangely, after writing this lecture I found that Umberto Eco had used precisely this sort of example for precisely this purpose in his postscript to *The Name of the Rose*. There is a *Zeitgeist* after all.)

1 'Shall we go then?'
    'Well… all right.'

2 'Shall we go then?' said Jack.
    'Well… all right,' said Jim.

3 'Shall we go then?' said Jack.
    'Well… all right,' answered Jim.

4 'Shall we go then?' asked Jack hesitantly.
    Jim was tight-lipped. 'Well… all right,' he said at last.

5 'Shall we go then?' asked Jack, letting a note of hesitation creep into his voice.
    Jim was tight-lipped. His face remained expressionless. 'Well…' His voice trailed away. Then, pulling himself together, he said firmly: 'All right.'

You see how many choices are involved, even in a simple exchange like that. It all depends on what the writer wants or thinks he wants to achieve. It all depends on how much information he thinks his reader needs in order to experience the scene as he wants him to experience it. As we read most novels we are completely unaware of the writer's having to make choices, but if you're writing you come up against it every second.

If I can write a tiny fragment of dialogue in so many different ways, how am I going to decide which is the right way? If each decision merely depends on how I happen to feel the day I am writing, or what books I have read, or (which amounts to the same thing) how I imagine novels *ought* to be written, then what happened to the desire to speak with which I began? For that was something intensely personal and urgent, which seemed to have nothing to do with books and to be too deeply rooted to be dependent on daily fluctuations of mood.

I suppose this doesn't much matter if you think of yourself as a professional writer, that is, as someone who happens to write in order to earn a living as others mend roads or deliver milk or teach in universities. But if you have turned to writing because of a need, then the implications of this are very worrying. For there seems to be a need but no way of satisfying it. Is there a way out of this contradiction?

I think there is; or rather, there are as many ways as there are real writers. Let me try to explain this by presenting you with another example, not one made up for the occasion this time, but an autobiographical one.

When I wrote my first novel, in 1966, I faced a crisis. I didn't know if I had it in me to do what I had always felt I would do one day, that is, write a novel. At that point many pressures converged which ensured that the novel did in fact get written, not the least of which was *fear* – fear that I might never get it written. Yet even when I could see my subject clearly, felt the shape of it, knew the different characters and the setting, I still couldn't get the opening right. I knew just where I wanted to start: a solicitor arrives at a house to make an inventory of the possessions of a man who has just died. There he meets the man's family, and the book is about the relations of these people to each other and especially to the dead man whose possessions lie about, waiting to be inventoried.

I could visualise the house and the street it was in. I knew exactly where I had to go from there. But every time I tried to write the opening scene I found it collapsing under me. Other novelists, as far as I knew, had never had that sort of problem. They might rewrite a scene several times, spend days, even weeks, searching for precisely the right word. But with me it wasn't a question of the right word. There seemed to be an unbridgeable gap between what I visualised, what I sensed was *needed*, and my ability to put it into words at all.

Was I not a writer then? Perhaps I had been fooling myself all these years? Perhaps this was the moment to recognise the fact and give up. Yet the need to speak, and now to speak about this particular subject, was overwhelming.

My problem seemed to have to do with description. Should I describe the house in one sentence? One paragraph? Two? Ten? I had never given this any thought when I was coming to grips with the theme of the book, but now here it was, blocking my way. The trouble was that whatever it was I wanted to do, I was not doing it. Yet surely I was only writing in the first place because it was something I wanted to do. So what was going wrong?

The question I had to ask myself was: What was it I *really* wanted to do? And it seemed I could only answer that negatively. I found that each time I described the scene I was doing something I *didn't want*. At first I thought it was that each time I found myself mimicking the tones of all the other descriptions I had ever read, and I didn't want that. This was my book, there was something special I had to say, and I didn't want to say it in other people's phrases. But what were *my* phrases?

And suddenly it came to me. It was not that I didn't like the *forms* of description I was using; I didn't like any form of description. What's more, I suddenly realised, I didn't *need* it. What had happened was that I had adopted not just the tone and manners of every book I had ever read, I had also adopted their assumptions. Chief among these was the assumption that if someone, in a novel, arrives at a house or enters a room or meets someone for the first time, then that house or room or person must be described. But why must they? Was this an absolute law of narrative? No, of course not. It was a convention, it was the way you told a story. But, as my struggle with it has just demonstrated, conventions are never 'mere' conventions. Till you have moved outside them they seem absolutely *natural*. But now that I *had* moved outside this particular convention I saw that all the time I had been struggling in vain to climb over a wall when I could simply have stepped sideways and walked round it. I could in fact get on with what really interested me, which was the introduction of the solicitor into the family of the deceased, *without* having to describe the house at all. All I needed to do was to start the characters talking. (In the end this scene became the opening not of the book but of the second chapter):

'Mr Stout?' said the woman who opened the door.

'Hyman,' said Joe. 'Mr Stout's on holiday. In Corsica.'

'Gill said it would be Mr Stout,' said the woman doubtfully.

Joe shrugged.

'They could at least have sent one of their permanent staff,' said the woman.

'I am one of their permanent staff,' said Joe.

'You look like a student,' the woman said.

'As a matter of fact,' said Joe, 'and if you want me to be quite precise, I *am* their permanent staff.'

'You'd better come in,' said the woman.

'Thank you,' said Joe.

'I'll lead,' said the woman. 'Close the door behind you and give it a push or it won't stay shut.'

'I'm afraid,' he said to the woman, 'I stepped on something which gave a kind of squeak.'

'What kind of squeak?'

'Well... sort of high-pitched I suppose.'

'Don't worry,' she said. 'That was probably one of Mick's toys. He leaves them about everywhere. I hope you broke it.'

'I rather think I felt it move,' he said.

'Some of them even do that,' she said. 'But it may have been Oscar.'

'It felt more like Oscar,' he confessed.

I had made a fantastic discovery, you see. I had discovered that I did not *have* to do what I didn't *want* to do, and at the same time that I could *do* something which a moment before I had had no idea I *could* do. I had discovered that I was not so much interested in telling a story as in *making a story happen*. There was something dead, I realised, in recounting a story, describing the scenery and places for my readers as though they were blind. I wanted something which would be alive from the first word to the last. Now I found I could actually create my characters *and* move my story forward using nothing but dialogue and — I suddenly realised this too — my inventory lists. So that, instead of being something within me which I couldn't get out, the novel had become something which I found a growing excitement in *making*. The challenge was what spurred me on and brought me pleasure: the challenge to create a novel using no description but only dialogue and lists of objects. And of course as I slowly made it I found myself growing in understanding of the theme which had set the whole thing off: the relations between subjective fantasy and objective fact, between invention and inventory.

The first lesson I learned then was that there are no short cuts where art is concerned. You have to discover everything for yourself, and each time you have to go all the way back to the beginning. It is not a struggle between convention and sincerity, as Romantic theories of art suggest, but rather a struggle to discover what it is one wants to be sincere about. And to do that no amount of thought or reading will help, only work, the making of things.

And yet of course, while other artists can never act simply as models, they provide an indispensable help. Their own struggles, their own solutions, even the paths they *didn't* take – all these can help. Just as one discovers who one is not by introspection but through acting, and not only through acting but through love and friendship and enmity, so one discovers what it is one wants to be sincere about at least partly through what one reads.

Often this is negative: I *don't* want to do this. And, indeed, looking back now, I see that the main impact of other writers upon me was entirely negative. I read Tolstoy and Stendhal and George Eliot with different degrees of interest, but they failed to engage me at the deepest level. And the same is true of the paintings of Leonardo and Rubens and Delacroix, the music of Beethoven and Brahms and Wagner. At the time I didn't realise it. It was only when I encountered works of art which really *did* engage me that I realised what I was missing in the others, just as it is only when one really falls in love that one realises that what one had hitherto taken for love was not the real thing at all.

The moment of truth came for me with the reading of Proust's great novel. As soon as I began it I knew that it was *real* for me in a way that Tolstoy and the rest never had been. And for one simple reason: it dared to talk about failure. Not simply talk about it either, but demonstrate it occurring in the very writing of the book I was reading. Proust conveys miraculously both the sense of pleasure Marcel takes in the world about him and his intense desire to transmute that pleasure into something permanent by writing about it; but he also conveys the *failure* of such attempts. I cannot tell you how exhilarating I found this. Instead of feeling that the failure I was experiencing daily was a purely personal one, I now saw that it had to do with the nature of the project itself. And, if that was so, then it was something that could be lived with and, by being accepted, be overcome. Overcome not by being left behind but by being *incorporated* into whatever had to be said.

You see, in those works, by Dickens and Conrad, Jane Austen and George Eliot, which I was repeatedly told were the summit of narrative art, there was a closed, a sealed-off quality. They shut me out. There they were, supremely confident, supremely articulate, even in their narration of failure and frustration and incomprehension. But Proust was different. And I felt, reading him, that he was talking about things that were familiar to me; not, as I felt with the other great novels of Western culture, that I was listening in on the rites and rituals of some utterly remote tribe.

Years later I came across the work of Wittgenstein and realised why philosophers of many different persuasions warmed to him. For here too was someone willing to say: 'I don't know.' 'I'm puzzled.' 'I can't.' 'When I try to think this through I grow dizzy.' The long tradition of Western philosophy, which has, at least since Plato, taken it as axiomatic that if the mind encounters a problem then it is its task to *overcome* it, was here being quietly put in its place. Wittgenstein was in fact saying: 'If the mind finds problems coping with this particular subject then that *in itself* is perhaps interesting and meaningful.' In a similar way I found Proust saying: 'There is the desire to speak and, often, the impossibility of speaking. That is a fact about human life. Why does it exist? How do we cope with it?'

Of course one only responds to a writer if one finds one can trust him over details. It was because Proust was such a marvellous observer of human nature, such a mimic of human speech, such a wonderful craftsman with language and narrative, that I could take courage fom his central insights. In a similar way, I found, reading Kafka and Eliot, that they were speaking to me in a way that suggested that they too understood me in a way I felt no writer I had so far read, did. 'Someone must have been telling lies about Joseph K.' 'On Margate sands./I can connect/ Nothing with nothing./The broken fingernails of dirty hands.'

'Words strain,/Crack and sometimes break under the burden,/
Under the tension, slip, slide, perish,/Decay with imprecision,
will not stay in place,/Will not stay still.' What a relief these
words were after the great, confident – and of course magnificent – novels and poems that are the staple of the European and
English heritage. Not all writing, it seemed, belonged to some
great tradition to which I did not have the key.

Let me read you a poem. It is a short poem by the Israeli
poet Yehuda Amichai. Its qualities survive, I think, even in
translation:

When a man has been away from his homeland a long
                                                    time,
his language becomes more and more precise
less and less impure,
like precise clouds of summer
on their blue background
which will never rain.

Thus, all those who were once lovers
still speak the language of love, sterile
and clear, never changing, and never
getting any response.

But I, who have stayed here, dirty my mouth
and my lips and my tongue.
In my words there is garbage of soul
and refuse of lust and dust and sweat.
Even the water I drink in this dry land,
between screams and memories of love,
is urine recycled back to me
through complicated circuits.[1]

1   Yehuda Amichai, from *Time*, tr. by the author with Ted Hughes, Oxford,
1979, p.69.

This poem, like most of Amichai's, is at once simple and profound. The poet has stayed in Jerusalem, 'in this dry land'. Here there is nothing new, and even water is so scarce that recycled urine has to be used. But of course the poem – no less than Yeats's 'Circus Animals' Desertion', which it resembles in many ways – is both lament and celebration. More celebration than lament. The poet has remained close to his roots, his feelings, however confused and inarticulate these may be. Those who move away find a more precise language, but this very precision is a sign of its artificiality, like those summer clouds which are in a way not really clouds since they bring no rain.

In this poem, as in so much of Amichai and of the Israeli novelist Aharon Appelfeld, I find again what first moved me in the work of Proust and Kafka and Eliot. Here is something which connects with my own experience as 'Lycidas', 'Ode to Autumn' or 'Dover Beach' do not. Here is something which speaks to me and gives me a sense of how I might myself speak in turn. There is no key here to a mysterious power, 'genius' or 'tradition', but rather the acceptance of the lack of a key; words are recognised not as clear, forceful and exact, but as parts of the 'garbage of the soul'; and the life-giving water, I realised, could still be life-giving even if it was only my own urine recycled back to me through complicated circuits.

I come now to a crucial question. It is one I have often asked myself and to which I still don't have an answer. The question is this: how far was my response to the work of the writers I have just mentioned due to purely personal and arbitrary factors? Was it just because I was born in one country and have had to move on to two others, because I am a Jew with a typically Jewish ancestry – with ancestors, that is, coming from many different countries and cultures, none West European – was it because of this that I was touched to the core by Kafka but not by Milton, by Proust but not by George Eliot, by Amichai but not by Arnold or Hardy?

There is of course nothing wrong with that. We all find pleasure and comfort in authors who speak to our condition, who write out of traditions we have been brought up with and about places and people we are familiar with. That is why the whole notion of a canon of literature is nonsense. A Victorian gentleman will respond to Horace and Pope in a way that a child from a northern mining community or from a Sephardic Middle Eastern family obviously will not. An Anglican will respond to Herbert and Coleridge in a way that a Moslem or a Jew will not, and so on. So perhaps my own response to Kafka and Proust, my sense that here were writers speaking to me as George Eliot and Tolstoy never had, was simply the result of my own historical circumstances.

But of course that is only half the answer. Art is precisely that which speaks *across* cultural divides. I can respond to Dante and Herbert though I don't share their system of beliefs. And though Proust was indeed half Jewish, I am not going to commit the absurdity of suggesting that he is a Jewish writer.

Historical circumstances, while they can never be discounted, are not paramount. But I would put it more strongly. I would say that while historical circumstances may blind us to some areas of art and culture, they may also *help us* to see what had been hidden to those with different backgrounds. We should, I am suggesting, think of our personal circumstances not as disadvantages but as a privilege. In other words, there were perhaps forms of art which my personal circumstances had given me insights into, insights which might have come with more difficulty to those who, for example, had never left their native country except to go on holiday.

So, what had my particular circumstances enabled me to see about the art of the past which the scholars and critics I read as a student failed to see or, seeing, had misunderstood?

The *Sunday Telegraph* reviewer of my last but one novel, the writer Thomas Hinde, reprimanded me severely for abruptly changing tack in the middle: 'The author arrives in one chapter,' he wrote, 'to wander about the setting of the novel, tediously complaining that till now he hadn't been able to get a word in. If this were true... it would be a confession of failure, since speaking through his characters and their actions is the novelist's business.'

Thomas Hinde may not be a bad novelist but he is certainly a bad reader. Because a character says 'I' in a novel it doesn't mean he's the author, as every schoolboy knows. But I quote this passage because of the sentiments with which it concludes: 'speaking through his characters and their actions is the novelist's business.' But why should Hinde think he knows just what is and is not the novelist's business? Imagine a music critic telling a composer that it's his business to write good tunes (actually such reviewers existed until fairly recently), or an art critic telling a painter it's his business to produce life-like images (we haven't heard from those for a long time).

My answer to such accusations is that if this is indeed the novelist's business then I am happy to be in another sort of business. In that first novel I was telling you about, the issues I was concerned with were issues like: what is left of us when we are stripped of our possessions? What kinds of creatures are we, who put clothes on our bodies and live in houses and accumulate objects about us and who, when we die, expect to be buried or burned? Why do we live more forcefully in the hearts and minds of those who are closest to us when we are dead than when we are alive? Looking back at the seven novels I have published since *The Inventory*, I see that these are the questions that have gone on obsessing me. Like recent French historians I am interested in the *longue durée*, in seeing human beings and their actions in a longer perspective than that of a single set of actions, in trying to catch the slow transformations wrought by time but not normally perceptible. Not that I am interested in the *roman fleuve*, for one can speak about the work of time in quite short books, as Virginia Woolf has done, or even in a page or two, as Borges has done. And not that I am uninterested in stories; but there are stories and stories. Braudel thought he was a historian even though he wasn't much interested in recounting the political intrigues of the court of Philip II, and I still think I'm a novelist even though I don't want to write the kind of novel that Thomas Hinde writes.

Let me remind you of an experience you must all have had. You come down to breakfast on an early summer morning and in the fruit bowl in the kitchen you see a melon. It is early, very quiet. The light is uniform, slightly misty. One side of the melon glints as the light catches it. Why does your heart leap? Why does it go out to the melon the way it does? Why do we want to draw the fruit or put down the experience in words?

I think the answer is that by doing so we would in some way possess it. But there are many kinds of possession. There is the buying of the melon; the eating of it; and this other thing I am talking about. And I think artistic possession is the most satisfying. For what happens when we sit down in the silence of that early morning and start to draw the fruit? We begin to discover its otherness. We begin to learn, in our bodies, through our fingers, what its breath is, we begin to feel the stream of life in which it floats. We begin to experience that stream as other than ours, and yet by the activity of hand and eye and mind and body we begin to partake of that stream. And as we do so we are more possessed *by* the melon than possessing it. And in that state we start to discover something about ourselves, about the stream of life in which *we* float. We start to experience ourselves not, as we ordinarily do, from the inside, but from some point outside ourselves, we start to sense ourselves as having no more but also no less right to exist than the melon before us, the cat lying asleep on the table beside it, the tree that can be seen through the window.

But, it will be objected, that is all very well for the painter, but what about the writer? Surely, as Thomas Hinde says, the novelist's job is quite different. But why? Does it have to be? If I am drawn to the melon, to that early morning scene, and if my gift is for writing and not for painting, why should I hold back? If I feel that the melon calls forth a certain confused speech within me to which I desperately need to pay heed, why then should I deny myself just because Thomas Hinde tells me to? But I want to go even further than that. I want to say that the kind of novel Hinde is advocating is one which leaves out so much. I want to insist that most of our experiences are closer to the one I have just described than to any we find in the traditional novel. I want to assert that the kind of novel Hinde appeals to actually imposes on its readers a thin and unreal view of life. John Mepham, in a beautiful essay on Virginia Woolf, has put it better than I ever could:

> The traditional novel [he writes] is a form of representation which involves the creation of an imaginary but well-ordered fictional space... The orderliness of the fiction involves not only this internal orderliness but also an orderliness in its telling. For a story to be told there must be, implicitly or explicitly, a teller of it, a narrator, or a narrative voice, the voice of one who knows. The narrator who tells the story does so in order to speak his knowledge. The story is thus teleological both formally and substantially. The fiction has an end in terms of which its beginnings and middle make sense. And the telling of the story has a purpose, a purpose which is prior to and independent of the fiction itself.
>
> But what if we lack this sense of epistemological security? What if our experience seems fragmented, partial, incomplete, disordered? Then writing might be a way not of representing but of creating order. This would be a specifically literary order and it would not be parasitic

upon any belief in an order existing prior to it. For example think about the memory one might have of a person one has loved. It is possible, quite independently of literature, to give shape to, to fill out, this memory. It might be assimilated into some religious vision of life. Or it might be brought into relation with one's commitments to some very elaborated system of values, concepts and symbols ... But without such frameworks, without such means of thought and expression, we might have the feeling that the remembered person escapes us, is ungraspable, cannot be contained in our minds except as a disordered flow of particular fragments of memory... Then we should feel, as it were, that there is something that needs to be said but that we lack the means of saying it. If writing could be the means of completing the half-finished phrase, of bringing together and thereby enriching the fragments, then writing would not be primarily the telling of a story, but the search for a voice. Narration would not be the embodiment of some pre-existing knowledge, but the satisfaction of the desire to speak with appropriate intensity about things of which our knowledge is most uncertain.[2]

This puts marvellously well what I have been striving to say. It may be that few people will feel that need or will respond to the forms of art which articulate it. But it may be too that the dominant traditions of art in the West since the Renaissance have, for complex reasons, played down or denied this need outright, and so made us forget that it exists in all of us, and forget too that there are other traditions of art which *do* recognise it. It may be that the interest of Proust in medieval cathedrals and the paintings of Vermeer, of Eliot in Dante and

---

2 John Mepham, 'Figures of Desire: narration and fiction in *To the Lighthouse*', in Gabriel Josipovici, ed., *The Modern English Novel*, London, 1976, pp.149–85, pp.149–50.

Donne, of Van Gogh in Japanese prints, of Webern in late medieval polyphony, of Stravinsky in riddles, charms, and the ancient rituals of the Orthodox Church, of Picasso in African and Iberian art – it may be that all these things were not haphazard but grew out of the sense these very different artists all had that if they were to discover what they really wanted to say then the dominant traditions of Western art since the Renaissance would be of no use to them. They would have to look behind and beyond for models and inspiration. And by doing so they have made us, their public, aware of the fact that for four centuries we had been living with an unduly restricted and impoverished view of art.

The first thing everybody learns about the history of art is that some decisive change occurred at the time of the Renaissance. Exactly what that change consisted of is more debatable. The old story went that it led to the rise of realism, the acceptance of the human form and the disappearance of an inhuman, church-dominated art. But that story has looked more and more unconvincing as we have learned to look at other traditions than those dominated by the Renaissance ideals themselves. I simplify, but I don't think I distort unduly, when I say that in painting the change led to the development of the window effect – that is, the viewer is placed centrally and looks into the painting as if through a window at a drama being enacted in an enclosed space outside; in music it led to the expressive use of the voice in opera and the forward drive of sonata form, with its dramatic clashes and eventual resolution; in literature it led, in the end, to the kind of novel Thomas Hinde was appealing to. In all these instances the two key points are: (1) the teleo-logical drive of the work, and (2) the careful excision of anything that might ruin the illusion.

These two developments were enormously powerful and

mutually reinforcing, and they help account for the majority of
the masterpieces of Western art between 1600 and 1900. But
there was a price to be paid. I have already mentioned one: the
inability of fiction to deal with what John Mepham called 'the
satisfaction of the desire to speak with appropriate intensity
about things of which our knowledge is most uncertain.'[3] But
there were others. Take opera. In the nineteenth century more
and more elaborate sets and costumes were made to body forth
a drama which was growing more and more fantastic. But do
we need all these cardboard ships and temples and palaces, all
these rich costumes, in order to respond to what happens on a
stage, even in so unrealistic a medium as music-theatre? When
Stravinsky wrote *Renard* and *L'Histoire du soldat* he required no
set, the minimum of props and, above all, he used singers to
sing and actors to act. In so doing he was going back to an age-
old tradition of popular drama, where travelling players would
set up a simple stage in a village square and perform upon it,
showing the audience their skill but never trying to overwhelm
them with illusion or exoticism. The audience, needless to say,
had no difficulty in responding. The great early film comedians
worked in much the same way, in contrast to the producers of
the Hollywood spectaculars, which merely extended the nineteenth-century operatic tradition. When Harpo moves away
from the wall against which he has been leaning and it collapses
behind him, we love it. We respond at one and the same time
to our own foolishness at having forgotten that what we were
seeing was no wall but a stage prop and to the film's wit at
exposing this. Soon, though, we are once again absorbed in the
adventures on the screen.

Since the Renaissance, Western art has been obsessed by the
twin notions of imitation and expression. What Stravinsky and

3   *Ibid.*

the Marx Brothers do is remind us that art has always and every-where, apart from a brief span of time in a tiny corner of the globe, been seen less as the imitation of reality or the expression of profound truths than as a kind of *toy*.

The idea of a work of art as a toy is one that may offend the more high-minded among you. But I think I need hardly invoke the name of Winnicott or any other child psychologist to remind you of the fundamental, perhaps sacred importance toys had for us in our childhood. And what is a toy? It is and it is not. A toy bear does not pretend to be a bear; it is a toy bear or teddy bear; a toy horse does not pretend to be a horse, it is a toy horse or a hobby-horse. As such it can be invested by the child's imagination with the properties both of animals and of inanimate objects. It can be named and hugged, but it can also be thrown about and kicked.

It is of course no coincidence that two of the greatest modern poets, Baudelaire and Rilke, both devoted essays to toys, and that one of the greatest modern writers of fiction, Kleist, has written an essay on puppets. There are really three aspects of the toy analogy I would like to bring out.

The first is that both toys and artefacts are always double: objects and living beings. A novel is words on a page *and* the world those words evoke; a painting is marks on the canvas *and* the world those marks evoke; a piece of music is sounds made by instruments *and* the form those combined sounds create. Recently it has become fashionable for both artists and theorists to insist on the material side of the equation: a book is *only* words on pages; a painting is *only* marks on the canvas; and so on. This is of course part of a reaction to the nineteenth-century insistence on the opposite. What that gave us was the aesthetic of realism; what we have now is the aesthetic of abstraction. Neither in its pure form seems to me very interesting. The works I respond to are those which move between the two, those which, like toys, can take on a full life and engage our imaginations precisely because they do not try to hide the materials from which they are made.

Once this doubleness is accepted a new sense emerges of the possibilities of art. Art is no longer a poor imitation of life; it can do things life cannot. Why, for example, force a good singer to act when he will do it badly? Why not, as Stravinsky did, double singer with actor? Why limit what goes on in a painting only to what one would see looking out of a window? Why n ot, as in medieval paintings or in R.B. Kitaj's magnificent *Cecil Court* painting, include past and present, those who could have been there and those one wishes might have been there? Why try to reproduce in words a description of something which will always be infinitely richer than words? Why not use the possibilities of narrative to explore the intermingling of past and present and future which we think and dream about but which does not occur in real life. Why, on stage, stick to one plot, one story? Why not have five quite different stories existing simultaneously? A stage need not be a room into which we look as through a fourth glass wall: it can be a laboratory in which we can experiment. And the same is true of a book.

And this brings me to the second aspect of the toy analogy. A wooden toy is a complicated little object. It is more than the sum of its parts, but its parts and how they are put together are clearly visible. So too with artefacts. Actually, I dream of a novel not so much like a wooden toy as like those great nineteenth-century machines you see in the Science Museum or in the Brighton Transport Museum, those gleaming pistons and spinning wheels. Why should a novel not be as complex as that and yet made up of such essentially simple elements? As we work on it we discover that it can do things we never dreamed it could; yet this is the result not of genius or inspiration but of quiet humble work with nuts and bolts and levers. If there are thirteen ways of looking at a blackbird there are also no doubt thirteen ways of making a mechanical blackbird, and each way reveals a new aspect of the bird to us.

But, ultimately – and this brings me to the third aspect of the toy analogy – toys, no less than tribal masks, are mysterious and powerful presences. They are mysterious and powerful because of, rather than in spite of, their materiality. Picasso's great portraits of the early 1930s, Stravinsky's *Octet* or *Symphonies of Wind Instruments*, the early novels of Robbe-Grillet and the chilling later plays of Beckett pack an enormous, a frightening power into quite a small compass. Yet there is nothing hidden about their production. Everything is there for us to see. Yet there is of course a miracle here: the miracle of the artist's skill and resourcefulness. As we look we respond to the object but we also come to see that with a little effort we too could make something of the same sort: not as good, obviously, but of the same kind. It brings us to an awareness of all the wasted potential in our lives and shows us how to use it.

Now, if it is true, as I have been arguing, that the predominant art traditions of the West have for the past four hundred years taken a direction quite different from that of other cultures, and if this has meant the shutting out of certain possibilities, as well as the dramatic development of others, then the question arises: why should this have happened?

That, of course, is a big question, and many of the best historians of ideas and culture have written big books trying to answer it. We have been told about the printing revolution, the religious revolution, the scientific revolution, the rise of the bourgeoisie, the rise of the novel, and so on. The real difficulty lies in the fact that we are the heirs of those revolutions and find it very hard to think in any terms other than those they have made current. Some of the best recent work on the subject, such as Svetlana Alpers' book on seventeenth-century Dutch art or Peter Brown's collection of essays on society and the holy in late antiquity, have been successful precisely because the authors have managed to project themselves imaginatively into cultures not dominated by assumptions derived from these revolutions.

I hope that my first critical book, *The World and the Book*, flawed and often naïve as I now frequently find it to be, belongs to this tradition. In it I set out to explore what had got lost when the Renaissance turned its back on the Middle Ages and how some of those elements survived, though in transmuted form, in a few writers, and then resurfaced in this century. I tried to show how writers like Rabelais, Swift and Sterne had kept before us the idea of a work of art as a toy in a culture which was progressively narrowing the boundaries of the concept of play.

I do not want to rehearse these arguments here. I mention that book because it is part of my theme that it is out of my own preoccupations as a writer that my criticism has emerged. Any insights I might have had in that book into Dante and Chaucer, Swift and Nabokov, as well as its central theme, was the direct result of discoveries I had made in the course of struggling to write the novels, stories and plays which I was mainly interested in producing.

All artists are solitary beings. All artists have to find their own way. But none of us can do that entirely on his own. So we look around for help. And we become rather good at sensing what will be of use to us and what won't. I said earlier how much we owed to the great Modernists, not just for their own wonderful works but for making it possible for us once again to appreciate forms of art which had been forgotten or ignored for centuries. Proust and Eliot are among the greatest critics as well as the greatest writers of our century just because it was vital for them to understand the past in order to go forward in their own art. When Schoenberg was asked how he had come to work out his radical compositional methods he answered: 'I was thrown into violent seas and I had to swim.'

The critical and historical insights of a Schoenberg or an Eliot cannot be taken out of the context of their own struggles. Unfortunately, that is exactly what happens when these insights are transferred to the academies. When that happens personal insights and polemical positions are reified into a canon of literature or a great tradition. And this is perfectly natural, for academies perhaps need to think in terms of fields of study and cannot tolerate the idea that the nature of the field might itself be in question. Thus the Oxford English syllabus in the 1920s would have made sense to Matthew Arnold. It made no sense to Auden, who did no work and got a bad degree. The very same syllabus didn't make much sense to me either, thirty years later, though it did leave me plenty of time to read the books I wanted.

Perhaps that is the best a writer can expect from a university. Perhaps there will always be a conflict between literature as an academic subject and literature as a living force. But there is also a historical dimension to the problem. Though universities emerged in the Middle Ages, the attitudes we associate with the study of the Humanities in universities itself goes back to the Renaissance. In other words the study of the Humanities in the universities is itself complicit with those attitudes to art whose limitations I have just been trying to sketch in. No wonder Eliot said: 'Oxford is very beautiful but I don't like to be dead.'

Though, as I say, Oxford left me plenty of time to read what I wanted, I was glad to get out. Its values were too much those of George Eliot and Matthew Arnold, and though I could respect and even admire these, I did not feel they were mine. How fortunate I was, though, to have Sussex to come to. For what I found here and what I have tried to perpetuate in my own teaching was an openness *within the academy* to precisely those kinds of re-evaluation I have been discussing. The arts syllabus here does not reflect the vision of George Eliot or Matthew Arnold – a watered-down version of which lies behind Thomas Hinde's remarks –

but rather, in spite of all the revisions of the past twenty-five years, that of Proust and Eliot and Kafka and Stravinsky.

I don't know how many of you realise how extraordinary this is. How much we owe to the vision of men like David Daiches, the first Professor of English, Martin Wight, the first Dean of the School of European Studies, Tony Thorlby, the first Professor of Comparative Literature, and John Cruikshank, the first Professor of French. These men were imaginative enough to see that the Renaissance Humanist traditions in which they themselves had been educated were, despite their virtues, severely limited, and that here, in the first of the new universities, there was the chance to introduce into the academy some of that rethinking of both the history and the function of art and culture which Modernism – the thought and work of Kierkegaard and Nietzsche, Proust, Eliot and Kafka – had brought with it.

That is why teaching here at Sussex has meant far less of a clash between my own concerns as a writer and my duty as a teacher than I could ever have thought possible. I have found an atmosphere here open to the views of art expressed above. And, amazingly, I have been able to teach here what I love and not what I have been told I should admire. I hope I have been able to persuade my students also to love and not simply to make gestures of obeisance towards a range of works and authors no one would have dreamed of putting on the Oxford English syllabus in my day: biblical narratives, Dante, Kierkegaard, Thomas Mann. I hope that in spite of these times of government-induced crisis in the universities, in spite of the blindness of the UGC, who are making every effort to undo all that Sussex has created and turn us into just another university, safe, solid, and dull, a place no artist would want to come within a hundred miles of – I hope that in spite of all this Sussex will be able to go on offering its students just that.

But it would be wrong to end there. I began, after all, by

asserting that there was an unbridgeable gap between the making of art and all talk about art. I have tried to show that every writer has to be a reader; has, that is, to find what help he can in the masters of the past. But I have also insisted that the critical activity must come second. That is the danger of talking about the subject as I have done this evening. And it is of course a danger inherent in all teaching, even when that teaching is most congenial. For there is knowledge and knowledge. Each work is a struggle to discover what it is one knows, what it is one wants to say. And when it is done it is all to do over again. And if artists are better than scholars at rediscovering the riches of the past, they also secretly long for amnesia. History, for all of us, is a nightmare from which we are forever trying to awake. If the work I am currently engaged upon is to be any good then I have to forget all I ever knew. Then, in time, the work itself may teach me to remember.

That is why I should now like to stop talking about art and end by reading you a story. It is the shortest story I have ever written, barely a page long. I want to read it partly as a commentary on this lecture and partly as an experiment, to demonstate that though it will still be my voice that you will be hearing, and though that voice will still be speaking words intended by me, the story is both much more and much less my own than the lecture. The precise nature of that 'much more' and 'much less' is what I hope you will ponder as you leave this hall.

The story was sparked off by the title of a picture by Paul Klee, 'At the Edge of the Fertile Land'. I didn't know the picture, but when I came across the title I found I couldn't rest until I had somehow made it my own. When I had finished the story I found that Klee's title wasn't quite right for it, so changed it to 'In the Fertile Land'. Not very logical, you will say, if the story was only written to try and make sense of Klee's title. But who ever gave you the impression that making artefacts was a logical business?

In the Fertile Land

We live in a fertile land. Here we have all we want. Beyond the borders, far away, lies the desert where nothing grows.

Nothing grows there. Nor is there any sound except the wind.

Here, on the other hand, all is growth, abundance. The plants reach enormous heights, even we ourselves grow so that there is absolutely no stopping us. And, when we speak, the words flow out in torrents, another aspect of the general fertility.

Here, the centre is everywhere and the circumference nowhere.

Conversely, however, it could be said – and it is an aspect of the general fertility that everything that can be said has its converse side – conversely it could be said that the circumference is everywhere and the centre nowhere, that the limits are everywhere, that everywhere there is the presence of the desert.

Here, in the fertile land, everyone is so conscious of the desert, so intrigued and baffled by it, that a law has had to be passed forbidding anyone to mention the word.

Even so, it underlies every sentence and every thought, every dream and every gesture.

Some have even gone over into the desert, but as they have not come back it is impossible to say what they have found there.

I myself have no desire to go into the desert. I am content with the happy fertility of this land. The desert beyond is not something I think about very much, and if I occasionally dream about it, that contravenes no law. I cannot imagine where the limits of the desert are to be found or what kind of life, if any, exists there. When I hear the wind I try to follow it in my mind across the empty spaces, to see in my mind's eye the ripples it makes on the enormous dunes as it picks up the grains of sand and deposits them in slightly altered patterns a little further along – though near and far have clearly a quite different meaning in the desert from the one they have here.

In the desert silence prevails. Here the talk is continuous. Many of us are happy even talking to ourselves. There is never any shortage of subjects about which to talk, nor any lack of words with which to talk. Sometimes, indeed, this abundance becomes a little onerous, the sound of all these voices raised in animated conversation or impassioned monologue grows slightly disturbing. There have even been moments when the very abundance of possible subjects, and of available directions in which any subject may be developed has made me long for the silence of the desert, with only the monotonous whistling of the wind for sound. At those times my talk redoubles in both quantity and speed and I cover every subject except the one that obsesses me – for the penalty for any infringement of the law is severe. Even as I talk, though, the thought strikes me that perhaps I am actually in the desert already, that I have crossed over and not returned, and that what the desert is really like is this, a place where everyone talks but where no one speaks of what most deeply touches him.

Such thoughts are typical of the fertility of our land.[4]

4 'In the Fertile Land', in *In the Fertile Land*, Manchester, 1987, pp.61–2.

Acknowledgements

The pieces printed here were in the main written in response to invitations from editors, publishers and institutions. To all of them I am grateful for the original impetus and for allowing me to reproduce them. I list below the titles, dates and places of publication or delivery.

1 'The Bible Open and Closed'. The first Amos Wilder Memorial Lecture given at the University of Boston on 23 October 2002.
2 'Vibrant Spaces', in *Sense and Sensitivity: Essays on Reading the Bible in Memory of Robert Carroll*, ed. Alastair G. Hunter and Philip R. Davies, Sheffield Academic Press, Sheffield, 2002, pp.358–73.
3 'Singing a New Song'. A lecture delivered at the 35th annual Jewish-Christian Bible Week in Bendorf, Germany, July 2003, printed in *PN Review* 155, Vol. 30, No. 3, 2004, pp.18–22.
4 'The Opinion of Pythagoras'. A lecture delivered in New College, Oxford, on 2 October 2004 at a seminar on Shakespeare and Philosophy in honour of the retirement of Professor A.D. Nuttall.
5 'I Dream of Toys'. A lecture delivered in Berlin in November 2000 to the group Paragrana at the Centre for Historical Anthropology of the Free University, as part of a conference on games.
6 'In Time'. Review for *Modern Painters* of 'Rembrandt by Himself', National Gallery, London, Autumn 1999, pp.23–5.

7 'Escape Literature: Tristram Shandy's Journey Through France', in *L'Invitation au voyage: Studies in Honour of Peter France*, ed. John Renwick, Voltaire Foundation, Oxford, 2000, pp.157–64

8 'Dejection'. Talk given on BBC Radio 3, 21 October 1989, printed in *PN Review* 22, Volume 18, No. 5, 1992, pp.22–5.

9 'Kierkegaard and the Novel', in *Kierkegaard: A Critical Reader*, ed. Jonathan Rée and Jane Chamberlain, Blackwell, Oxford, 1998, pp.114–28.

10 'Kafka's Children'. Introduction to *Franz Kafka: Collected Stories*, Everyman's Library, London, 1993.

11 'The Wooden Stair'. Preface to *Franz Kafka: The Collected Aphorisms*, Syrens, Penguin Books, London, 1994.

12 'Listening to the Voice in *Four Quartets*'. Commentary on *Quatre Quatuors*, tr. Claude Vigée, Menard Press, London, 1992; English version in *PN Review* 87, Vol. 19, No.1, 1992, pp.44–51.

13 'Borges and the Plain Sense of Things', in *Borges and Europe Revisited*, ed. Evelyn Fishburn, Institute of Latin American Studies, University of London, 1998, pp.60–7.

14 'Aharon Appelfeld: Three Novels and a Tribute'. Prefaces to *The Retreat*, tr. Dalya Bilu, Quartet Books, London, 1985; *The Age of Wonders*, tr. Dalya Bilu, Quartet Books, London, 1993; *For Every Sin*, tr. Jeffrey M. Green, Quartet Books, London, 1995; tribute delivered in June 2001 at the University of Beersheba on the occasion of Appelfeld's retirement from thirty years of teaching there, and printed in *PN Review* 141, Vol. 28, No.1, 2001, pp.24–7.

15 'Andrzej Jackowski: Reveries of Dispossession'. Introduction to the catalogue for the exhibition of that name, Purdy Hicks Gallery, 1994.

16 'The Singer on the Shore'. A lecture given at a conference on morality and art, Senate House, London University, November 2000, and printed in *PN Review* 138, Vol. 27, No. 4, 2001, pp.16–20.

17 'Memory: Too Little/Too Much', in *The German-Jewish Dilemma: From the Enlightenment to the Shoa*, ed. Edward Timms and Andrea Hammel, Edwin Mellen Press, Lampeter, 1999, pp.317–27.

18 'This is Not Your Rest', in *Jewish Identity*, ed. David Theo Goldberg and Michael Krausz, Temple University Press, Philadelphia, 1993, pp.309–21.

19 'Writing, Reading and the Study of Literature'. Professorial Inaugural Lecture, University of Sussex, 6 March 1986, printed in *New Literary History*, Vol. 21, No. 1, 1989, pp.75–95.

Index

Abel 5–6, 7–8

Abraham 8–10, 11, 13, 40–1, 101, 139, 146–7, 251, 252, 295, 296, 297, 302

Absalom 20, 37–9

Achilles 251, 306

Acts of the Apostles 18–19

Adam 5–6, 12, 15, 16, 19, 23, 33, 53

Agamemnon 251

Agnon, S.Y. 299

Alter, Robert 46, 54
  The Art of Biblical Narrative 46n
  The Art of Biblical Poetry 54n

Amichai, Yehuda 221, 318–19, 320
  Time 318n

Amis, Kingsley 273–4
  Lucky Jim 273

Appelfeld, Aharon 221–53, 288, 305, 319
  The Age of Wonders 222, 229–35, 249–52, 305–6
  Badenheim 1939 222
  Beyond Despair 251
  The Conversion 245
  For Every Sin 236–42
  The Healer 245–9, 252
  The Retreat 222–9
  Tzili 222

Augustine, St 7, 22, 60, 184, 246
  City of God 7
  Confessions 247

Austen, Jane 317

Authorised Version 3n, 47n, 49, 50

Bakhtin, Mikhail 75–7

Balzac, Honoré de 243, 298–9

Barber, C.L. 64

Barker, Margaret 35
  The Revelation of Jesus Christ 35n

Barrés, Maurice 282
  Les Déracinés 282

Barthes, Roland 26, 42n, 72, 116
  Analyse structurale et exégèse biblique 42n
  Mythologies 116

Becket, St Thomas 109

Beckett, Samuel 52, 125, 128, 129, 132–3, 137, 144–5, 188, 193, 208, 212, 217, 244, 265, 300
  All That Fall 52
  'Dante and the Lobster' 144
  Endgame 132–3, 137, 265
  Waiting for Godot 184

Begin, Menachem 277–8

Ben-Amos, Avner 282

Benjamin, Walter 16, 79–80, 82, 117, 134–5, 136, 300, 301–2
  The Origins of German Tragic Drama 117n
  Selected Writings 80n
  'The Storyteller' 134–5

Berkeley, George 209

Berryman, John 78
  His Toy His Dream His Rest 78
  77 Dream Songs 78

Bible 1–24, 28–9, 37–45, 46–59, 222, 253

Blanchot, Maurice 168
  'Reading Kafka' 168
Boaz 29–30
Borges, Jorge Luis 121, 208–19, 322
  'Death and the Compass'
    213–14
  'Deutsches Requiem' 211
  Dreamtigers 217n
  Fictions 208, 211
  The Garden of Forking Paths 211,
    217–19
  'Tlön, Uqbar, Orbis Tertius'
    208–10, 219
Brecht, Bertolt 72
Brod, Max 150, 152n, 155, 158, 159,
  160, 162, 174, 179, 232
Brown, Norman O. 96
  Life Against Death 96n

Caillois, Roger 80
  Les Jeux et les hommes 80
Cain 5–6, 7–8, 12, 53
Camus, Albert 16, 212
Carroll, Lewis 264
Cash, Arthur 106
  Laurence Sterne: The Later Years 106n
Casella 260–2
Cassuto, Umberto 46, 46n, 57
  A Commentary on the Book of
    Genesis 46n
Cave, Terence 73
  Recognitions 73n
Celan, Paul 221, 288, 299–300,
  301–2
  Collected Prose 299
Cervantes, Miguel de 16, 94, 262
Cézanne, Paul 201, 300
Chardin, Jean 255, 258
Chaucer, Geoffrey 109, 163, 330
Christianity 139, 146, 181, 238, 246,
  248, 252, 257, 280
Chronicles 9
Coleridge, Samuel Taylor 120,
  122–4, 128, 320
  'Dejection: An Ode' 122–4

Conrad, Joseph 317
Contingency 15
Corinthians 92
Cruikshank, John 332

Daiches, David 332
Dante Alighieri 202, 260–2, 266,
  269, 290, 295, 320, 324, 330, 332
  Purgatorio 260–2, 295n
David 2, 3, 15, 20, 30–1, 34, 37–9,
  48, 54, 304
Dickens, Charles 151–2, 317
Donne, John 102, 167, 202, 324
Dostoevsky, Fyodor 75–6, 130, 201,
  265–8, 298–9
  Notes from Underground 130
  War and Peace 97
  A Writer's Diary 266
Dou, Gerrit 99
Douglas, Mary 32n, 35, 35n
  In the Wilderness 35n
  Leviticus as Literature 35n
Duchamp, Marcel 81, 82
Duras, Marguerite 243, 244

Eco, Umberto 311
  The Name of the Rose 311
Eliot, George 97, 243, 316, 317, 320,
  331
  Middlemarch 97
Eliot, T.S. x, 97, 122, 124–5, 132,
  151, 161, 183–207, 212, 224, 243,
  244, 268–70, 273, 298, 317, 319,
  324, 330, 331, 332
  Ash Wednesday 195, 270
  Four Quartets x, 122, 124,
    183–207, 270
    Burnt Norton 125, 183–196
    The Dry Salvages 198
    East Coker 197–9
    Little Gidding 199–207
  'The Love Song of J. Alfred
    Prufrock' 268–70
  Murder in the Cathedral 195
  'Preludes' 161

'Rhapsody on a Windy Night'
161
'Tradition and the Individual
Talent' 189, 196
The Waste Land 193, 195, 270
Enlightenment, 5, 11, 267
Epstein, Jacob 294
Esau 42
Eve 5–6, 16, 53
Everett, Barbara 85
Exodus 13, 14, 40, 42, 47

Farnaby, Giles 78
Ferrar, Nicholas 199
Flaubert, Gustave 26, 31
Fokkelman, Jan 3n, 47n
Major Poems of the Hebrew Bible
47n
Friedländer, Saul 287–8
Freud, Sigmund 21, 273
Frye, Northrop 17
Anatomy of Criticism 17n
The Great Code 17n

Galatians 87
Gandhi, Mahatma 12
Genesis 3, 6, 8, 12, 31–2, 33, 37,
42–5, 46, 56, 57, 295, 302
Ginzberg, Louis 9n
The Legend of the Jews 9n
Goethe, Johann Wolfgang von
163, 252, 285
Greene, Graham 224

Halbwachs, Maurice 278–80
Les Cadres sociaux de la mémoire
279
Harvey, Jonathan 308
Hebrew Bible 1–17, 19, 21, 29–36,
37–45, 46–59, 181, 243, 251, 279,
294–6
Hegel, Georg Wihelm Friedrich
138–40, 143, 215
Phenomenology 143, 215
Heidegger, Martin 180

Herbert, George 199, 262, 320
Hesse, Hermann 80
The Glass Bead Game 80
Hill, Geoffrey 288
Hinde, Thomas 321–3, 325, 331
Hölderlin, Friedrich 132, 180, 222
Holocaust 225–7, 230–4, 248,
275–89
Homer 1, 60, 244, 251, 280, 290,
306
Hugo, Victor 282
Huizinga, J. 80
Homo Ludens 80

Ibsen, Henrik 81
Isaac 40–1, 101
Isaiah 21

Jackowski, Andrzej x, 254–9
The Burying 257–8
Refuge/Refugee 254–5, 257
The Tower of Copernicus 255–6
Jacob 3, 9, 19–20, 40–1, 42–4, 47,
58, 101, 252, 304
James, Henry 200
'The Middle Years' 200
Jerusalem Bible 30
Jesus Christ 20, 21–2, 23, 107, 110,
133, 139, 147
Job 48, 56–7, 58
John, St 7, 21, 22–3, 294
Johnson, Samuel 128
Jonah 55, 108–9, 110, 232
Jonathan 2, 39, 48
Jones, Inigo 88
Jonson, Ben 79, 83–8
Bartholomew Fair 79, 83–8
A Tale of a Tub 88
Joseph 3, 4, 12–13, 15
Joyce, James 161
'Eveline' 161
Judah 3, 4, 12–13, 15
Judges 17, 53
Julius Caesar 281

Kafka, Franz 106, 121, 127–9, 132,
    137–8, 148, 149–78, 179–80, 193,
    197, 198, 201, 205–6, 222, 229,
    230, 232, 234–5, 236, 243, 244,
    253, 290, 295, 297, 298, 299–304,
    307, 317, 319, 320, 332
  America 151
  The Castle 198
  The Collected Aphorisms 179n
  Collected Stories 106n, 149–78
    'Absent-Minded Window-
        Gazing' 161, 165
    'The Bucket Rider' 170
    'The Cares of a Family Man'
        173–5
    'Description of a Struggle'
        157, 303
    'Eleven Sons' 149–50, 170
    'A Hunger Artist' 177
    'In the Penal Colony' 169
    'Josephine the Singer' 178
    'The Judgement' 164–5, 167,
        168, 177, 307
    'Metamorphosis' 152, 167,
        177, 303
    'A Report to an Academy'
        171–2
    'The Silence of the Sirens'
        106
    'The Stoker' 151, 164, 166,
        167
    'Wedding Preparations in
        the Country' 157
    'The Wish to be a Red
        Indian' 161
  A Country Doctor 170
  The Diaries of Franz Kafka 152n
  Letters to Friends, Family and Editors
    138n, 158n, 299n, 301n, 303n
  Letters to Milena 154n, 301n
  Meditation 161
  The Trial 303
Kant, Immanuel 26, 60
Keats, John 244, 319
  'Ode to Autumn' 319

Kermode, Frank 17
  The Genesis of Secrecy 17n
  Pleasing Myself 37n
  The Sense of an Ending 17n
Kierkegaard, Søren x, 12, 60, 96,
    130–48, 215–16, 235, 269, 332
  On Authority and Revelation 130–2
  The Concept of Irony 140
  Concluding Unscientific Postscript
        138–9, 140n, 141, 143–4
  Either/Or 136, 145–6
  Fear and Trembling 145–6
  Papers and Journals 135n, 138n,
        139n, 142n, 215n
Kings 53
Kirstein, Lincoln 291
Kitaj, R.B. 300, 328
  Cecil Court 328
  First Diasporic Manifesto 300
Klee, Paul 82, 333
Kleist, Heinrich 63, 222, 253, 327
Krauss, Rosalind 68, 69n, 76n
  The Picasso Papers 69n
Kugel, James L. 6n
  Traditions of the Bible 6n
Kundera, Milan 95
  Immortality 95

Lamentations 48
Lanzmann, Claude 288
  Shoah 288
Larkin, Philip 273–4
Lazarus 269, 294
Leah 252–3
Levenson, Jon 295
  Sinai and Zion 295
Levi, Primo 287, 288
Leviticus 14, 32n, 35
Lodge, David 243
Lot 8
Luke, St 10, 21, 22, 28
Luther, Martin 267

Mace, Thomas 79
Malamud, Bernard 227

Dubin's Lives 227
Mallarmé, Stephane 132, 201, 203–4, 300
Malraux, André 212
Mandela, Nelson 12, 286
Mann, Thomas 252, 332
Mark, St 20, 21, 22, 23
Marlowe, Christopher 84
   Hero and Leander 84
Marx Brothers 71, 72, 327
Matthew, St 1, 10, 18, 20, 21, 22, 23
Mepham, John 323–4, 326
Micah 294, 296
Midrash Tanhuma 7
Milton, John 128, 163, 320
   Lycidas 128, 319
Mitterrand, François 285
Modernism 212, 235, 243, 293, 300, 302, 303, 332
Montaigne, Michel de ix, 94
Moses 13–14, 20–1, 40–1, 42–4, 47, 51, 296
Mozart, Wolfgang Amadeus 60, 65, 67, 68, 77, 238, 241–2, 298
   Don Giovanni 60

Nabokov, Vladimir 154, 208, 244, 297, 330
   Lolita 154
Narrative 14–24, 36–45, 130–48, 208–20, 290–307, 311–33
New Testament 4, 18, 19, 29, 31
Nietzsche, Friedrich 60, 138, 235, 284–5, 286, 302, 332
   The Twilight of the Idols 285
   Untimely Meditations 284n
Nora, Pierre 282
   Les Lieux de la mémoire 282
Numbers 35
Nuttall, A.D. 61, 66

Old Testament 1, 18, 22, *see also* Hebrew Bible
Ovid 60, 91
Oz, Amos 221

Pagels, Elaine 35
   The Gnostic Gospels 35n
Pagis, Dan 221
Pascal, Blaise 256
Paul, St 11, 87, 92, 102, 109, 251
Perec, Georges 244
Phalti 2–4, 14–15
Philo of Alexandria 6–7
Picasso, Pablo 69, 81, 82, 97, 100, 325, 329
   The Absinthe Glass 81
   Mother and Child 81, 82, 97
   Mother with Pushchair 81
Piganiol, Jean Aimar 113
   Nouveau voyage de France 113
Pinget, Robert 292
Plato 60, 146, 252, 290
Poe, Edgar Allan 201
Pollack, Oskar 137
Postmodernism 128, 141, 302, 303
Powell, Anthony 243
Proverbs 57, 241
Proust, Marcel ix, 16–17, 25–9, 33–4, 36, 45, 77, 97, 126, 132, 151, 163, 188, 193, 197, 201, 205–6, 208, 230, 231, 235, 243, 244, 253, 290, 291, 298, 316–17, 319, 320, 324, 330, 332
   A la recherche du temps perdu 16–17, 26, 68, 126, 206, 230, 316
   Contre Sainte-Beuve 26
   'Journées de lecture' 25
Psalms 17, 23, 47n, 48–59
Pythagoras 70, 71

Raban, Jonathan 37
   Passage to Juneau 37
Rabelais, François 16, 94, 262, 330
Rachel 20, 252
Raphael 102
   Portrait of Baldassare Castiglione 102
Reformation 10
Rembrandt van Rijn 99–103
   Artist in his Studio 99–100, 103
   Portrait of the Artist at his Easel 100

Self-Portrait (The Hague) 102
Self-Portrait (National Gallery)
    102
Self-Portrait with Two Circles 102
Revelation 1, 17, 31
Rich, Barnabe 61–4
    Of Apolonius and Silla 61
Rilke, Rainer Maria 132, 180, 298,
    327
Rimbaud, Arthur 128
Robbe-Grillet, Alain 329
Robespierre, Maximilien 267
Rochefort, Henri 282
    L'Intransigànt 282
Romanticism 119, 123, 129, 213,
    266–8, 309, 315
Roth, Philip 242
Ruskin, John 25
    Sesame and Lilies 25
Ruth 3, 29–30

Sacks, Oliver 118, 286–7
    Awakenings 286
    *The Man Who Mistook his Wife for a
        Hat* 118n
Sainte-Beuve, Charles Augustin
    291
Samuel 2, 17, 31, 37–9, 53
Sarna, Nahum 50, 50n, 51
    On the Book of Psalms 47n, 50n
Sartre, Jean-Paul 16, 26, 212, 214
    La Nausée 16, 214
Saul 2, 20, 31, 34, 39, 48
Schoenberg, Arnold 161, 201, 330
Schwitters, Kurt 81
Septuagint 6
Shakespeare, William 60–77, 85,
    88–93, 96, 100, 265, 267–8, 281
    The Comedy of Errors 73
    Hamlet 267–8
    King Lear 265
    Macbeth 119
    The Merchant of Venice 68
    A Midsummer Night's Dream 64,
        85, 88–93, 97

'The Phoenix and the Turtle'
    85
Twelfth Night 60–77
The Two Gentlemen of Verona 68
Shaw, George Bernard 81
Shusterman, Richard 302, 306
Simmel, Georg 68, 69, 72
Simon, Claude 243, 244
Singer, I.B. 299
Snodgrass, W.D. 91, 92
    In Radical Pursuit 91
Socrates 140, 146, 267
Sophocles 41, 60
    Oedipus at Colonus 41
Spark, Muriel 65, 242, 253, 290
    The Bachelors 65
Stein, Gertrude 273
Sterne, Laurence 16, 83, 94–7,
    104–18, 130, 262, 330
    Tristram Shandy 83, 94–7,
        104–18, 130, 193
Stevens, Wallace 120–1, 124–7,
    128, 132, 170, 187, 208, 212, 217,
    219–20, 243
    Harmonium 121
    'The Man Whose Pharanx was
        Bad' 121, 125
    'The Plain Sense of Things'
        125, 127, 219–20
Stravinsky, Igor 81, 201, 291, 297,
    298, 325, 326, 328, 329, 332
    Agon 291
    L'Histoire du soldat 81, 326
    Octet 329
    Petroushka 81
    Rénard 326
    Symphonies of Wind Instruments 329
Sturrock, John 25n
Swift, Jonathan 83, 93, 96, 112, 262,
    330
    A Tale of a Tub 83, 93
Swinburne, Algernon Charles 269
Syntax 26–9, 31–2, 36, 309

Thorlby, Tony 332

Titian 102
  Portrait of a Young Man 102
Tolstoy, Leo 243, 316, 320
Torah 7, 17, 49, 51, 53, 57

Van Gogh, Vincent 325
Vermeer, Jan 99, 324
Virgil 60, 260–1, 281, 295

Wagner, Richard 138, 265–6, 316
Waldrop, Rosmarie 299
Waugh, Evelyn 270–3, 274
  Decline and Fall 270
  A Handful of Dust 271
  Vile Bodies 271
Webern, Anton 161, 324
Wight, Martin 332
Williams, William Carlos 125
Winnicott, D.W. 97, 327

The Piggle 97n
Wittgenstein, Ludwig 197, 198,
  201, 276, 317
  The Philosophical Investigations 198
Woolf, Virginia 77, 151, 242, 249,
  291–2, 322, 323
  The Waves 292
Wordsworth, William 123–4, 184,
  262–5, 267, 268
  'Ode: Intimations of
    Immortality' 123–4
  'Resolution and Independence'
    262–5

Yeats, W.B. 102, 126–7, 170, 190,
  192, 193, 202, 319
  'The Circus Animals'
    Desertion' 126–7, 193, 319
Yerushalmi, Josef Haim 284